The United States and Biological Warfare

The United States

Stephen Endicott
and
Edward Hagerman

Indiana University Press
BLOOMINGTON AND INDIANAPOLIS

and Biological Warfare

Secrets from the Early Cold War and Korea

This book is a publication of

Indiana University Press
601 North Morton Street
Bloomington, Indiana 47404-3797 USA

www.indiana.edu/~iupress

Telephone orders 800-842-6796
Fax orders 812-855-7931
Orders by e-mail iuporder@indiana.edu

The paper used in this publication meets the minimum
requirements of American National Standard for Information
Sciences—Permanence of Paper for Printed Library
Materials, ANSI Z39.48-1984.

Manufactured in the United States of America

Library of Congress Cataloging-in-Publication Data

Endicott, Stephen Lyon, date
   The United States and biological warfare : secrets from the early
cold war and Korea / Stephen Endicott and Edward Hagerman.
       p.   cm.
   Includes bibliographical references and index.
   ISBN 0-253-33472-1 (cloth : alk. paper)
   1. Biological warfare—United States. 2. Korean War, 1950–1953—
Biological warfare.   I. Hagerman, Edward.   II. Title.
UG447.8.E53   1999
358'.38'0973—dc21   98-29175

   1   2   3   4   5   04   03   02   01   00   99

This book is dedicated to
Dr. Joseph Needham
John W. and Sylvia Powell, Julian Shuman
and Dr. James G. Endicott

CONTENTS

MAPS

TABLES

PREFACE

In late February 1952, North Korean foreign minister Bak Hun Yung and Chinese premier Zhou Enlai accused the United States of using biological warfare in Korea. This charge drew worldwide attention after some American flyers who were Chinese prisoners of war confessed to having used biological weapons. When the flyers were subsequently released in the exchange of prisoners, they retracted their confessions—under threat of court-martial, as it turns out—and the U.S. government then and thereafter dismissed the charges as propaganda.

This incident focuses attention on what is perhaps the United States' best-kept military secret: the large biological warfare program developed on a crash basis between 1951 and 1953, and its antecedents in the germ war program developed in close cooperation with Great Britain and Canada during World War II. Documents declassified over the past twenty years or so have revealed the extent of the U.S. World War II program, as well as the secret deal to acquire the biological warfare technology employed by Japan during its invasion of China in 1937–45.

The slow flow of documents on the early Cold War biological warfare program has, until very recently, left many questions with few answers. But newly declassified American, Canadian, and British documents (many declassified at our request) and the cooperation of the Chinese central archives in granting us the first access by foreigners to relevant classified documents, have lifted the veil of secrecy to provide new evidence that the United States had an operational biological weapons system, and that it was employed in the Korean War.

For the first time, there is hard evidence that the U.S. government lied to both Congress and the American public when it said that the American biological warfare program was purely defensive and for retaliation only. To the contrary, a large and sophisticated biological weapons system was developed as an offensive weapon of opportunity. The U.S. Air Force had operational plans to use biological weapons in 1949 if the crisis surrounding the Berlin Blockade had led to general war, and later, during the Korean War, biological warfare was incorporated into the plans of the Strategic Air Command for general war, and into tactical plans for the U.S. Air Force in Europe. It is significant that this was the first time in modern military history that biological warfare was incorporated into doctrine as a weapons system. In addition, the United States had a technological capacity for the covert use of biological weapons, complete with a planning structure and operational capabilities.

Together, these U.S., Canadian, and Chinese documents provide strong corroborative evidence that the United States experimented with biological weapons during the Korean War.

Top secret internal documents of the Chinese public health agency responsible for reporting any evidence of biological warfare in areas bordering Korea provide a coolly professional and balanced record, complete with sardonic observations on the sometime overreaction of the population to fears of germ warfare. When this material is placed beside information drawn from the medical and operational archives of the Chinese and North Korean armies in the field, a pattern of disease and delivery systems is observed consistent with American capabilities, and yet anomalous with local incidence of disease. These top secret internal medical and intelligence documents leave the impression that the Chinese were deadly serious in their efforts to figure out what was going on in a time of confusion, and were not attempting to manufacture a propaganda case. Significantly, very little of the archival material was used in 1952 in publicly making the case for germ warfare, and it has remained classified ever since. One can speculate that the Chinese and North Koreans, then and later, did not wish to share intelligence information that the Americans might use in assessing their experiments. In the aftermath of the Cold War, we have entered the Chinese and North Korean documents into the record.

From the U.S. archives, this book unfolds the hidden story of the extension of the limits of modern war to include the use of medical science, the most morally laden of sciences with respect to the sanctity of human life. Though the story of U.S. biological warfare follows a carefully concealed path, this path was in fact heavily traveled from World War II through the Korean War. Picking up from where World War II left off, through the early Cold War, the conflict in Korea quickly resurrected a heavily funded program with top-priority status that deeply involved the presidential office, the Department of Defense, and several other government departments and agencies, as well as the military services and the medical, scientific, academic, and corporate communities of the United States. A joint effort enlisted Great Britain and Canada in secret research and looked forward to incorporating a biological weapons system in NATO forces.

Working on an A-1 priority status, frequently under highest urgency orders, the leadership and rank and file of this network came together to develop bacteriological agents, munitions, and logistical support for the strategic and tactical use of bacteriological warfare in a general war plan aimed at the Soviet Union. At the midpoint of the Korean War, in December 1951, the U.S. secretary of defense ordered that "actual readiness be achieved in the earliest practicable time" for offensive use of biological weapons. Within weeks, the chief of staff of the U.S. Air Force reported that such capabilities "are rapidly materializing." It was shortly after these secret communications had passed between the top U.S. generals that the North Korean and Chinese armies charged the United States with beginning a large-scale biological warfare experiment in Korea. The U.S. secretary of state flatly denied the accusation. Both sides maintain their positions to this day. Our research has been directed to investigating and resolving this contradiction.

The momentum of and mood surrounding U.S. bacteriological development, the level of concern over the need for human experiment, and the crisis atmosphere of the time—a time when the United States military had suffered "a series of disasters unequaled in our country's history" (Appleman, *Disaster in Korea*, p. 5)—compels the historian to ask, without prejudging the answer, why U.S. forces would not use bacteriological warfare in Korea. What military, political, or moral restraints applied in that moment of ideological and political passion and of military crisis?

Questions of moral scruple about using "public health and preventive medicine in reverse" largely disappeared in an early post–World War II decision that came as close to a pact with the devil as any in U.S. political or military history. On the initiative of the service chiefs, the United States granted immunity to a group of Japanese war criminals (who had conducted biological warfare experiments on Chinese cities and had murdered at least three thousand prisoners of war, including some Americans, in the course of "scientific" germ war tests) in return for their cooperation in sharing their knowledge of biological warfare. The Japanese program and the U.S. deal remained one of the best kept official secrets of the two countries for more than thirty-five years. The declassified documentary record remains conspicuously silent on how the Japanese program was integrated into the American.

Despite silence on the Japanese connection, gradual declassification over the past twenty years has revealed an expanding picture of policy, action, and motives about biological warfare. This book is an attempt to fill in this picture by bringing together our research in the United States, China, Japan, Britain, Canada, and Continental Europe, and the labors of others who preceded us. Our hope is to contribute to the historical understanding of a moment of crisis when the limits of modern war expanded into a fundamentally new form of violence.

ACKNOWLEDGMENTS

It is impossible to acknowledge properly the help of the many people who helped us over the twenty years that it has taken to prepare this book. To those not mentioned by name, we nevertheless express our sincere thanks. At the U.S. National Archives and Records Administration, we especially wish to thank Richard Boylan for his able assistance over many trips and many years. We wish to thank Dave Giordano for his help in leading us through the maze of USAF records; the late Eddie Meese, who pointed us in fruitful directions early in our research; and Will Mahoney, who filled gaps at the end. Researchers extraordinaire Eddie Becker and Joan Yoshiwara not only helped us sift through thousands of records but also made our extended stay in Washington, D.C., enjoyable and affordable by finding some foam mats, a bridge table and some chairs, pots and pans, and a contraption for making coffee that allowed us to turn a couple of spare rooms in their house into a comfortable bunker for the duration. There are also the military archivists and historians scattered around the United States who gave us information and assistance: Bill Sibert at the St. Louis Record Center; Mike Waesche at Suitland Records Center; Joyce Conyers-Hudson, Department of the Navy, Head of the Official Papers Unit, U.S. Marine Corps Historical Center in Washington, D.C.; Olthea S. Croom, Records Analyst, Pentagon Headquarters, U.S. Air Force; Herb Mason, Command Historian of the Headquarters, Air Force Special Operations Command; Stanley Sandler, historian for the U.S. Army Special Operations Command, Fort Bragg, North Carolina; and Archie DiFante in the Air Force Historical Research Office at Maxwell Air Force Base, Alabama. We thank Dennis Bilger at the Truman Library for guiding us through the records of the Psychological Strategy Board. At the Canadian National Archives in Ottawa, we are indebted to Paulette Dosois, Robert MacIntosh, Paul Marsden, and Norman Fortier for guiding us through the relevant collections, and to John Armstrong and others in the Access to Information Section for their work on our behalf. We express our gratitude to the research librarians of York University for their unfailing support, especially Anne Cannon, Grace Heggie, and Vivienne Monty for their assistance in ordering hard-to-find documents, and Gladys Fung for her patience and ingenuity in tracking down difficult-to-find materials through interlibrary loan. We thank Ken Kann, Mark Selden, and Carl Dow, who helped us by interviewing retired U.S. and Canadian air force officers, some of whom were prisoners of war during the Korean War, and who consented to interviews about their experiences. We wish to thank Bruce Cumings, John W. Powell, and Kei-ichi Tsuneishi for their careful readings of the whole or part of the manuscript. We thank Norman Endicott and Walton Rose Q.C. for their legal reading of the authors' handling of corroborative evidence.

In the course of several research trips to China, we incurred debts to many organizations and individuals, of whom we would specially like to mention Zhu Liang, chair of the Foreign Affairs Committee of the National People's Congress; Qian Liren, former director of the *People's Daily* and member of the Standing Committee of the Chinese People's Political Consultative Conference; Zhang Wenpu, head of the Chinese People's Institute of Foreign Affairs; and Liao Dong of the Chinese Association for International Understanding for their friendship, advice, and practical assistance in many matters. At the State Archives Bureau, we were received by director Liu Guoneng, Shen Zhengle, Long Baocun, and others who listened to our requests, helped us find relevant documents on the incidence of germ warfare during the war to "Oppose America, Aid Korea," and gave us permission to quote from them. Our thanks also to the Ministry of Defense for granting us access to certain important documents of the Chinese army, and for helping to arrange interviews with Colonel Qi Dexue, Research Fellow in the Department of Military History, PLA Academy of Military Science, and with Professor Zhu Chun, formerly a member of the Prison Camp Division Headquarters, General Political Department of the Chinese People's Volunteer Army in Korea, 1951 to 1953. Consul General Chen Wenzhao in Toronto and Colonel Lou Zhenquan, military attaché to the Chinese Embassy in Ottawa, also provided invaluable assistance. Special thanks to Xia Guang, Tsau Shuying, Donald Holoch, and Janice Matsumura for help with translating documents. And not least, in Beijing, our appreciation to George and Laura Huang for their warm hospitality, for time spent in argument around their kitchen table, and for help in translation work.

In Japan we are indebted to Masakatsu Ota of the Kyoto News Service for introducing us to researcher Ms. Fuyuko Nishisato and to Professor Kei-ichi Tsuneishi, experts on the history of Japan's biological warfare program. We are further indebted to all three for sharing their research, as we are to Professor Takao Matsumura of Keio University. In Britain we thank the Korea veterans of the Middlesex Regiment who generously corresponded with us; Jon Halliday, who pursued the question of biological warfare for many years; and Paul Lashmar, investigative journalist and TV producer, who shared with us the results of his research in the Public Records Office.

Two people deserving of special mention who pioneered the way during the difficult years of the Cold War to document and publicize the course of what they believed to be biological warfare experiments in East Asia were Dr. Joseph Needham, principal author of the International Scientific Commission Report, published in Peking in 1952, and John W. Powell, who, together with his wife Sylvia Campbell Powell and editorial associate Julian Schuman, was indicted for sedition by the American government for reports published in his magazine, the *China Monthly Review*, and who later exposed the deal that the United States had made with the war criminals of Unit 731 of the Japanese Army in China. Their work remains among the indispensable sources for scholars investigating the topic.

We thank John Gallman, director of Indiana University Press, for his commitment to this book. We are indebted to his staff who worked overtime to get the book to press, and especially to Jane Lyle for her diligent and careful copyediting.

We wish to acknowledge the financial support that we received from the Social Sciences and Humanities Research Council of Canada, from York University, and from Atkinson College, which made this extensive research project possible. Finally, our thanks to our spouses, Ann Eyerman and Lena Wilson Endicott, for their support, attentiveness to the excitement of new discoveries, and patience with the lengthy processes required to co-author a book of this nature.

30 January 1998
York University
Toronto, Ontario

INTRODUCTION
by Richard Falk

The aftermath of the Gulf War has brought to political consciousness the real menace of biological weaponry as a new, frightening dimension of warfare. The prolonged process of verifying Iraq's destruction of its capabilities and apparent willingness to wage war with weapons of mass destruction has produced a journalistic outpouring of concern about the recent spread of biological weapons to a series of Third World countries, including several in the Middle East. Usually this threat is associated either with sinister machinations of the dark forces of international terrorism or with the evil stratagems of allegedly pariah states. Unfortunately, this way of perceiving reality overlooks a much deeper narrative of involvement with the development of this weaponry that implicates most, if not all, governments on the planet, including that of the United States.

At present, the U.S. government is behind an international diplomatic effort to strengthen the Biological Weapons Convention of 1972, which prohibits the development, production, possession, threat, and use of biological weapons. President Clinton even singled out this effort as a priority of his administration in the area of arms control, and negotiations are currently under way in Geneva to strengthen the treaty regime, especially by providing for various forms of inspection to verify compliance. There are real questions as to whether this attempt to deal with the danger of a biological arms race will succeed. Pharmaceutical companies are opposed to inspections that might expose their trade secrets, and several key governments have made it clear that there will be no firm commitment to the renunciation of biological weaponry until the nuclear weapons states make a comparable commitment, which is highly unlikely in the foreseeable future.

But there are other concerns as well, especially the extent to which government—any government, including our own—can be trusted when it comes to matters of national security. There is, first of all, a thick veil of secrecy and deception that surrounds the undertakings of government in the domain of national security. In the American case, this opaqueness is reinforced by the doctrine of deniability, which authorizes lying to the extent necessary to resist unwanted disclosures. Second, there is the sense that the constraints of law and morality must be put aside in circumstances of warfare or in the pursuit of vital national interests. Third, there is a highly compliant mainstream media even in constitutional democracies that is deferential to the national security establishment, and generally succumbs to pressure in the unusual event of an unwanted revelation. And fourth, there is the fusion of militarist thinking that anything goes in war with the prevalent belief among political and military leaders that "saving American lives" is a justification for otherwise terrible deeds that brushes aside any moral and legal obstacles. Such a combination of circumstances suggests the breadth of the gap that separates the citizenry from its political and military leadership in the areas of war and peace.

It is against such a background of concerns that this disturbing and fine book by Stephen Endicott and Edward Hagerman assumes its great importance. The authors, experienced historians whose approach to their subject is impressively exhaustive and meticulous, explore one of the most notorious allegations of the Cold War era—that the United States used biological weapons on an experimental basis in China and North Korea during the Korean War. This allegation was dismissed by Western media as hostile propaganda at the time, and it was further discredited as relying on "confessions" allegedly obtained by North Korea from brainwashed captured American soldiers. These confessions were indeed later retracted, but under the suspicious circumstance that the released POWs otherwise faced court-martial proceedings.

Relying on a vast array of previously unavailable declassified sources and on access to archival materials in several countries, including China, Endicott and Hagerman reached the conclusion that circumstantial evidence strongly supports the allegation of use. It also implies a continuing high-level cover-up about the true relationship of the United States government to biological weaponry in general. The authors are scrupulous in their presentation, providing evidence and reasoning for each link in their argument and resisting generalizations that exceed what can be reliably documented. They also examine fairly the arguments and evidence that have been advanced over the years to discredit the central allegation of BW use, and find them thin and contrived. At minimum, this book raises the historical debate on the allegation about biological weaponry to a new and necessary level of scholarly seriousness that challenges the government to come forward with its own refuting arguments and evidence. It is of utmost importance to clear up the record. This is so not only because it is an essential item of Cold War history, but because it relates so closely to the credibility of the U.S. government as a diplomatic leader in the struggle to prevent any further moves toward a global biological weapons arms race.

In my view, the resolution of the sensationalist story line of whether biological weaponry was used in combat situations in China and Korea during the Korean War is of great interest and importance, but it does not begin to exhaust the real significance of this book. What I find so vividly present in this work is the revelation of the war mentality that guides the thinking of those responsible for the national security of this country, and of such kindred states as Canada and Britain. It is here that one's worst fears and apprehensions are unfortunately amply upheld. With respect to biological weaponry, even at a time when it was generally considered to be both immoral and illegal, the United States government was energetically exploring the offensive possibilities. And by authoritative decision at command levels, it was prepared to use biological weapons as a weapon of choice whenever military circumstances so warranted. Such an internal governmental approach, clearly documented in a seemingly incontrovertible manner for the period 1950–1953, contradicted the general claim then made, and subsequently reaffirmed, that the U.S. program in biological weapons was maintained solely for defensive purposes, and as a backup retaliatory threat in the event that such weaponry was used by adversaries. Endicott and Hagerman also show that support for building up a combat-ready massive biological weapons capability was abandoned only because it became clear by 1953 that the problem of effective delivery could not be successfully resolved. It is chilling to speculate on what might have followed if genetic engineering had then possessed the capabilities it seems presently to possess, which might well have produced a satisfactory solution to the delivery problem.

This pattern has many important implications beyond the reconstruction of history. There is no reason to suppose that current thinking within the national security establishment proceeds on any other basis than a continuing adherence to the tenets of ultra-realism. As such, it makes the legal undertakings of the United States government (and of others) very unreliable under any sort of geopolitical pressure. It also makes a mockery of pious protestations about the immorality of biological weaponry. It makes it grossly hypocritical to attack foreign governments that are supposedly exploring the military utility of this weaponry. Perhaps most of all, the elaborate process of cover-up and concealment depicted in this book is one more indication that citizens in the United States (and elsewhere) are naïve if they rely upon and trust the claims of government in relation to national security policy. One lesson that could be learned is that democracy is dangerously vulnerable unless it disallows its leaders and officials to hide their deeds behind a cloak of secrecy. Trust is essential for participatory citizenship in America, and it is now evident that trust is impossible without far greater transparency than currently exists.

Stephen Endicott and Edward Hagerman deserve our gratitude for producing such an important study based on prodigious research, but even more for their courage in taking on such a delicate theme. There are likely to be recriminations and countercharges hurled in their direction, highly orchestrated responses designed to divert attention from the substance of their analysis. Such a prospect is hardly fanciful. Consider the backlash a few years ago when the prestigious Smithsonian Institution sought to mount an exhibition on the fiftieth anniversary of the dropping of atomic bombs against Hiroshima and Nagasaki. The end result of the incident was that the director of the museum was dismissed and the exhibition was scaled way back to deprive it of any elements of overdue atonement for the prolonged damage inflicted on Japanese civilian society. In this instance, unlike that pertaining to the biological weapons narrative, the essential facts were known (although the bureaucratic rationale for the use of atomic bombs at that stage in the war remains a matter of controversy and concealment), and it was patrioteering elements of the citizenry who apparently self-mobilized (with notable congressional and Pentagon backing) to safeguard their own consoling version of history, thereby avoiding the anguish of self-examination with respect to responsibility for having crossed the nuclear threshold.

Or consider the furor generated by the CNN programs in June of 1998 on Operation Tailwind, in which it was alleged that sarin gas (CBU-15 or GB) was used to kill a group of American defectors resident in Laos during the Vietnam War. Despite the care and skill with which these experienced television journalists proceeded, a massive counterattack was immediately launched that led to their dismissal and an abject CNN retraction. The focus on the sensationalist element of sarin gas was natural, because of its lethal character, yet somewhat misleading. Aside from whether or not sarin gas was actually used, what became clear beyond a reasonable doubt in the CNN programs and research was that U.S. military commanders, at the highest levels, initiated and carried out an operation to kill Americans in neighboring Laos on the basis of a secret program that was never revealed even to Congress. In a series of interviews with the CNN correspondents, Retired Admiral Thomas Moorer, Chairman of the Joint Chiefs of Staff at the time of Tailwind, clearly and repeatedly confirmed the main and most controversial elements of the story. As with biological and atomic weapons, those who justified such action, including Admiral Moorer, were content at the time, and even now in retrospect, with the essentially empty assertion that the undertaking "saved American lives," which seems to operate within American military circles as an uncontestable argument for weapons and tactics that would otherwise be deemed reprehensible.

In all of this, there is no reason to suppose that the United States is behaving any worse than other states. Its behavior is the focus of such attention here because of the nature of the particular inquiry, but also because the U.S. government is so quick to seize the high moral ground in diplomacy, and because its role in global security policy is so prominent. But the issues raised are far broader and more profound than the criticism of a particular country with respect to a given line of policy. If what is revealed is "the normalcy" of the United States with respect to the global agenda on security and war/peace issues, then the idea of relying on international treaties and arrangements is most precarious as a means to avert tragedy and catastrophe in the future. What is ultimately at issue is the entrenchment in government of a war mentality that overrides the major premises of both elemental morality and civic democracy. Unless this mentality is effectively repudiated and abandoned in the inner circles of government, we should expect more in the future of what Endicott and Hagerman have documented in relation to the Korean War period. What is at stake, of course, is the urgent need for the drastic revision of our understanding of human security as we embark on this transition to a new millennium. It has become far too unreliable and dangerous to rely any longer on the sort of militarist approaches that have guided statecraft in Machiavellian directions for the past several centuries. A preferred alternative would be to move with resolve toward a human-centered view of security that is infused with a belief in the sanctity of every person's life.

5 August 1998
Istanbul

ABBREVIATIONS

AFB	Air Force Base
AFOAT	Code for the assistant for atomic energy responsible for biological warfare
AMC	Air Materiel Command
ARCW	Air Resupply and Communications Wing
BW	Biological warfare
CAT	Civil Air Transport
CCRAK	Combined Command for Reconnaissance Activities, Korea (also referred to as Covert, Clandestine, and Related Activities, Korea)
CEBAR	Chemical, biological, and radiological warfare
CGFEAF	Commanding General Far East Air Force
CIA	Central Intelligence Agency
CINCFE	Commander in Chief Far East
CINCUNC	Commander in Chief United Nations Command
CW	Chemical warfare
DEPTAR	Department of the Army
DOD	Department of Defense
FEC	Far East Command
FRS	Fellow of the Royal Society
G-2	U.S. military intelligence
GHQ	General Headquarters
ICRC	International Committee of the Red Cross
JCS	Joint Chiefs of Staff
JSPC	Joint Strategic Plans Committee
NA	National Archives of the United States
NAC	National Archives of Canada
NCNA	New China News Agency (Xinhua)
NSA	National Security Archive, George Washington University, Washington, D.C.
OPC	CIA Office of Policy Coordination
PLA	People's Liberation Army
POW	Prisoner of war
PSB	Psychological Strategy Board
RG	Record Group
SCAP	Supreme Command Allied Powers
SCMP	Survey of China Mainland Press
SOD	Special Operations Division, U.S. Army Chemical Corps
WBC	Bacteriological Warfare Committee
WRS	War Research Service Committee
WSEG	Weapons System Evaluation Group

The United States and Biological Warfare

1 Aches and Fevers in China and Korea

I went to China in 1952 wanting to assess the assertions of germ warfare being one reason. Without going into the evidence, I came away convinced that Chinese officials believed that the evidence was conclusive. On returning, Alan Watt, my successor as permanent head of the Australian Department of External Affairs, informed me that in the light of my public statements he had sought a response from Washington and was informed that the United States had used biological weapons during the Korean war but only for experimental purposes.

—Dr. John Burton, letter of 12 April 1997[1]

The dropping of insects from the air is entirely feasible.

—Dr. G. B. Reed, Canadian expert in biological warfare, 15 May 1952[2]

Let us get mobilized, attend to hygiene, reduce the incidence of disease, raise the standard of health, and crush the enemy's germ warfare.

—Mao Zedong, Inscription for the Second National Health Conference, 1953

Discharged soldier Shi Hongru, 25, left his native place in the early morning hours of 10 March 1952, carrying a sturdy travel bag, half empty. He was bound on a journey of filial duty to Changde, a fabled city of imperial palaces that lay beyond the Great Wall, some three hundred miles from his starting point in Shandong province.

His father, a traveling merchant, had died there five years earlier of dysentery. Because of the civil war in northern China between the Nationalists and the Communists, the family had been unable to make proper funeral arrangements. Now the son was going to find his father's remains and bring them back to the family burial ground.

Shi arrived in Changde, capital of Rehe province, eleven days later, on 21 March. On the way he had walked, probably hitched rides on barges in the Grand Canal, and ridden on a horse-drawn cart. In Changde he rented a room in a guest house next to the 5th District police station, a room whose previous occupant had been a man selling pig bristles. After making some inquiries, Shi went to the suburbs on the 23rd to dig up his father's bones. He hired a man to help him. This man wore gloves, but Shi did not. After digging up his father's remains, he returned to the guest house in Changde. There, on the 28th, Shi fell ill. He got worse the next day: chest ache, high fever. At the provincial hospital where he was taken, they said it was pneumonia. At 4 A.M. on 1 April, Shi died. An autopsy showed fluid in his chest. His blood was cultured: the ASCOLI test reaction was positive; microscopic examination of a specimen showed a chain bacillus. White mice were inoculated, and they died after three days. Another specimen was made: anthrax bacillus.

Public health authorities could not determine the source of this infection. The police made inquiries at the guest house. Shi had not worn gloves at the graveyard, but his father's bones tested negative. Anthrax usually affects animals. Yes, a man selling pig bristles had stayed in Shi's room. Other people at the inn recalled Shi telling of riding horse-drawn carts on his way from Shandong. But there was no conclusion about the source of the bacteria that had caused his fatal illness.[3]

Two hundred and fifty miles east of Changde, in the suburbs of Shenyang city, Wang Zhibin, 47, a pedicab driver, became nauseated on 22 March 1952. He felt stuffy in the chest in the early hours of the 24th. At 6 A.M. that morning he fell unconsious, vomiting white fluid. Three hours later, he died.

The autopsy pathology report mentioned hemorrhages in the brain and respiratory system and in the lymph and adrenal glands, and the presence of a bacillus similar to anthrax bacillus. "Therefore we assume that this case is anthrax which entered through the respiratory system," wrote Chen Yingqian, leader of the medical research group. "We used his spleen and heart muscles to culture the bacteria. We inoculated white mice, which died within 3 days, and we found the same bacteria. A further ASCOLI test was positive; therefore our final decision in the case was anthrax bacillus." Again the medical research team did not determine the origin of the disease. Their report merely said, "Three or four days before the illness occurred, outside the courtyard wall of his residence many flies were found.

It may be related to livestock. We have not found any other sources because the patient was a pedicab driver. Possibly the source of his infection cannot be determined."[4]

Sudden deaths from respiratory anthrax also struck down a railway worker of Manjing train station in Changtu county, Liaoxi province, on 16 March 1952, a young schoolteacher in Liaoyang county on 8 April, and a housewife in Anshan city on 14 April.[5] In Jin county, a donkey fell ill on the evening of 12 March, refusing to eat grass, and died the next day. An autopsy showed hemorrhage of the heart and spleen, the result of anthrax bacilli.[6]

All these occurrences were in widely separated places, seemingly unconnected by any spreading epidemic pattern from a central point. What was their origin? A clue to this mystery was offered in the case of the stricken railway worker, Qu Zhanyun. According to the summary of this incident prepared by the provincial epidemic disease prevention committee, U.S. aircraft flew over Manjing railway station on 16 March. Following this occurrence, another railway worker, Liu Zhongguo, while checking the tracks found a large number of black beetles 1.5 kilometers north of the station. He brought samples back to the station. His fellow worker, Qu, had contact with the bugs. "Liu went to the disease prevention post for disinfection. Qu did not. He fell ill on the 19th with headache, [illegible] pain; the second day he had nausea. Hospitalized on the 21st at the Siping Railway Hospital with high fever, continuous vomiting, weakness, insomnia, incontinence, a high white blood count, large bacilli in the sputum. Died on the 22nd; autopsy . . . determined anthrax." Bacterial samples made from the beetles showed the presence of anthrax bacillus. Qu had no history of contact with animals, and no animal diseases were found in the village where he lived. "Before Qu fell ill, he ate pork with his family; nothing happened to the other family members."[7]

Another illness, acute encephalitis, made its appearance in northeast China in the early spring of 1952. The virus causing this deadly disease of the cerebral cortex was not unknown to the northeast, but when it surfaced, it normally struck in the spring and summer, and was associated with bites from ticks in the remote forested areas of Songjiang and Jilin provinces. Known as "spring and summer" or "forest encephalitis," it affected forestry workers.[8] But in large cities such as Shenyang, Anshan, and Fushun in the industrial heartland of Liaoning province, next door to Korea and in the center of China's heavy industrial belt, people now began to succumb to an encephalitis-causing virus in alarming numbers.

Medical workers were mobilized to investigate a flood of sudden deaths.

Their reports show remarkable caution in making a diagnosis. They took their time about it, because in their experience, encephalitis was new to the area. The leader of the pathology group, Dr. Li Peilin, a graduate of Mukden Medical College in 1927 who had earned his Ph.D. at the University of London in 1939, was at the time professor and head of the department of pathology at the National Medical College in Shenyang. A person well acquainted with the local environment, he was a distinguished medical scientist, the author of half a dozen published papers on pathology and anatomy.[9]

One of the first cases was in Fushun city in early March 1952, when three children died acute deaths. Dr. Li Peilin's medical research group went to the site without delay to investigate and made their report:

> 1. Clinical evidence of sickness:
>> i) Illnesses:
>>> a) Xing Defu, male, 5. Fell ill on the evening of 5 March, vomiting, unconscious, short of breath. Died at 7 A.M. on the 6th.
>>> b) Bao Lirong, female, 9. Visited Xing Defu's house on 6 March, fell ill at 1 on 9 March . . . she got fever, became delirious, spit yellow fluid, fell unconscious. Died at 5 P.M. the same day.
>>> c) Zhang Jingyuan, female, 15 months. Fell ill at 3 P.M. of 9 March, fever, vomiting yellow fluid and white foam, unconscious, short of breath. Died at 0:30 A.M. on the 10th.
>>> *Notes:* (1) The three cases all drank from the regular water supply line and did not eat any special food. (2) The nearby domestic animals had no plague or pestilence.
>> ii) Site investigation:
>> The three all lived in the Xinfu district of the city, and the sanitary conditions there are bad. Insects were found in four places. The living conditions in that district are very poor; the residences and courtyards and streets are narrow, and there was a large trash pile in front of Bao Lirong's gate. When cleaning up the trash on 5 March, they saw more than ten mosquitoes and other insects.
>> iii) Deductions:
>> According to the above, it is possible that it is a contagious disease, and its spread is closely related to the density of insects.
> 2. Autopsy report:
>> i) Bao Lirong: mainly we saw that the cerebral cortex nerves were affected . . . the result of phagocytotic cells [literally: swallowing cells]; the intestines had no special indications.

ii) Zhang Jingyuan: hemorrhaging of the adrenal gland was clearly seen; the cerebral cortex cells showed degenerative change from phagocytosis. . . .

Deduction: According to the above and other cases in Shenyang districts, the main symptoms are toxic degeneration of cerebral cortex cells and a phagocytotic phenomenon similar to a special toxic degenerative encephalitis, but it is not the same as the epidemic encephalitis of the northeast district in the past. Possibly it is:

a) Food poisoning: meat poison can cause this symptom . . . but why was it limited to a few people, and why did it not become epidemic? This needs further study.

b) An unknown toxic poisoning disease of the cerebral systems that causes a special form of encephalitis. The loss of consciousness by the above patients can be explained thus. The next step should check the intestinal system lymph glands for salmonella, and also look for a virus in the cerebral cortex to further determine the cause of the disease.

In general, in the past this kind of encephalitis was never seen in the northeast region, and this time, since the American imperialists have used germ warfare and we found a few cases, it needs special attention.

Signed: Pathology group leader, Li Peilin and Chen Yingqian[10]

During the last three weeks of March 1952, the medical research group was called to examine the circumstances of twenty-four sudden deaths in the industrial belt of the northeast. In sixteen of these cases the pathology diagnosis was acute toxic encephalitis or "suspected as similar to encephalitis," with most patients dying within twenty-four hours of the onset of the illness. By and large, the doctors could still only speculate on how the virus had entered the victims' bodies: from the clinical evidence, insect bites seemed less likely; infection through the digestive system or the respiratory tract was more probable.

South of the Yalu River (the boundary between China and North Korea), especially near the battlefront at the main line of resistance on the 38th Parallel, the North Korean and Chinese armies had become aware in January–February 1952 of an unusual array of health problems among their soldiers in the Ichon, Chorwan, Kumhwa, and Pyongyang areas. They also noticed that U.S. aircraft were dropping strange objects, including tree leaves, soybean stalks and pods, feathers, cotton batten, and cardboard packages and bombs containing live insects of various descriptions and rotten fish, decaying pork, frogs, and rodents.[11]

The Commission of the Medical Headquarters of the Korean People's Army issued the following report on 29 January 1952:

> On the morning of January 28, 1952, an enemy aircraft flew over territory in the district of Ichon two or three times and then made off in a southerly direction. On that morning, the weather was calm and misty. Towards noon, the mist dispersed and on the snow at various points on the territory flown over by the enemy aircraft, the Chinese People's Volunteers found insects—flies, fleas, ticks and spiders. About 14 hours, fleas, flies and spiders were found in the Evondi district. There was a greater number of fleas than other insects; on one square metre, up to 10 could be counted. The appearance of these insects in winter conditions on the snow seemed extraordinary to the Chinese volunteers. Interested by this fact, medical instructor Chang Chva Sin collected several species of insects and took them to Im Guk Mo, the chief of the regiment's medical centre. The latter decided to verify the discovery of the insects and in the company of medical instructor Chang Chva Sin, set out at 17 hours for the place of the discovery.

Dr. Im confirmed the discovery, and in conversation with local inhabitants, he learned that they had never before seen insects in the snow. Pursuing this information further, investigators heard that on the same day, 28 January, insects had been found where other units of the Chinese army were located. Stringent measures were taken to prevent the spread of any disease the insects might carry, while tests were conducted on specimens. Also, it was established that from 1 January to the time of the incident, there had been no cases of infectious disease in the Chinese army or among the adjacent population; nor had medical personnel found any disease-carrying rodents. The records of the Medical Center of Unit N of the Chinese army indicated that air temperature during the month of January had varied between −15 and +1 degree centigrade, too low normally to allow activity or reproduction of insects. Tests conducted on 29 January by the bacteriological laboratory of the Medical Headquarters of the Korean Army found the tests of fleas and spiders to be negative, but the flies tested positive for cholera, which, apart from an outbreak in South Korea in 1946, had been unknown in Korea for sixty years. An entomological investigation found four groups of flies—classis: insecta pterygota; ordo: diptera; subordo: cyclorapha; familia: anthomyiidae—all having great resistance to low temperatures, and the first three not known in Korea. The ticks belonged to a type unknown in Korea but capable of conveying "spring and summer recurrent fever" and encephalitis.[12]

The Korean Medical Headquarters investigated another incident affecting the Chinese army on 11 February 1952. Soldiers in Unit N in the region of Cheumdon in the Chorwon district, not far from the main line of resistance, reported three F-51 aircraft flying low past Hill 342.20 dropping gray cylindrical objects almost 10 centimeters in diameter and almost 20 centimeters long, and packets of yellow colored paper. The wrappings were already torn. They were found to contain flies, fleas, ants, and other insects, which were already beginning to spread by the time the soldiers reached them. The chief medical officer of the unit collected several insects for laboratory analysis and organized the burning of the packets and the disinfecting of the area. It was established that in recent months no infectious disease had been reported among the civilian population in the area or in the army. There were no cases of infected rodents found in recent years, and no infectious diseases reported among domestic animals. Records of the Medical Center of Unit N of the Chinese army indicated that the temperature between 21 January and 14 February had varied between −21 and +5 degrees centigrade. The bacteriological examination of flies, ants, spiders and mosquitoes at the laboratory of the Korean army's medical headquarters showed negative results, but a flea specimen tested positive for plague bacillus. The test was confirmed by a biological test on guinea pigs and agglutination tests with specific serum.[13]

A few days earlier, on 8 February, the Chinese army had captured Corporal James Chambers, No. 123621632, of the U.S. 2nd Division, 38th Regiment, and discovered that he had been inoculated against plague. About the same time the inoculation certificates of two captives from the South Korean 2nd Division, Nan Guanqi and Chen Xiasan, also showed inoculations against plague.[14]

A worried Chinese General Staff sent experts to investigate the situation at the battlefront. The average temperature there in the first part of February was between −7.2 and −9.2 C, frigid temperatures at which insects could not normally survive or propagate naturally; the specialists satisfied themselves that the insects had appeared after the passage of enemy airplanes. On 18 February more insects, including fleas, appeared near the rail center of Anzhou in northwestern Korea, and some were diagnosed with plague.[15] That same day the acting chief of staff of the People's Liberation Army, Nie Rongzhen, reported to Mao Zedong, chairman of the Central Military Commission, and to Premier Zhou Enlai:

> In addition to sending experts to the spot for investigation, we sent specimens to Beijing for cultivation and testing; it will take two more days to find out which kind of germs these insects

brought. According to the estimates of the experts, the possibilities of cholera, typhoid fever, plague, and recurrent fever are highest. If confirmed by testing, our epidemic prevention and elimination work should be conducted immediately and effectively . . . and we need support of personnel and materials from the Soviet Union.[16]

Chairman Mao minuted this report: "Ask Premier Zhou Enlai to attend to this matter and deal with it." Two days later, after getting a preliminary report on the insects and the bacteria they carried, Zhou Enlai put forward a six-point plan: (1) Strengthen testing of the contaminated insects sent from the battlefront; according to preliminary tests, plague, cholera, and other germs were present. (2) Send an epidemic-prevention team and vaccines, powder, and other materials to the battlefield. (3) Publish a statement denouncing the crimes of American germ warfare, and demand that the United States be held responsible. (4) Through the Chinese People's Committee for Defending World Peace, suggest to the World Peace Council that it initiate a campaign against U.S. germ warfare. (5) Telegraph an order to the battlefront in Korea to mobilize epidemic prevention, and to strengthen vigilance in northeast China. (6) Telegraph a request for help to the Soviet government. After receiving Mao's approval, the Chinese government, together with the government of North Korea, began an all-out campaign of preventive measures and political diplomacy.[17]

On 22 February 1952, Bak Hun Yung, foreign minister of the Korean Democratic People's Republic, issued a "serious protest" to the United Nations against the germ war crimes of the Americans and appealed "to the people of the whole world to check the outrages of the interventionists." Two days later, Premier Zhou Enlai followed up with his angry denunciation of the U.S. bacterial warfare experiments with an appeal to "the peace-loving people all over the world" to put an end to the criminal acts of the U.S. government. He claimed that this was not the first time the Americans had used bacteriological weapons in the war. As early as December 1950, when the U.S. troops were retreating hastily southward, according to Zhou Enlai, they had disseminated smallpox virus in the northern provinces of Korea. Furthermore, he said, in preparing to use bacterial weapons, the U.S. government had employed the expertise of General Shiro Ishii and several other Japanese bacteriological warfare criminals "whose hands have long been stained with the blood of the Chinese and Korean people."[18]

In the meantime, on 21 and again on 25 February, the Central Military Commission telegraphed urgent directives to the Chinese army in Korea commanding immediate action at all levels of organization for epidemic prevention in military and civilian units.[19] The first of three million doses of plague vaccine were on the way to the battlefront, and on 28 February, although as yet there had been no recorded cases of army personnel affected by plague, the Chinese army in Korea began inoculating its troops against plague.[20] Another two and a half million doses of five-in-one vaccine and five million of cholera vaccine would follow as soon as possible; specific hospitals were to be assigned "to receive, heal, and isolate the patients," to create mobile epidemic prevention teams to strengthen work on collecting information and on germ testing, to conduct epidemic-prevention education among the soldiers and civilians, and "to pay special attention but not create panic or confusion."[21]

Though plague was endemic in parts of northeast China, none had been reported in Korea since 1912. Until the end of February 1952, contagious diseases such as recurrent fever, smallpox, and typhus existed among civilians and in some individuals in the army, according to the headquarters of the Chinese army in Korea, but "the serious contagious diseases, plague and cholera," were not found among army personnel or civilians. But a month later, the Chinese army in Korea had diagnosed sixteen cases of plague "or something similar to plague" among its personnel in widely scattered areas. They occurred in seven of its armies—the 20th, 27th, 39th, 26th, 40th, 12th, and 67th. A number of dead rats or live rats that died suddenly were found, and in three cases they were diagnosed with plague.[22] Among civilians, in a single village populated by six hundred people in Anju prefecture, fifty people became infected by plague between 25 February and 11 March 1952, thirty-six of whom died.[23] In March there were forty-four cases of encephalitis and meningitis in the army, of which sixteen were fatal, five cholera cases were discovered near Pyongyang, with three deaths. Aside from these diseases, there were forty-three people with acute diseases in March, of whom twenty died—some within thirty hours after falling ill, others after eight, six, or even two hours. "As to what this illness was," the army reported, "we cannot make an accurate diagnosis, and whether or not it was related to the enemy's spreading bacterial war is under further investigation."[24] According to the official history of the Chinese army in Korea, "The enemy's germ war once endangered the Chinese and Korean armies . . . to a certain extent [and] created psychological tension among our soldiers and the civilians for a while."[25]

The deputy chief of staff of the Volunteer Army, General Deng Hua, took charge of combating the threat of epidemics in cooperation with the logistics department of the army. A massive health campaign got under way, with an emphasis on catching mice, exterminating insects, safeguarding water resources, and sanitizing living quarters. One million three hun-

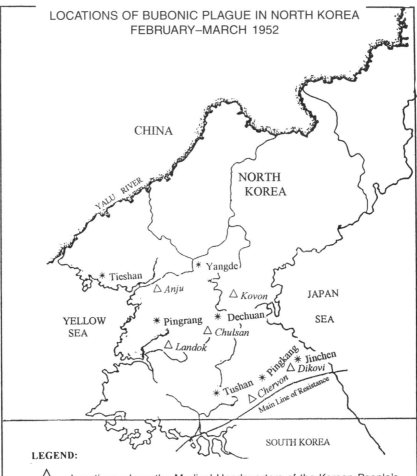

LOCATIONS OF BUBONIC PLAGUE IN NORTH KOREA
FEBRUARY–MARCH 1952

LEGEND:

△ Locations where the Medical Headquarters of the Korean People's Army reported finding fleas infected with plague bacilli (*P. pestis*) following bombing raids by U.S. aircraft during the period 11 February to 2 March 1952. *Source: Documentation on Biological Warfare,* File 50208-40, Pt. 1.1, Vol. 5919, RG 25, NAC.

✳ Places where the Chinese army diagnosed "sixteen cases of plague or something similar to plague" in the last half of March 1952. JW-1 1952, Vol. 107, Doc. 14, PLA Archives (Chinese spelling).

dred thousand Koreans living in residential areas in the war zone and within one kilometer of major transportation routes were also inoculated. Therefore, according to the official history of the Chinese Volunteer Army, "the epidemic situation was rapidly controlled." It says that in 1952, 384 Chinese soldiers in Korea were infected by the U.S. germ warfare, 258 of whom recovered.[26]

In the first week of March 1952, the New China News Agency reported a new trend: the Chinese Air Observer Corps recorded increasing enemy air intrusions over northeast China. On the ground, people began to discover insects and other vectors of bacterial warfare similar to those found at the battlefront south of the border.[27] To deal with this development, the Chinese government, on 14 March, formed a central epidemic prevention committee in Beijing, with Zhou Enlai as chair and Guo Moro, president of the Chinese Academy of Science, and Nie Rongzhen, acting chief of staff of the People's Liberation Army, as vice-chairs. The full-time office of this high-powered group included officials from the Ministry of Health, the Ministry of Public Security, and the General Staff of the Army.

A few days later, the new committee sent out a lengthy, top-secret telegram to provincial and local people's governments and to army headquarters in the coastal areas of China from the north to the far south, announcing its formation, giving anti–bacterial warfare instructions, and telling them to establish local epidemic disease prevention committees.

"Since 28 January," the telegram began, "the enemy has furiously employed continuous bacterial warfare in Korea and in our Northeast and Qingdao areas, dropping flies, mosquitoes, spiders, ants, bedbugs, fleas . . . thirty-odd species of bacteria-carrying insects. . . . They were dropped in a very wide area. . . . Examination confirms that the pathogenic microorganisms involved are plague bacillus, cholera, meningitis, paratyphoid, salmonella, relapsing fever, spirochaeta bacteria, typhus rickettsia, etc. . . . Now that the weather is turning warm, contagious disease and animal vectors will be active without restraint, and serious epidemic diseases from enemy bacterial warfare can easily occur unless we immediately intensify nationwide work on the prevention of epidemic disease." Everyone receiving this message knew immediately that there was no room for complacency or business as usual; the high-ranking cadres in the provinces and in the localities realized that they were expected to play a leading role.

The telegram signaled the disease-prevention targets in order of precedence: plague, cholera, smallpox, paratyphoid, relapsing fever, meningitis, encephalitis, and yellow fever. "After new laboratory results are obtained, adjustments [in this order] will be made." District boundaries were stipulated: Korea as an epidemic disease district; northeast China as an urgent epidemic disease-prevention district; the north, east, and central South China coastal areas were observation districts; inland areas were preparatory districts. Each district was assigned its priority task, ranging from health reconnaissance, preventive vaccinations, and preparation of hospitals to receive epidemic disease patients, to controlling communication and transportation lines and keeping watch on the maneuvers of enemy planes. All personnel entering or leaving certain critical railway and highway junctions had to have certificates of vaccination; "otherwise they must receive injections from the station's quarantine organization."

Epidemic disease prevention was to take the form of a mass movement involving all citizens: Flies, mosquitoes, fleas, lice, rats and mice, and other animal vectors were to be eliminated and burned. Water sources were to be protected, and tap water management was to be reinforced; indoor and outdoor toilet sanitation was to be maintained. Vendors and foodstuff shops were to use glass covers; people were warned not to eat raw or cold foods. Contagious patients were to be strictly quarantined; corpses of contagious patients were to be buried locally: "It is not permitted to ship them to other places; if necessary, autopsies should be performed." Evildoers were to be prevented from spreading insects or poisonous medicine on the ground; health knowledge was to be popularized. In accordance with requirements, disease-prevention pledges were to be instituted.

The committee directed all scientific institutes, universities, and colleges in the various districts to participate in anti-bacterial warfare research work. The guidelines suggested that attention be paid to such issues as investigating how the enemy was spreading bacteria (whether it was being dropped from planes, shot with artillery shells, or spread through enemy agents); finding out the time, area, insect density, and type of insect; recording in detail the damage to farm crops, and the sicknesses and deaths caused by the enemy's spread of bacteria; and preserving live insects for further study. The research experts and professors were to maintain detailed scientific records, with signatures, which were to be properly preserved. "Thus, the process of epidemic disease–prevention work will have sufficient basis, and also will give concrete proof of the enemy's crimes."[28]

With the help of the mass media, the patriotic health campaign was soon in full swing throughout the country. By the end of March 1952, the Central Epidemic Disease Prevention Committee had organized 129 epidemic prevention brigades involving 20,000 medical workers. Within two weeks, 4,850,000 people were inoculated with anti-plague vaccine in the northeast and along transportation routes in other areas.[29]

The Medical Research Group concluded that the first proven case of a U.S. germ warfare attack on northeast China took place on 12 March in Kuandian county, some twenty-five miles north of the Yalu River.[30] Kuandian is an important railway and highway junction on one of the main transportation routes between China and North Korea. Just after noon on that day, the New China News Agency reported that inhabitants of the county town saw eight American fighter planes pass over the city. The Chinese Air Observer Corps identified them as F-86 Sabrejets. Observers saw a bright cylindrical object fall from one of the planes. Immediately afterward, and during the following days, townspeople organized searches outside the East Gate, where the object appeared to have landed. They collected flies, spiders, and fowl feathers.

Nine days later, a schoolboy found fragments of a container (pieces of metal and bits of a thin, porous substance) around a shallow crater at the point of impact in the middle of a corn field.

The New China News Agency reported that the site was visited the next day by an anti-epidemic corps led by the local magistrate and by Professor Liu Zhonglo, a Ph.D. graduate of Cornell University (1926), director at the time of the Institute of Entomological Research, and professor and head of the Department of Entomology at the Peking College of Agriculture. Professor Liu had searched the neighborhood four days earlier, picking up insect samples. The team found feathers scattered around, "singly and in heaps, including yellow and white short down and black feathers; the quills of the feathers were clear of any flesh or mud; there were no remains of any fowl in the vicinity." Fifteen metres from the bomb crater there were scattered several hundred bomb fragments of different sizes, "silvery gray in colour, made of a substance like plaster."[31] Entomologists collected more flies, spiders, and feathers around the "bomb" crater "and carefully assembled as many container-fragments as possible, melting the snow with the help of hot water."[32] Biological testing revealed the insects, spiders, and feathers to be carrying the anthrax bacillus. No cases of anthrax were reported in or around the town as a result of this incident.

During this same time, up to 5 April 1952, there were four other cases involving anthrax and encephalitis, in which similar direct evidence convinced the Chinese scientists of the presence of U.S. biological weapons in attacks on targets in northeast China.[33]

The scientists also found many instances in which perceived evidence of germ warfare proved to be unfounded or was the result of panic reactions to naturally occurring events. Dr. Qin Yaoting, a distinguished scientist with six published papers on parasitology, a professor of biology at

Mukden Medical College from 1930 to 1948, and then head of the Department of Biology at National Medical College in Shenyang, received for examination seven hundred insects collected between 5 and 12 March from anti-epidemic corps in five of the industrial centers in southern Liaoning province. He analyzed and categorized them all, cultured sixty-one of them, and inoculated fifty white mice with the cultures, but he discovered no evidence of germ warfare. Most results showed ordinary colon bacillus, *kucaojun* ("bacteria causing hay fever"), and amoebic bacteria. Plague, typhoid, dysentery, and anthrax bacteria were not found. Five of the mice died within one or two days, but he had not detected the cause. "We need to continue our observations because not enough time has elapsed," he wrote in his report. "We can't yet make a definite decision or come to a conclusion about these tests."[34]

In the spring of 1952, the daily summaries from localities to the Northeast Epidemic Disease Prevention Committee reported on all kinds of diseases and on every death: 60 families in one county with measles, 16 deaths; 89 with paratyphoid in another county; 5 cases of malaria, 3 of scarlet fever, 2 of typhus; 389 in Jilin province with "blood dysentery." There were, as well, incidences of anthrax, encephalitis, and plague that were thought to be connected with the enemy's biological war.

The Liaodong Provincial Epidemic Disease Prevention Committee sent an alarming report: 38 percent of the territory was affected by the activities of enemy planes that had dropped infected insects, and "disease is spreading through the whole province." In the forty days between 6 March and 14 April, 2,000 people fell ill, of whom 140 had died. While most of the illnesses were admittedly from common epidemic diseases such as measles, whooping cough, and influenza, 589 were unidentified acute ailments. In addition, 558 domestic fowl and animals died.[35]

On more than one occasion, the Research Group of the Northeast Epidemic Disease Prevention Committee became exasperated by time wasted on panic reactions. Called to the suburbs of Shenyang, where black powder had been found, they determined it to be locally made gunpowder. Jian county reported three children with suspected cases of encephalitis; one had died. The Research Group rushed a team to investigate: the death was from tubercular meningitis, one of the others had had mumps and recovered, and the third was not sick at all, but had cried a lot one evening. A village in Dehui county reported ten children ill, of whom one had died, and a local autopsy reported a suspected case similar to encephalitis. When the Research Group arrived, it found that the autopsy on the corpse had been done several days after death, and the diagnosis was incorrect. The other children had said they were dizzy. Now, only one still had some

Table 1
Summary of Zhou Enlai's Brief Report on U.S. Germ Warfare

	April/May 1952			
ITEM	APRIL CASUALTIES		ACCUMULATED TOTALS	
	No.	Deaths	No.	Deaths
Volunteer Army in Korea				
Plague	9	2	18	8
Suspected plague	8	3	8	3
Northeast				
Encephalitis	18	6	42	20
Suspected encephalitis	40	7	43	8
Anthrax	4	4		
Paratyphoid	4	4		

Notes:
1. "Aside from these contagious diseases, others are diphtheria, dysentery and epidemic meningitis . . . not increasing from last year."
2. Other contagious disease bacteria mentioned as having been discovered by bacterial examination on, or in, various vectors are cholera, typhoid, dysentery with blood in the stool, hemorrhagic "bashite," septicemia bacteria, and "baixuezheng."
3. "Although plague and encephalitis continue to occur, they are still of a spreading nature, not yet an epidemic. Other contagious diseases are not increasing from last year. This demonstrates that our disease-prevention work has obtained results."
4. The report does not include information on North Korean military or civilian casualties from germ warfare.

Source: Liaoning Archive, Vol. 62, permanent, Telegram: "A brief report by the Central Epidemic Disease Prevention Committee on anti–germ warfare epidemic disease-prevention work situation of May."

fever. Preliminary conclusion: an ordinary cold. There were no other epidemic signs. A village doctor in Chaoyang county reported seventeen cases of cholera, two of them fatal. This proved to be a false diagnosis, but by the time the medical experts arrived, the two had been buried, so there was no autopsy. Everyone else recovered. One report sardonically noted, "Some who had been making coffins for the dead felt jittery and thought they were seriously ill, too."

"The investigations of groundless epidemic reports from Chaoyang, Jian, and Dehui," wrote Chen Yingqian, leader of the Research Group, "were a waste of time and resources. We hope that in the future we can improve on the system with timely, accurate, dependable reporting on epidemic disease conditions."[36]

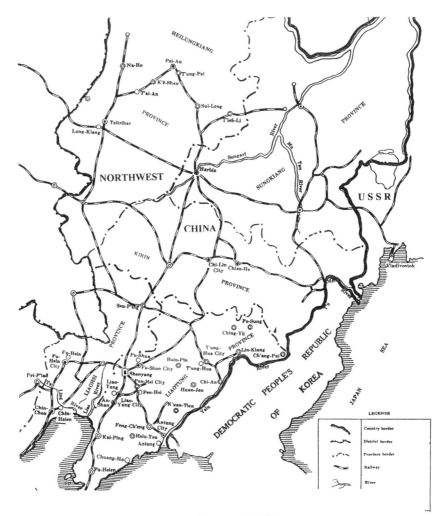

CHINESE MAP

Naming localities in Northwest China "into which United States planes intruded and disseminated insects and other objects from February 29 to March 21, 1952."

Source: Adapted from Joseph Needham et al., *Report of the International Scientific Commission for the Investigation of the Facts Concerning Bacterial Warfare in Korea and China,* 61 pp. plus 600 pp. of appendixes (Peking, 1952), Appendix Gb.

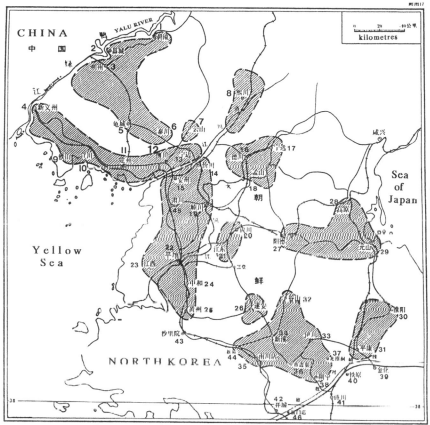

"Sketch Map of Regions on the Korean Battleground Where
American Military Forces Spread Bacteria in 1952"

Note: This map originally appeared in *Dui dijun yanjiu* [Regarding Research on
Enemy Forces], which was one volume of a still-classified series of books edited for the
General Staff of the People's Liberation Army in 1956 by Peng Dehuai and Deng Hua.
The series is titled *Kangmeijuanchao zhanzhen jingyanzhongji* [The Oppose America,
Aid Korea War: A Summing Up of Experience]. This map is "No. 17" as published in
Zhongguo renmin zhiyuanjun kangmei yuanchao zhanshi [History of the Chinese
People's Volunteer Army in the Resist America, Aid Korea War] (Beijing, 1990). English
place names and numbers added.

1. Bitong	16. Dechuan	31. Pingkang
2. Changcheng	17. Ningyuan	32. Gushan
3. Shouzhou	18. Mengshan	33. Yichuan
4. Xinyizhou	19. Shunchuan	34. Xinxi
5. Yucheng	20. Chengchuan	35. Nanchuandian
6. Qinchuan	21. Jiangdong	36. Shibianli
7. Yunshan	22. Pingrang	37. Longzhaodong
8. Xichuan	23. Jiangxi	38. Shuoning
9. Tieshan	24. Zhonghe	39. Jinhua
10. Xuanchuan	25. Huangzhou	40. Tieyuan
11. Dingchuan	26. Suian	41. Lianchuan
12. Bochuan	27. Yangde	42. Kaicheng
13. Ningbian	28. Gaoyuan	43. Shaliyuan
14. Jiachuan	29. Yuanshan	44. Xinmu
15. Anzhou	30. Huanyang	45. Suchuan
		46. Banmendian

Three months after the start of what they became convinced were U.S. biological warfare attacks, Zhou Enlai and the Central Epidemic Disease Prevention Committee calmly evaluated the situation up to May 1952: enemy planes were continuing to spread poisonous insects in Korea and in the northeast, and were expanding their experimental area to include central and south China; there had been 358 enemy sorties into Guangdong province during April. In Korea, the major problem was plague; in the northeast, encephalitis. "In particular, the cause of encephalitis and the means of contagion still have not been found." Although plague and encephalitis continued to occur, they were "still of a spreading nature, not yet causing an epidemic. Other contagious diseases have not increased from last year. This demonstrates that our disease-prevention work has obtained results."

The preventive health campaign had achieved much: the masses had caught and destroyed millions of insects and rodents. Great piles of trash had been cleared—almost 3 million tons in the northeast alone. "Some of the trash had been piled there since the warlord period, through the Japanese, Jiang [Chiang Kai-shek], and now—four dynasties. This time we cleaned it all up." The recipients of preventive inoculations included 11.4 million people vaccinated against plague and 3.5 million people given four-in-one and five-in-one vaccines.[37]

A year later, in the spring of 1953, and until the end of the war that summer, the Chinese authorities in the northeast continued to think that the U.S. Air Force was "brazenly waging bacterial war in the northeast." Every week, F-86 and F-84 jet planes, and occasionally some B-26 and B-29 bombers, were seen intruding into Chinese airspace. According to eyewitness reports, they dropped "four-part bacterial bombs" and other receptacles containing insects and spiders in feathers, balls of cotton batten, and sorghum leaves, or they spread powder compounds and insect vectors in vapor through spray tanks.[38]

Apart from respiratory anthrax and encephalitis, there was a new condition, a new source of about 100 acute deaths from January to April 1953—"a special type of pneumonia," "a congestion and swelling of the lungs," ("xiaoyuer" and "jianzi" pneumonia)—that had drawn attention since the previous year and was also thought to be closely related to American bacterial warfare. With respect to the spread and occurrence of this disease, and the question of prevention and treatment, the health authorities regretted that "because of lack of knowledge, we find it very hard to pin this down, to prevent or cure this disease."

In its review of the general state of contagious diseases in the northeast in the first part of 1953 (i.e., those not thought to be linked to germ warfare), the health authorities list measles (82,882 cases), whooping cough, diphtheria, flu, five cases of smallpox, and 100 cases of malaria—in all, 89,812 cases of contagious diseases, of which 2,662 had been fatal, a death rate of 2.96 percent. The report mentions the occurrence of plague in certain counties of Rehe and Heilongjiang provinces (the Inner Mongolia area); "plague-carrying rats have been discovered, but in this review the outbreak is not attributed to U.S. aerial activity."[39]

Mixed in routinely and matter-of-factly with basic disease data were reports from Chinese health authorities on evidence of agents, munitions, and disease that they attributed with greater or lesser assurance to bacteriological warfare. This evidence included routine reports of enemy aircraft sightings and the finding of bacteriological bombs.

One report described a plane dropping metal canisters near a railroad station which spread flies and mosquitoes over an area of 700 square meters.[40]

Another account told of an enemy plane that had strafed a passenger train, then dropped "sticky objects that resembled nasal mucus, it turned white in the snow, but turns brown on a stove and on wood; it burns when lit on fire." Specimens were sent for testing, but the documents do not include the results. A report of a sudden infestation of small black bugs (which were found to carry plague bacillus) after a passenger train had passed aroused concern about enemy agents, as did the discovery of bags filled with fleas.[41]

Several reports of the proliferation of disease-infected insects in proximity to railway stations passed without comment as to their source, including the discovery of several heaps of locusts not naturally found in the cold weather.[42]

A bag found at a bridge with "twenty-odd flies in it" was considered suspicious and sent for tests. The results are not in the documents, but nine of the twelve bridge guards came down with an undiagnosed disease.[43]

Twenty-one students of the Kainan Railway School were reported to have fallen ill with an unspecified disease on the same day as a localized spread of mosquitoes and flies, mostly along one street. No comment is made as to the source of the mosquitoes, nor as to the source of a plague that broke out around three railway stations.[44]

On 6 and 13 March 1953, two soldiers of the guard battalion at Shenyang air base were reported to have died "sudden acute deaths" from a "special kind of pneumonia and encephalitis" that were deemed suspicious.[45]

Other reports indicated a sudden infestation of flies and mosquitoes out of season. In a related report by the New China News Agency, in March 1952, a Japanese nurse at Chinchow City Hospital recognized a mosquito carrying salmonella typhus as a species of "snow mosquito" common to her home region in Japan.[46] This was presumably the "overwintering mosquito" upon which the U.S. Army Medical Corps' 406 General Medical Laboratory in Japan did extensive research before and during the Korean War period.[47]

Health authorities reported the first confirmed dropping of a bacterial feather bomb in a suburb of Kuandian. The feathers tested positive for "bacteria similar to respiratory anthrax bacillus" which were "under further research." The fifth confirmed case of bacteriological warfare in northeast China reportedly took the form of chicken feathers infected with encephalitis and myocarditis.[48]

The official health reports on epidemic disease prevention come as close as the scholar is likely to get to critical dispassionate accounts of how the Chinese authorities viewed the possibility of a U.S. biological warfare campaign. The confidential to top secret reports between internal cadre, extending to Zhou Enlai and Mao Zedong, indicate a matter-of-fact approach to facts and cases such as might be expected from the personnel of a public health system.

There is an impression that Mao and Zhou, after cautiously watching and waiting, had decided by the end of February 1952 that the U.S. forces were in fact using biological weapons. The historian of Chinese decision making in the Korean War, Colonel Qi Dexue, described what his research had unveiled:

> In the first part of February, Mao and Zhou Enlai were not convinced that there was anything, but by mid-February they were certain that cholera and plague existed in Korea. . . . The information upon which Zhou Enlai based his public statement came from Acting Chief of Staff Nie Rongzhen to Mao and Zhou on 18 February 1952. This report shows that there was an initial hesitation about the matter in the first part of February, but a firm conclusion was reached by the middle of the month. It was the 42nd Army that discovered the first batch of insects; by the middle of the month, they had found out what diseases the insects carried: plague and cholera.[49]

Once convinced, Mao instructed Zhou to create an epidemic disease–prevention organization that Zhou would head. The organization functioned with equal caution, following the routine of health professionals in patiently gathering information on disease in general, while observing any unusual patterns or explicit evidence that the enemy was waging germ warfare. Though there is little question that everyone from Mao and Zhou on down used the threat of germ warfare to whip up support and volunteers for the public health effort against epidemic disease, there also is little question that the evidence convinced those in the field and Mao and Zhou Enlai that the Americans were experimenting with biological warfare, targeting armies in the field, the population, and the communications system.

How do the Chinese who participated in the effort against bacterial warfare think and feel about it almost fifty years later? In the spring of 1952, China organized the Commission for Investigating the American Crime of Bacteriological Warfare. This large commission, one part of which went to North Korea and the other to northeast China, consisted of two sections. The first had a sociopolitical content, including journalists and representatives of trade unions, the women's and youth movements, and religious and other public bodies, while the other included more than forty Chinese scientists and specialists in various branches of medicine.[50] The first section was to visit the localities and interview witnesses, while the second was to look into the scientific aspects, checking the evidence, identifying specimens, and conducting tests and autopsies. The leaders of the commission were Madame Li Dequan, minister of health, director of the Chinese Red Cross Society, and formerly general secretary of the Young Women's Christian Association of China; and Mr. Liao Chengzhi, a leading member of the new government whose family had been closely connected with Sun Yatsen's attempt to establish the first republican form of government in China. With such prominent leaders, the commission was clearly intended to become a credible witness around which to focus public awareness.

Many members of that commission have passed away, but three scientists and a historian were located in Beijing in 1994, and were interviewed for this book. All of those interviewed have traveled freely abroad, but they have all chosen to work and live out their lives in China. What follows is a condensed account of these interviews, of what they each had to say about themselves and about their experience, and their opinions of what they still consider to have been U.S. biological warfare in 1952.[51]

Professor Qiu Weifan

Professor Qiu (W. F. Chiu), a plant pathologist, has an international reputation in his specialty: purple spot disease on soybeans. He wrote the chapter on China in volume 4 of R. G. Milne, ed., *The Plant Viruses* (New York, 1988). He studied at the University of Wisconsin from 1945 to 1948. He was interviewed at Beijing Agricultural University, a sprawling institution in the suburbs of the city, out near the Summer Palace. It took more than an hour to get there from Tiananmen by taxi.

He said, "I'm eighty-two now. I was young back then, only forty. I had come back from the U.S. in 1948 and started working at the Beijing Agricultural University in 1949, after Liberation. . . . When I was in the U.S., I already knew that they were training technicians for biological warfare. One of my colleagues, Dr. James Walker, left suddenly for secret work. They were studying to see what kind of disease on rice is the most destructive, rice blight.

"At the end of 1951, the U.S. Air Force dropped leaflet-type bombs, the kind that 'open without exploding,' which contained, among other things, plant residue—leaves, stems, roots, etc., along with insects. Different specialists worked on studying these things. Our scientists isolated bacteria from the insects and found various diseases. We made cultures of them, which are preserved.

"I isolated only the plant residue. I found fungi. I saw a parasitic fungus on soybean plants of a kind that is especially damaging to soybean production in two ways: first, it decreases production, and second, it creates a purple spot on the beans, which means you can't export the product; nobody wants to buy it. This disease would create a long-term effect. They wanted to experiment to see if they could successfully spread an epidemic of the disease.

"I was in Beijing. Then I went to Harbin for about a week; I think it was in November 1951. I didn't go to North Korea. Many other of my scientist colleagues went into the field and saw the bombs come down; the materials from the bombs were sent to me for testing. I isolated these materials in the laboratory.

"We also found bacteria infectious to human beings. In many villages there were epidemics of cholera, typhoid, and plague. Teams of physicians were sent there to help stop it. The evidence is that the U.S. Air Force dropped lots of these non-explosive bombs carrying bacterial war. I have no doubt about that, even now.

"Toward the end of 1952, several specialists, myself included, went to Eastern and Central Europe with an exhibition to display the evidence of U.S. germ warfare. We went to East Germany, Czechoslovakia, and Vienna, Austria. Three kinds of people came to this exhibit: some believed that the U.S. did it; others didn't believe it; others had doubts—why use biological warfare when they have so many other terrible weapons already? I answered their questions about the agricultural material. I know that area. I saw such specimens.

"Purple spot disease became an epidemic in some local areas. We've changed seeds so this doesn't happen much. New seeds are resistant to purple spot. But once the parasite has been introduced, the disease will surely develop."

Professor Qiu did not personally see U.S. aircraft dropping things. "I worked in the laboratory; the specimens were brought in to me."[52]

Professor Shen Qiyi

Professor Shen, also a plant pathologist, is a former president of Beijing Agricultural University. He was a deputy general secretary of the Investigation Commission in 1952 and a leading member of the China Association for the Dissemination of Scientific Knowledge.

Professor Shen said, "I am eighty-five years old. I helped to organize a group to investigate the biological warfare. I went to northeast China. The same thing occurred there as in North Korea. Professor Liu Zhonglo, an entomologist from this university, who has since passed away, was one of the most important scientists. Since the bacterial war was secret, we weren't sure what was happening, and so we went to investigate. The plant materials weren't so prevalent—there were leaves and other things difficult to identify. Professor Liu saw a container with evidence of infected insects. We cultured samples of the things that had been dropped. Professor Qiu Weifan was in the laboratory to check and confirm our findings. He found some fungi new to China—so they were likely dropped in from the air. I am not an expert on biological warfare.

"At that time the biological warfare was a unique thing, and the enemy wanted to learn about the results. We had to be careful. Eventually we helped produce a big black book with all the evidence. Premier Zhou Enlai reviewed everything carefully. Because it was an international affair, we also invited Joseph Needham and others to come. That Black Book carried their names. We submitted all our evidence to them, and they included it in their book. Joseph Needham and the other members of the International Scientific Commission condemned the U.S.

"Later Professor Qiu Weifan took a group abroad with the evidence— if memory serves, they went to East Germany, to Leipzig. That evidence was factual.

"Our work lasted about two months. We went to Shenyang (Mukden) and Andong and into the adjacent countryside. I never saw any airplanes, but we talked to local people who testified that they had seen aircraft and showed us the objects that had been dropped. Mainly there were diseases that affected people. The U.S. biological warfare cannot be denied. Even though our group collected only part of the evidence, it was enough to prove it. I would say the same thing whether I was outside China or inside the country. It was true. Of course, biological weapons were only supplementary to the other weapons that the U.S. was using; they were only part of the U.S. effort, and not the main part. After the war we did not continue the work."

Dr. Yan Renying

Dr. Yan is a graduate of Peking Union Medical College specializing in women's diseases. She went to the United States for postgraduate training at Columbia University in 1948–49 and returned to China in 1949. In 1952 she represented the China Medical Society on the commission investigating germ warfare.

In 1994, Dr. Yan was director of the Mother and Child Health Center of Beijing Medical University, an organization that had been working with the World Health Organization for the previous twelve years. Because it took some time to locate her, there was no opportunity for a meeting, so she was interviewed over the telephone.

Dr Yan went to Korea twice—once with the Chinese investigation mission, and then later with Dr. Joseph Needham. She acted as translator for Madame Li Dequan and took part in collecting samples and in interviewing people.

Dr Yan said, "The Chinese scientists who took part in our investigative work were people of high reputation and integrity. I have not a single bit of doubt about the existence of a U.S. biological warfare campaign in northeast China and Korea in 1952."

Professor Liao Gailong

Professor Liao, 76, is a research professor of history at the Chinese Academy of Social Sciences and a senior fellow at the Communist Party Research Center in Beijing. In 1994 he was completing a biography of Deng Xiaoping. Liao was appointed in 1952 to join the commission on germ warfare by the Chinese Peace Committee, where he was deputy head of the Public Education Department of the All-China Federation for Resisting America and Aiding Korea.

He said, "We left Beijing on 15 March 1952 to investigate the crimes of U.S. biological warfare. We divided into two groups, one going to Korea and the other to northeast China. I went to the northeast, where I worked with people older than me. It wasn't easy to collect the evidence to pinpoint the U.S. responsibility for diseases and plague at certain places.

People went out trying to find the bombs and other vectors. I remember well one investigation in Kuandian county in southern Liaoning province. We had with us a scientist named Liu Zhonglo, an expert on insects, an entomologist; he found a pottery container that was partly intact, oval-shaped and bigger than a basketball. There were insects in and around it laden with germs; I think it was anthrax. We talked a lot about that. We went to places along the Yalu River for about two weeks and found other evidence. I never saw a U.S. plane because they came mainly at night, when we were sleeping.

"As for the consequences of the biological warfare epidemics, it's hard to say. It did lead to epidemics, to plagues, in Korea as well. It was our judgment that the U.S. was trying to gauge the effectiveness of this type of weapon. Their efforts aroused our attention. On the Korean side of the Yalu River and on our side, we developed a system of prevention. People were vigilant, and as a result the epidemics didn't spread far. But I cannot doubt that it happened. I am still convinced that the U.S. conducted biological warfare, but not on a massive scale.

"I can't say much about casualties. We weren't really aware of how many casualties there were; we weren't concentrating on that aspect in our investigation.

"The United States has never admitted to it, and it never will until pushed down to the last nail of evidence. According to the evidence we found, we say that the germ warfare did take place, even though the casualties weren't as high as the U.S. expected them to be. Their efforts failed.

"There were two other investigations. The first was by Ives Farges of the French Socialist Party, minister of food in the coalition government in Paris. He went to Korea, and I accompanied him. That was in June. We saw U.S. planes every night. Farges interviewed a pilot who was shot down, and who admitted to having dropped germ bombs that didn't explode. Farge proposed that the man's family, lawyer, and minister be invited to come and hear what he had to say. But Zhou Enlai was cautious. He feared that the man might recant, and then we'd be in trouble. The pilot might say that he was instructed to say these things. Then later there was a delegation of international scientists, and they also affirmed the U.S. use of germ warfare.

"In August 1952 we sent a delegation to Canada, to the International Red Cross Conference at the Royal York Hotel in Toronto, to explain what was happening. At that time I met Mary and James Endicott, who had been in China that spring and had reported on the U.S. germ warfare.

"I also went with Liao Chengzhi and some others to Pyongyang to see evidence, and it was convincing. We sent filmmakers to take pictures. Zhou

Enlai looked at the rough cuts and took me along, too, to make sure that the film would be a good one, to see what the loopholes might be."

Just as no Americans who might have been involved have affirmed the use of germ warfare during the Korean War, no Chinese who were involved in opposing it have acknowledged that they were witness to anything other than the real thing.

One Allied serviceman was reported to have witnessed bacteriological warfare in Korea and to be willing to talk about it, but that trail led to a dead end.[53] Credible testimony from a former official on the Allied side in Korea comes from the permanent head of the Australian Department of External Affairs at the beginning of the Korean War, Dr. John Burton. Burton later resigned his position, at least in part over Australia's decision to become involved in the Korean War against his recommendation that it could not be won. He subsequently visited China during the war and was confronted with the claim of germ warfare. Burton has long publicly maintained that Sir Alan Watt, his successor in External Affairs, told him that the department had been informed that germ warfare was used but has been unable to substantiate his claim because "there are no documents."[54]

With this thread of testimony, supported by the recently released Chinese documentation from the Liaoning Archives and the archives of the People's Liberation Army, our trail leads to the development and planning of the U.S. bacteriological warfare program, from the early Cold War years culminating in the Korean War, to the course of that war, and to those who had the capability and the motive to use biological weapons during the Korean War.

2 World War II Origins

Those disease producing bacteria which seemed to offer
some promise were assigned to various university and private research laboratories for extensive experimentation.
—George W. Merck,
Special Consultant on Biological Warfare, 1946

Chinese and North Korean allegations of bacteriological warfare raise a question about one of the United States' most closely
guarded military secrets: its biological warfare capability during the Korean War. Did it have such a capability? The answer is to be found in a
story that began during World War II.

Early U.S. studies into the feasibility of bacteriological warfare failed
to endorse biological weapons. Especially influential in downgrading germ
warfare was a brilliant paper in 1933 by Major Leon A. Fox, chief of the
Medical Section of the U.S. Chemical Warfare Service (later called the
Chemical Corps), which argued that for the near future, problems with
delivery and with the ability of scientifically organized countries to immunize their populations would rule out biological warfare.[1] But with the
United States' entry into World War II in 1941, an alliance of military,
industrial, and political interests called for a re-evaluation.[2] In a period of
impending crisis, the call received a hearing. The immediate incentive was
reports by 1939 of Japanese and German developments in biological warfare. It was also difficult to ignore the fact that Italy, as well as the Soviet
Union, France, Great Britain, and such minor powers as Canada and Po-
land, had active biological warfare programs.

By August of 1939, the Chemical Warfare Service had concluded that
nine diseases were a possible germ war threat.[3] Two years later, on 15 July
1941, the surgeon general of the Army recommended another study, which
was conducted by Colonel James S. Simmons, a long-time advocate of a
bacteriological warfare program and a critic of the position presented by

Fox. Simmons made the most of his opportunity, marshaling the data available in the Office of the Surgeon General to make his case supporting a biological warfare program to Harvey H. Bundy, special assistant to Secretary of War Henry Stimson.

Simmons called for a study of the offensive as well as the defensive potential of germ warfare, leaving for others the decision of whether it should be used only in retaliation or also as an offensive weapon of opportunity. In addressing the ethical dilemma of the Army Medical Corps, which was caught between the Hippocratic oath and military duty, Simmons wrote, "Since the primary function of the Medical Department is to preserve life rather than to destroy it, should it be deemed advisable to develop facilities of this type of [offensive] warfare this should be accomplished through the activities of some branch of the service other than the Medical Corps."[4]

A month later, on 20 August 1941, Bundy called together leaders in U.S. military medicine, medical and scientific researchers, and military intelligence to consider Simmons's recommendations and to deal with moral concerns. Present were representatives from the Office of the Surgeon General, the Chemical Warfare Service, the National Research Council, the Committee on Medical Research of the Office of Scientific Research and Development, and G-2 (military intelligence). It did not take long for the committee to adopt Simmons's recommendation that an offensive capacity be developed for bacteriological warfare.

The moral quandary of the Medical Corps was more difficult to resolve. In recommending the development of both an offensive and a defensive capacity, the Simmons committee conceded that the Office of the Surgeon General and the Army Medical Corps could not be involved in offensive development. It put forward a hypocritical "solution" to this problem, proposing that one committee handle defensive, another offensive warfare, while noting that the two committees would "in effect be one." The committee on offensive germ warfare would be staffed by civilians— "experts . . . in fields of human and veterinary science . . . in entomology, plant pathology, toxicology and soil chemistry." Military service members would participate in meetings of this committee "but should not be members"; there would be separate reports for offensive and defensive warfare. The former would go to the Chemical Warfare Service, and the latter to the surgeons general of the Army and Navy. The Simmons report did not address the fact that the Chemical Warfare Service was the creation of the Army Medical Corps, or of its officers who were also medical doctors.[5]

The secretary of war, Henry Stimson, quickly lined up an array of distinguished scientists and academicians to direct the biological warfare program. He set the wheels in motion on 1 October 1941 when he requested that the president of the National Academy of Sciences appoint a civilian Bacteriological Warfare Committee.[6] In what appears to have been a deliberate obfuscation, the name was changed to the WBC Committee. The scientists of this committee immediately established liaison with the biological warfare programs of Great Britain and Canada.

In February 1942, the WBC Committee concluded that bacteriological warfare was feasible and recommended that all defensive and offensive possibilities be explored. Stimson passed the recommendations on to the Joint Chiefs of Staff, who responded favorably, but stated that they preferred not to be in direct control. They wanted to prevent the public's being "unduly exercised over any idea that the War Department might be contemplating the use of this weapon offensively."[7] Stimson followed up with a lengthy memo to President Roosevelt urging the vigorous and secret pursuit of a biological warfare program through a civilian agency. Roosevelt, some two weeks later, wrote Stimson that he had not had time to read the memo but was directing them to proceed.[8] Though on the record he considered bacteriological warfare repugnant, a sentiment that Stimson appeared to share,[9] Roosevelt evidently was persuaded by the weight of expert advice and concern about Japanese and German bacteriological development. The president and his secretary of war gave in to arguments of national security.

Just as the chemical industry had lobbied for an active chemical warfare policy during the interwar years, the pharmaceutical industry was conspicuous in promoting bacteriological warfare development during World War II. George W. Merck (head of the pharmaceutical giant Merck & Co.) was recruited by the Roosevelt administration to head the civilian War Research Service (WRS) Committee (successor to the Branch of War Research in Chemistry). Created in March 1942, the WRS Committee was to coordinate biological warfare work. With Merck at its head, it came to include Dr. Edwin B. Fred as its director of research and development, and the novelist John P. Marquand as its director of information and intelligence. Intelligence information on enemy bacteriological warfare development was to be provided by the Army, the Office of Naval Intelligence, the Office of Strategic Services, and the FBI. Public relations were handled in cooperation with the Bureau of Public Relations of the War Department, the Office of War Information, and the Office of Censorship. In an attempt to ensure its secrecy, the WRS was buried in the Federal Security Agency, that part of the social service infrastructure that, among other things, handled social security.[10]

The role of the WRS was to organize a program of research and development to extend the boundaries of knowledge concerning the use of pathogenic agents as a weapon of war and the means of protection against possible enemy use of these agents. Merck's committee further expanded the circle by asking the National Academy of Science for assistance. The academy appointed a National Research Committee of advisors, code-named the ABC Committee. It drew on leading medical scientists from the faculties of Yale, Columbia, Johns Hopkins, Vanderbilt, Pennsylvania, and Illinois, as well as from the Mayo Foundation, the National Research Council, and the National Academy of Sciences. There were representatives from the Army and Navy, and one representative each from the Public Health Service and the Department of Agriculture. General Simmons, who had led the fight for recognition of the importance of biological warfare from within the Chemical Warfare Service, was a liaison officer for this committee. The chair, Dr. W. Mansfield Clark, managed to represent a remarkable cross-section of the committee in those heady early days of biological warfare development and civilian cooperation. A faculty member of the Johns Hopkins University Medical School, he also was a member of the National Academy of Sciences and chairman of the Division of Chemistry and Chemical Technology of the National Research Council. As he assumed the chair, the ABC succeeded the WBC. The scientific community was in place.[11]

Having signed up the relevant public institutions to get the biological warfare program off the ground, the War Department took it back. Spurred by intelligence information in December 1943 that Germany might be considering the use of biological rocket attacks against Britain, as well as by "concrete information . . . on work carried on in the United States, the United Kingdom, and Canada that attack by biological weapons was feasible," the War Department and the president expanded the program. To that end, Roosevelt in June 1944 transferred the assignment to the War Department, working in close collaboration with the Navy Department.

George Merck's War Research Service continued to sponsor research at the universities and helped to secure scientific personnel and equipment, and the secretary of war appointed Merck as his special consultant on biological warfare. Civilian contact was further strengthened through a committee created by the National Academy of Science and the National Research Council. But the military was now fully in charge. Primary responsibility fell to the Medical Corps and its creation the Chemical Warfare Service, headed by General William Porter. A newly appointed

Biological Warfare Committee, composed of ten high-ranking officers, advised the War and Navy departments.

Begun with an initial grant of $250,000, modest by wartime standards, the biological warfare program quickly grew to be one of the largest wartime scientific projects in American history, second only to the Manhattan Project, which had created the atomic bomb. Granted top-priority status, the program employed approximately four thousand people by the end of the war.[12] The center of activity was the Special Projects Division of the Chemical Warfare Service and its new research and development center located at Camp Detrick, Maryland.

Camp Detrick was established in April 1943 when it became obvious that the Chemical Warfare Service's Edgewood Arsenal, also in Maryland, could not handle the expanded activity. By the end of that year, Detrick was well into large-scale research. In addition, a small test site was established at Horn Island, Mississippi, and work began in the summer of 1944 on a large, sophisticated operation at Granite Peak, Utah, a substation of the existing Dugway Proving Ground.

The Detrick scientists cast a wide experimental net. They studied anthrax, brucellosis (undulant fever), botulinus toxin, plague, ricin, southern blight of grains, potatoes, and sugar beets (*Sclerotium rolfoil*), late blight, late blast, brownspot of rice, plant growth inhibitors, rinderpest, glanders and melioidosis (pseudoglanders), tularemia (rabbit fever), mussel poisoning, coccidioidomycosis, rickettsia, psittacosis, neurotropic encephalitis, Newcastle disease, and fowl plague. They monitored independent studies of cholera, rinderpest, and foot-and-mouth disease, and a Canadian study of typhus. They then got involved in the project on ricin, which involved Johns Hopkins, Procter and Gamble, and the British at Suffield, Alberta. By the end of 1943, the team working with ricin had concluded that it was as deadly as botulinus and cheaper and easier to produce. Beyond these projects, other agents were investigated. (Merck reports that all potential agents were evaluated.) The first to receive concentrated attention at Detrick were anthrax and botulinus toxin. These were agents on which the British and Canadians had done a good deal of work, including extensive field tests both for the agents and for the related munitions. Also, the Chemical Warfare Service had conducted some field tests using botulinus at Horn Island.

It also was Detrick's mission to mass-produce agents for operational use. It was this consideration that helped influence General William Porter of the Chemical Warfare Service to select Dr. Ira Baldwin from the University of Wisconsin as the laboratory's first science director. Among his other credentials, Baldwin was an agricultural bacteriologist who specialized in large-scale commercial production of bacteria. Baldwin believed that some early discussions with the Chemical Warfare Service, in which he had indicated that he could produce bacteria safely and efficiently in 10,000 gallon tanks, had influenced the decision to hire him.

Detrick scientists also worked on munitions, including cooperative work with the British and Canadian programs. They worked mostly on burster type and gas expulsion bombs, but as with agents, no possible munitions were overlooked. They experimented with aerosol cloud production and with smoke bombs. They also worked with artillery munitions. At the Horn Island testing site in Mississippi, they experimented with insect vectors, including cooperative work with the Canadian program that had originated such work.

But the delivery system that had undergone the most testing and was most readily available to become an operational weapon was a British 4-pound aerosol bomblet that could be adapted to the standard 500-pound cluster bomb. Each cluster carried 106 of the bomblets. A U.S. variation was developed later which carried fourteen 30-pound bombs. The cluster was set to explode above the ground, distributing the bomblets over a considerable area in a controlled pattern.

The British did live tests with this bomb armed with anthrax on the uninhabited island of Gruinard off the coast of Scotland. The disease spread to a neighboring island, at which time Britain ended the testing; the island had to be quarantined for the next four decades. But the British tests produced the first practical biological bomb developed by the Allies, a bomb that could spread anthrax in a cloud of spores. The Canadians conducted further trials with the anthrax bomb at Suffield. Cluster bombs were later tested with a variety of fills, including botulinus toxin and tularemia, but the anthrax bomb emerged as the weapon of choice.

The Americans, British, and Canadians also worked on ointments and vaccines to protect military personnel and civilians. Technicians developed protective masks and clothing. Detrick's Special Projects Division defined its mission as large-scale studies spread across this wide range of experimentation.

But when General Porter took over the direction of research and development in bacteriological warfare from Merck and Baldwin in June 1944, he focused on anthrax. Overriding safety regulations issued by Baldwin, who had resigned, Porter expanded and sped up the project to mass-produce enough anthrax agent to fill a British order for 500,000 of the British 4-pound bombs. Thus the anthrax bomb was operational as a weapon of mass destruction when the war ended. At the time of the Normandy landings, both anthrax and botulinus toxin, to quote Detrick's Dr. H. I. Stubblefield, "could be produced in sufficient quantity for retaliatory use in a minimum time."

And what could be used in retaliation also could be used as a weapon of opportunity—the more so since the scientists at Detrick had produced effective toxoids, tested in human experiments, for the immunization of American troops against type A and B botulinus toxins, as Canadian scientists had developed immunizations for Canadian and British troops. There was sufficient quantity on hand to immunize all troops involved in the invasion.

To add to the offensive potential of biological warfare, the British invention of penicillin and its development for mass production in Canada and the United States gave the Allies an antidote for anthrax not available to the Axis powers. The Detrick scientists also were confident about their progress in immunization work for tularemia, brucellosis, and glanders. The Medical Corps and the Chemical Warfare Service may have been overly optimistic about their progress in weapons and immunization, but by the end of the war they had persuaded themselves, as well as high policy makers, that bacteriological warfare had a future, as had their counterparts in Canada and Great Britain.[13]

There is reason to believe that the United States and its allies would have used bacteriological warfare offensively had it been operational at the time of a crisis that other weapons could not have handled. The moral argument against the use of biological weapons from the disarmament talks of the interwar years faded when it became a feasible way to wage war.[14] The president who used the atomic bomb against Japan implied in a letter written in 1953 that had the war in the Pacific not ended by mid-August 1945, he would have used biological as well as chemical weapons.[15] Roosevelt and Stimson may have been reluctant, but Roosevelt approved the wartime program. And Roosevelt listened, without comment, as his closest advisors weighed the prospect of waging biological warfare against Japan's rice crop in 1944.[16] The very creation of so large a scientific program to develop a new weapon implied an intention to use it.

Reservations on the part of some military officers that chemical (and by implication biological) weapons would degrade the professional military art[17] did not extend to the Army Medical Corps and its offshoot the Chemical Warfare Service. The nature of their job was to advance the value of chemical and bacteriological agents for military use. Those medical doctors who chose to work with bacteriological agents compromised their Hippocratic oath. Many doubts probably gave way to interest. Admiral William D. Leahy and a few others remained isolated if significant voices against the use of biological warfare. Proponents of its use sought rationalization in the higher duty of the fight against Fascism. As one leading Detrick scientist retrospectively observed, "We were fighting a fire, and it seemed necessary to risk getting dirty as well as burnt. . . . We resolved the ethical question just as other equally good men resolved the same question at Oak Ridge and Hanford and Chicago and Los Alamos."[18] It is difficult to argue that any of these people expected that the fruits of their work would not be employed offensively in war, in a U.S. and Allied strategy moving toward total war.

Even with the moral reservations of men such as Admiral Leahy brushed aside, however, there remained certain constraints on the use of biological and chemical weapons. One was the lingering fear that U.S. and world opinion would morally condemn this extension of the limits of war. The burden of using chemical weapons was politically great because the United States had ratified the 1925 Geneva Protocol against chemical weapons. Its failure, along with Japan, to ratify the protocol banning biological weapons relieved the U.S. from arms-limitation obligations in that direction, but it raised nagging questions about U.S. intentions before the international community.

Another constraint was the fear of retaliation and whether the military objective necessitated taking that risk. This was not an issue with Japan by the time of the campaign against its island defenses, though it was a concern at the time of the Normandy invasion in Europe. As the war moved closer to Hiroshima, U.S. intelligence confirmed that the Japanese had the capacity for bacteriological warfare and had used it in China. There was also a flurry of speculation when the Japanese launched hundreds of balloons, many of which reached the United States, some traveling as far east as Illinois. But the U.S. government felt confident that the Japanese lacked the capacity to retaliate against American territory with their bacteriological weapons.[19]

General William Porter was eager to have chemical and biological weapons tested in battle, and he tried hard to have them introduced into the waging of World War II. Stanley P. Lovell, the scientific advisor to the Office of Strategic Services, supported his enthusiasm, and in several tight situations the military leadership contemplated taking the leap.

The first situation in which the U.S. military is known to have contemplated the use of bacteriological warfare was in the wake of General Erwin Rommel's pummeling of U.S. forces at Kasserine Pass in North

Africa in February 1943. The Americans became concerned that this victory might encourage Fascist Spain to join the Axis alliance. Lovell, together with scientists of the Canadian bacteriological warfare program, came up with a scheme in which mixtures including grains attractive to houseflies would be molded into the shape of goat dung, infected with psittacosis and tularemia bacteria, and dropped from planes throughout the country. The resultant preoccupation with disease was intended to draw attention away from interference with the U.S. war effort. Before the military command had to make a decision on what may have appeared at the time as a rather bizarre plan, Rommel was in retreat and the plan was dropped. Pertinent to the North African incident was the experimentation with disease-inoculated fly bait both in Canada and in U.S.–Canadian experiments at Horn Island.[20]

In another incident the U.S. Joint Chiefs of Staff agreed to a gas attack on Iwo Jima in the aftermath of the bloodbath in the Battle of Tarawa, only to be vetoed by President Roosevelt.[21]

By 1944, General Porter considered that advances in the development of bacteriological weapons made them more deadly than gas,[22] and he sped up the program in hope of getting into the war. His acceleration began in early 1944, when the OSS bit on faulty intelligence that Germany was planning to use germ warfare in the form of botulinus toxin to counter an invasion of Europe. It was in response to this possibility that the U.S. and Canadian bacteriological warfare programs pulled off the remarkable feat of preparing enough botulinus toxoid to immunize the invading armies. Later firm intelligence that the Germans were not planning germ warfare did not slow Porter in getting rid of Baldwin and pushing forward. He was no doubt looking ahead to the Pacific war, and perhaps he was hopeful that Churchill would give bacteriological warfare its chance in Europe.

Porter probably knew that Churchill's personal scientific advisor, Lord Cherwell, had convinced the prime minister that bacteriological warfare had potential as a superweapon at least equal to atomic warfare, and that Churchill had presented Cherwell's conclusions to the British chiefs. He may not have appreciated the fact that the British Chiefs of Staff had a close harness on Churchill in bacteriological as well as chemical warfare, and that Churchill lacked their endorsement. So when the British order for 500,000 anthrax bombs arrived in conjunction with the invasion of Europe, Porter no doubt was hopeful that the British contemplated using them.[23]

When the European opportunity failed to materialize, Porter made one last attempt to get his laboratories into the war. In the summer of

1945, shortly before the atomic bomb was dropped, he revised an old proposal. He again proposed poisoning the Japanese rice crop, no doubt hoping that Truman would be more receptive than Roosevelt. But the military chiefs, anticipating Japan's surrender, questioned the plan on the grounds that its effects would not be felt for a year, leaving the United States to feed a starving population after the surrender. Nevertheless the Air Force, with Secretary of Defense Lovett's endorsement, began work on a plan that was subsequently put aside following Japan's surrender.[24] Had the European invasion bogged down, had his competitors in the Manhattan Project not succeeded, or had Japan not surrendered by August, Porter might have had his chance. The test of intent would have to await another war.

3 The Japanese Connection

ISHII, Shiro may be wanted in China as a war criminal because of his bacteriological experiments upon Chinese and Americans as human guinea pigs.
—U.S. Military Intelligence report, 6 September 1947

The United States interrogated some twenty others who were directly connected with the actual experiments and as a result the United States alone is in full possession of all the details of this work.
—Colonel McQuail, Report on General Ishii's biological warfare experiments, 10 June 1947

Resurrecting the biological warfare program was an attractive option for U.S. military planners in the years immediately after World War II. Uncertainty about Soviet biological warfare development during the early Cold War years reinforced an argument that U.S. national security required that the World War II program be continued in order to hold the lead in this form of warfare. The relatively low cost of a bacteriological weapons system (about $60 million spent in World War II, compared to $2 billion to develop the atomic bomb) and the rapid development of biological warfare research caught the attention of political and military leaders faced with postwar budget cuts. The opinion that air-dropped biological weapons could be efficiently combined with strategic atomic bombing further encouraged their promotion. Some strategists also expressed the opinion that in the face of international pressure to limit or ban weapons of mass destruction, biological agents held considerable potential for covert, strategic and tactical operations.

The decision of the U.S. government in 1947 to grant participants in the Japanese bacteriological program immunity from war crimes prosecution in return for exclusive acquisition of the results, especially results of deadly experiments on human subjects, indicated how intent policy makers were on pursuing the possibilities of biological warfare.

U.S. leaders acknowledged among themselves that the Japanese experiments were actually war crimes deserving of punishment, and they contemplated the risks of the U.S. and international public's discovering the deal. There was a high risk that the Soviets, who had also captured some Japanese biological warfare personnel, and had overrun the smoldering remains of germ warfare facilities in Manchuria, would expose any U.S. cover-up. The Soviet government eventually put captured participants of the Japanese biological warfare program on public trial as war criminals at Khabarovsk, Siberia, not far from the Manchurian border, and called upon the United States to do the same with members of the Japanese units who had made their way back to Japan and into American hands. They were especially interested in the fate of Lieutenant General Shiro Ishii, head of Unit 731 and the driving force behind the development of Japan's biological warfare program.

Having weighed the risks, the U.S. Joint Chiefs of Staff, General Douglas MacArthur, and the Army's Chemical Warfare Service nevertheless decided that the Japanese data was so valuable as to be worth the hazard that a secret deal would be accidentally discovered.

What the U.S. wanted most was Japanese experimental evidence from the testing of agents on human subjects; there was considerable interest as well in Japanese delivery systems and field tests.[1]

In October 1945, President Truman sent Dr. Karl T. Compton, president of the Massachusetts Institute of Technology, as a presidential emissary to review Japanese scientific development, including biological warfare. By 1947 the Joint Chiefs of Staff struck a deal with Lieutenant General Ishii, placing information divulged into "intelligence channels" rather than turning it over to the War Crimes Tribunal, thus guaranteeing immunity from prosecution,[2] a clear indication that the U.S. president and Defense Department agreed with the urgency of acquiring Japanese information.

In this fashion began one of the great cover-ups in U.S. history. Despite some memoirs of Japanese ex-servicemen published in the 1950s, Sei-ichi Morimura's best-selling historical novel on the subject, *The Devil's Gluttony*, published in 1981, and—perhaps most dramatic—an hour-long television documentary about Unit 731 produced by Haruko Yoshinaga and aired by the Tokyo Broadcasting Company in 1976, the first documentary evidence of the deal became public only thirty-five years later, in 1980, through the untiring efforts of John William Powell, a much-prosecuted American journalist with a long history of inquiry into the American biological warfare program.

Powell, who was born in China in 1919, the son of a famous American editor, J. B. Powell, had served with the U.S. Office of War Information in that country during World War II. A member of the U.S. National Press Club, he continued his father's work after the latter died of maltreatment in a Japanese internment camp. The younger Powell was editor and publisher of the *China Monthly Review* in Shanghai from 1947 to 1953. When he criticized the U.S. and United Nations role in the Korean War and supported the North Korean and Chinese charges that the United States had used biological warfare, the U.S. government banned the *Review* from the American mails in 1953. With this loss of its main readership, Powell closed down the *Review* and returned home the same year. After refusing a CIA invitation to spy on China,[3] Powell was hounded by Congressional committees, kept from finding employment, and finally indicted for sedition in 1956, along with his two editorial assistants, his wife, Sylvia Campbell Powell, and assistant Julian Schuman. They faced twenty-year terms in prison for "deliberately false reporting," according to the U.S. government, about events in China, including reports on germ warfare during the Korean War. With the help of legal counsel from members of the National Lawyers Guild, the editors of the *Review* put up a strong defense, which included precise requests for secret U.S. government documents. The prosecution backed down. When John F. Kennedy replaced General Eisenhower as president in 1961, the case was dismissed at the government's request.

Years later, after the dust had settled, Powell began some research on the U.S. bacteriological warfare program. In one of those lucky accidents that sometimes befall researchers, he uncovered evidence of the U.S. deal with the Japanese biological warfare criminals by getting his hands on an exchange of memoranda involving General MacArthur; his intelligence chief, General Charles Willoughby; his legal section chief, Alva Carpenter;[4] and the State–War–Navy Department Coordinating Committee. Powell's exposure of the cover-up appeared first in the *Bulletin of Concerned Asian Scholars* and later, in abbreviated form, in the *Bulletin of the Atomic Scientists*.[5] The U.S. government continued to make denials, but two years later, Japan officially acknowledged its World War II biological warfare program, as well as the fact that General Ishii had received a large retirement pension.[6]

What the two countries had been hiding was the record of the first major biological warfare program in the world, which had begun in 1932 and included operational use of biological weapons against Chinese armies. More significantly, they were hiding a history of tests on at least ten thousand prisoners of war—mostly Chinese, but including some Russians and probably Americans, in the judgment of U.S. intelligence[7]—who were put to death after hideous experiments. Some of these experiments later came to light in all their gruesome detail: Some prisoners were given inoculations of lethal bacteria and their health was monitored; if they survived, the experiments continued until death occurred. Other prisoners were tied to stakes five meters apart in a field, then fragmentation bombs loaded with anthrax, cholera, plague bacilli, or gas gangrene were exploded by an electric current about fifty meters away; some died immediately from bomb splinters, but others lingered in severe torment while medical scientists recorded the course of their vital functions until they too expired. In these death factories in Manchuria, vivisections took place on living human beings. For purposes of secrecy, the people designated for experiments were kept in a special prison, and the medical scientists usually referred to them as "logs."[8]

The program was created under the cover of water purification units. At its heart was Unit 731, led by Shiro Ishii, a medical doctor, a Ph.D., and a career officer whose efforts had carried him to the rank of lieutenant general in the Japanese army. Ishii's ideas served the interests of the Japanese Kwantung Army in Manchuria. Intensely anti-Communist and convinced of the inevitability of war with the Soviet Union, the Kwantung leaders advocated a "strike the north" strategy. Opposing a move southward against the colonies of the western powers, the army envisioned conquests in northern China and Siberia. Its leadership accepted Ishii's arguments that biological warfare was a potential equalizer against superior Soviet numbers at the same time that it was a deterrent against what the Japanese believed was a Soviet biological warfare program. The "water purification units" in Manchuria were created by royal decree and had the personal involvement of members of the imperial family.[9]

Personal assessments of Ishii by U.S. intelligence officers prepared the way for his exoneration from war crimes. In a 1947 report they describe him as "studious, sincere, benevolent, and kind." Furthermore, they wrote, "he is pro-American and respects the mental culture and physical science of the U.S."[10]

To acquire Japan's knowledge of germ warfare, the U.S. Chemical Warfare Service, the Far East Command, the adjutant general, the Joint Chiefs of Staff, the War, State, and Justice departments, and the U.S. chief war crimes prosecutor all played a part in giving General Ishii and his accomplices a promise of immunity from prosecution. They knowingly implicated themselves in hiding the kind of activity that U.S. representatives on the other side of the world, at the Nuremberg trials in Germany, were then denouncing as crimes against humanity.[11] As for the Soviet trial of Japanese germ war criminals in Khabarovsk, where the evidence of Japanese experiments was revealed to the world in all its detail, the U.S. military, political, academic, and journalist communities managed to dismiss it at the time as a "show trial," "a lot of baloney," "a dead issue," and a stage for propaganda purposes.[12]

What did the United States get from the deal? The record—so far as it is available in U.S. archives—indicates that at least two dozen interviews were conducted with General Ishii and his scientists, interviews that were backed up by retained or reconstructed records and photographic materials. Ishii gave reports on his own work on botulism, brucellosis, gas gangrene, glanders, influenza, meningococcus, plague, smallpox, tetanus, and tularemia. Another major figure in the Japanese program, Lieutenant General Masaji Kitano, gave statements on songo (hemorrhagic fever), bubonic plague, anthrax, tick encephalitis, typhus, dysentery, and typhoid. There were also statements on undulant fever, cholera, fugu toxin, mucin, salmonella, toutsugamushi (scrub typhus), tuberculosis, and plant diseases. The Japanese, like the Americans, had investigated a wide range of agents but focused on only a few. Plague was emphasized at all facilities, and anthrax, cholera, and typhus at most. The Japanese scientists submitted more than thirty-five reports to the Americans accompanied by some 8,000 slides detailing more than 800 human tests, along with three autopsy reports on glanders, plague, and anthrax ranging from 350 to more than 800 pages.[13]

U.S. scientists, in turn, produced more than twenty reports using the material gathered from the Japanese. Returning from Japan in November 1947, Dr. Edwin V. Hill, chief of basic science at Fort Detrick, the research center for the U.S. biological warfare program, observed, "Evidence gathered in this investigation has greatly supplemented and amplified various aspects of this field."[14] Another U.S. expert described Japanese experiments with fleas as "excellent."[15] Ishii had a special enthusiasm for bubonic plague bacilli spread by fleas, and his munitions people developed the explosive porcelain bomb in part to provide an effective delivery system.[16] With such a wide range of experimentation, especially in areas of mutual concentration, the elaborate Japanese records on human testing enhanced U.S. knowledge, both to confirm speculation where combined U.S., Canadian, and British work was more advanced, and to enhance data with respect to which the Japanese were ahead of the Allies.

There also was something to be learned from Japanese munitions development. The Allied delivery systems probably were more advanced by the end of the war, but the Japanese had tested their munitions against live subjects. They passed on their work with aerosols and feathers as carriers of biological warfare agents.[17] Although a Japanese attempt to develop an anthrax bomb apparently failed, in 1944 Kitano conducted highly success-ful field tests with plague by aerial spraying. Documents declassified in the U.S. National Archives to date do not reveal what the Japanese learned from the Kwantung Army's operational use of biological warfare against the Chinese. Nor is there a record of whether Ishii fulfilled his promise to share his tactical and strategic ideas about biological warfare, including its use in cold climates. Nevertheless, there is evidence that Japanese infor-mation helped the United States to develop a biological warfare bomblet that was designed and tested after 1947.[18]

4 The Secretary of Defense and Revival of a Program

A fallacious concept has been developed that weapons can be divided into moral and immoral types.
—Stevenson Report to U.S. Secretary of Defense, 30 June 1950

An adversary which is inferior to the United States in productive capabilities may more rapidly be brought to a condition of industrial exhaustion as the number and variety of effective weapons employed in war is increased. —Ibid.

Secret maneuvering to acquire the results of Japan's work on biological weapons accompanied a postwar restoration of activity in all areas of the U.S. bacteriological warfare program. The scientific and corporate communities again signed on, public institutions mobilized anew, policy emerged, research and development heated up, strategic and tactical theory, doctrine, and plans were developed, strategic missions were assigned, and services moved to operational readiness.

Under the direction of the War Department,[1] shortly after the defeat of Japan, the Chemical Warfare Service, later the Chemical Corps, formulated a rather general plan for continuing the bacteriological warfare program. Following revisions of the plan by various interested agencies, the director of the New Developments Division of the War Department Special Staff approved it, called for its implementation, and assigned responsibility for it to the Chemical Warfare Service, with assistance from the Surgeon General in respect to medical matters.[2]

The first to test public opinion on the renewal of bacteriological warfare development was George Merck, head of the Merck pharmaceutical business empire and a major organizer of the World War II program. In 1946 the War Department declassified a summary of the report he had prepared for the department on the biological warfare capability of the

United States. The Merck Report gave a brief history of the development of the World War II program, acknowledging the existence of parallel British and Canadian programs but concealing the degree to which the United States had committed itself to an integrated program with those countries.[3] Merck argued that bacteriological weapons had great military potential, and that their presence in the world's military arsenals was a reality of life. National security, he wrote, required that the United States be prepared.

Merck probed public reaction to this extension of war by claiming that bacteriological weapons were simply another type of weapons system, with no distinct moral issues involved in their development or use. His report also advanced the argument that biological warfare work brought subsidiary benefits to humanity "in public health, agriculture, industry, and the fundamental sciences."[4] It was this message that the War Department hoped to sell to the public. But critical reaction and the growing tensions of the Cold War caused policy makers to quickly reclassify the report. It was not released again until 1974.

Behind the scenes, there was considerable movement toward resumption of the joint program involving the U.S., Canada, and Britain. On 14 June 1945, slightly more than a month after the surrender of Germany, the three nations signed a statement of intention to continue their cooperation in the development of biological warfare. The British Chiefs of Staff Committee recommended that the program be continued in a December 1945 report containing a strong endorsement of the perceived potential of bacteriological weapons over the next ten years, emphasizing their advantages in relation to the atomic bomb as weapons of mass destruction. Beyond the potential of biological warfare as a complement to atomic warfare, the British endorsed "its use in minor wars on which it was not worth using atomic bombs; or major ones in which they were being barred." The British report echoed the concern of Merck that public opinion be turned around on biological warfare: "Biological Warfare need not remain a method of warfare repugnant to the civilized world . . . ," it reasoned. "Informed guidance of the public might well result in it being regarded as very humane indeed by comparison with atom bombs."[5]

Several initiatives emerged from the Defense Department in the late 1940s, especially from its Research and Development Board, which was responsible for guiding the Chemical Corps in its work.[6] From its beginning in 1947, the board's Committee on Biological Warfare (originally referred to as Committee X) called for a strong program. It was instrumental in organizing ad hoc committees of the Defense Department, the

Noyes and Haskins committees of 1948 and 1949, and the Stevenson Committee of 1950 to reinforce support for the biological warfare program.

The timing was ripe for the Stevenson Committee, which produced a highly influential report. This committee was initiated by Dr. Karl T. Compton, the former president of the Massachusetts Institute of Technology, Truman's personal emissary to investigate the Japanese biological warfare program, and now secretary of the Research and Development Board. Acting for the defense secretary, Compton solicited Earl P. Stevenson to chair the committee. Eight months later, Stevenson briefed Secretary of Defense George Marshall on its recommendations.[7] By coincidence, the report appeared 30 June 1950, less than a week after the outbreak of the Korean War.[8]

Like the Noyes and Haskins committees and the Research and Development Board itself, the Stevenson Committee represented a regrouping of the interests that had initiated the program during World War II. Earl Stevenson was president of Arthur D. Little, Inc., a consulting firm in Cambridge, Massachusetts, that was to play a role in the development of bacteriological warfare delivery systems. Other members were Dr. Willis A. Gibbons, associate director of research and development for the U.S. Rubber Company; Arthur W. Page, former vice-president of the American Telephone and Telegraph Company; Dr. Eric G. Bell, a professor of biological chemistry at Harvard Medical School; General Jacob L. Devers, USA (Ret.); Frederick Osborn, former deputy U.S. representative to the United Nations Committee on Atomic Energy; and R. Gordon Arneson, special assistant to the undersecretary of state, and his alternate from the State Department, Joseph Chase. The committee's secretariat was drawn from the Defense Department, the Research and Development Board, the Chemical Warfare Service, and the Air Force.[9]

This committee reaffirmed the direction taken in World War II. It first of all recommended an offensive as well as defensive policy, and revocation of the interim policy of "use in retaliation only" that applied at the time to chemical warfare (and, by implication, to biological warfare). It countered any objection to biological warfare on moral grounds with an appeal to the realities of modern total war:

> A fallacious concept has been developed that weapons can be divided into moral and immoral types. . . . It is not a fact that these or other modern weapons in themselves have increased the horrors of war. From the time that wars became total struggles between peoples, wars have gone on until the suffering and losses of the people on one side or the other have been sufficient

> to produce surrender or collapse. . . . Whatever methods or weap-
> ons are used, wars between peoples are terrible wars, and if the
> people, whether from wisdom or ignorance, firmly embrace a
> cause, the ensuing war will be one of general destruction. . . .
>
> Neither the people who defend liberty nor those who would
> destroy it can limit their efforts or their weapons in the contest;
> nor, as a matter of fact, have they.[10]

It was a grim if realistic statement of the Cold War mentality of much of the U.S. leadership during the crisis years of the early fifties. The committee's words reflected a world view reinforced by the experience of a world war just ended—or, in the minds of many, just suspended.

The Stevenson Committee extended this mentality to reject efforts at the United Nations in 1948 to limit weapons of mass destruction. The committee claimed that there was no satisfactory definition, in absolute terms, of this concept. Even ancient weapon fire, it argued, if used in suitable quantity, or in accordance with a suitable plan, could effect indiscriminate damage. The basic logic of the committee was that "modern total war itself is a 'weapon of mass destruction' as applied to the economic resources or social structure of a nation." Therefore the concept of "weapons of mass destruction" did "not appear to have any practical significance and should not pervade our thinking on these or any other weapons."

As for any attempt to classify biological agents as weapons capable of mass destruction, that would have to "rest largely upon conjecture":

> No data exist which permit an authoritative assay of the lethal
> scope of these agents when disseminated in a willful manner.
> The opinion of experts is that there is no procedure which is
> certain to produce large-scale epidemics among human beings.
> The extent to which a disease may spread through a community
> or nation is largely governed by factors still unknown. The direct
> contact of an individual with the disseminated material itself ap-
> pears to be required if a reasonable degree of success in caus-
> ing an infection is to be expected. Thus, except to the extent
> that the use of crop and animal agents may result in serious
> deprivation of food supplies, the classification of biological agents
> as "weapons of mass destruction" is unwarranted.[11]

Yet despite the assertive mood of its policy recommendations for offensive biological warfare, the Stevenson Committee acknowledged that it was going beyond the public consensus. The public had not yet accepted the idea that there were no limitations on the drift to total war, and that biological weapons were just a weapons systems without moral connotations. The committee therefore called for a carefully coordinated program of public information stressing defensive activities, in order to prepare the public for "intelligent action" and to minimize the adverse opinion "at home and abroad."[12]

In advocating a capability for biological as well as chemical and radiological weapons, Stevenson's committee used the strategic argument that the United States' advantage over the Soviet Union and its allies was its superior technical knowledge and its industrial capacity to counter the enemy's superiority in manpower. Expanding on this general strategic position, the committee argued that "an adversary which is inferior to the United States in productive capabilities may more rapidly be brought to a condition of industrial exhaustion as the number and variety of effective weapons employed in war is increased."[13] Seeing biological weapons as contributing to this shift in the strategic balance to the advantage of the United States, the committee advocated their development as offensive weapons of opportunity.

The Stevenson Committee recommended an increase in funding for research and development to bring biological weapons to operational readiness as soon as possible. It gave high priority to the construction and operation of one production unit as a pilot line, to be followed by the construction of a large-scale weapons plant once the necessary data on standardized agents was available.[14] In effect the committee was recommending official sanction for a policy that would lend a sense of urgency to getting the World War II program, reduced from almost four thousand personnel to fewer than four hundred in end-of-the-war cutbacks, out of mothballs and up and running.

After considering the matter for four months, Secretary of Defense George C. Marshall approved most of the Stevenson Report on 27 October 1950, two weeks after the Chinese army entered the Korean War. As a principal architect of U.S. strategy in World War II and one of America's most prestigious soldiers, Marshall was a natural choice as secretary of state and then secretary of defense for the Cold War, particularly with the possibility of a renewed general war. The military world view expressed in the Stevenson Report was compatible with that developed partially under Marshall's leadership as army chief of staff during World War II—and, one could surmise, was written with its recipient in mind.

For political reasons, rather than strategic disagreement, Marshall rejected the committee's recommendation to change the policy of "retaliation only" that applied to chemical and by inference to biological weapons. And deferring a recommendation on radiological warfare, he made the remaining recommendations items for action, specifically assigning responsibility for coordinating the proposals on chemical and bio-logical warfare to the secretary of the Army, who already had responsibility for research, development, and procurement in these areas.[15]

The Department of Defense boosted funding for biological warfare development to $345 million for the years 1951–53, from $5.3 million for fiscal year 1950.[16] The distribution of this large increase is shown in Table 2.

Table 2
Biological Warfare

Approximate Cost Summary
Fiscal Years 1951–1952–1953

Research and development	$58,500,000
Construction	
a. R & D facilities	56,334,000
b. Testing facilities	12,859,000
c. Production facilities	87,000,000
	156,193,000
Production and procurement	131,160,000
	$345,853,000

Source: Attachment to Memorandum for the Secretary of Defense, Subject: Chemical, Biological and Radiological Warfare, Top Secret, 15 Dec. 1951, TS-A94-0125, R1 Doc. 9 (also identified as Doc. 941196, p. 170), CD 385 (General), RG 330, NA. These figures do not include operating costs, i.e., maintenance of installations, pay of military personnel, etc. For the same period, the budget for toxic chemical warfare (GB nerve gases, mustard, and phosgene gas) was $419 million.

Prior to the declassification of top secret Defense Department composite figures for the Korean War period in 1996, historians were vexed by the difficulty of determining expenditures for toxic chemical and biological warfare, which had to be gathered from various appropriation bills and other released numbers. As a result, they greatly underestimated the amount that was spent for these weapons. The conclusions of two well-known historical studies dating from 1973 and 1990 (dealing solely with aspects of research and development) are compared with the latest U.S. Defense Department figures for the same aspects in Table 3.

The biological department of the Chemical Corps more than doubled its personnel, to 885, in 1952. Forward budgetary planning called for personnel to be expanded two and a half times by 1954.[17] Equally significant

Table 3
Toxic Chemical and Biological Research and Development Funding
U.S. Department of Defense for the Korean War period

Different estimates, in millions of dollars:

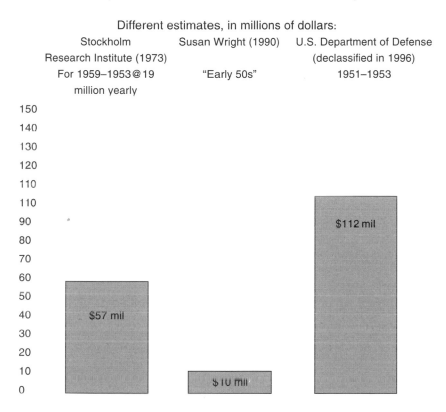

Stockholm Research Institute (1973) For 1959–1953 @ 19 million yearly	Susan Wright (1990) "Early 50s"	U.S. Department of Defense (declassified in 1996) 1951–1953
$57 mil	$10 mil	$112 mil

Sources: Stockholm International Peace Research Institute, *The Problem of Chemical and Biological Warfare,* Vol. 2 (Stockholm, 1973), pp. 204–205. Funding for 1946 to 1957 is averaged at $19 million annually; Susan Wright, "Evolution of Biological Warfare Policy: 1945–1990," in *Preventing a Biological Arms Race* (Cambridge, Mass., 1990), p. 33; Attachment to Memorandum for the Secretary of Defense, Subject: Chemical, Biological and Radiological Warfare, Top Secret, 15 Dec. 1951, TS-A94-0125, R1 Doc. 9 (also identified as Doc. 941196, p. 170), CD 385 (General) RG 330, NA: CW $53.6 million, BW $58.5 million, for a total of $112.1 million.

were the research contracts—more than two hundred by the end of 1951—with universities, colleges, medical schools, and commercial businesses to conduct research and development "on warfare phases of the biological agents, munitions and defensive program."[18]

The most striking note of urgency came from Secretary of Defense Robert Lovett at the end of December 1951, when he ordered the three services to increase their support for the recommendations of the Stevenson Committee so that "actual readiness [could] be achieved in the earliest practicable time."[19] Fifty experts in the Department of Defense worked on the preparation of this directive.[20] It called for the Joint Chiefs of Staff to provide "appropriate guidance, in emergency war plans and supporting logistics plans, for the employment of chemical and biological weapons." As a further impetus to prevent foot dragging, Lovett demanded that while

> the lack of conclusive information as to the capabilities of weapons prevents preparation of complete doctrine, concepts, and operational planning for biological warfare, both offensive and defensive . . . nevertheless, preparation of interim doctrine and plans for employment of . . . these weapons should not be held up pending their final evaluation, but rather these subjects should go forward hand-in-hand, each benefitting from and influencing the other."[21]

The Joint Chiefs of Staff responded to this order by placing biological warfare in strategic category number 1, and toxic chemical warfare in strategic category number 2, concluding that a secret first use policy for biological warfare, if militarily advantageous, could be pursued without political risk even though official doctrine for biological warfare remained undefined.[22]

The Biological Warfare Laboratories at
Camp Detrick, in Frederick, Maryland,
were established in 1943.

As chief of the U.S. Army's Chemical
Corps, Major General Egbert F. Bullene
was responsible for this top secret germ
warfare center during the Korean War
era.

SC 419068, Box 246, RG 111, NA

George W. Merck
Head of the Merck pharmaceutical corporation, a major contractor in the biological warfare program. He was special advisor on biological warfare to President Truman.
SCA, World War II, Album 211, RG 111, NA

Lt. General Shiro Ishii
Ishii headed Japan's Unit 731 in China during World War II. Members of this germ warfare unit performed horrifying experiments on Allied prisoners of war at Pingfan, northeast China. Ishii escaped punishment as a war criminal by making a secret deal with the U.S. government that provided the United States with the results of the experiments.

John W. Powell
Powell, the editor of the *China Monthly Review,* exposed the U.S.–Ishii deal in 1980.

The U.S. Navy sponsored the Stover Apparatus to research the technical aspects necessary to cause respiratory infections of Q fever and tularemia (rabbit fever) in human beings. Volunteers put their heads into this exposure chamber while an aerosol generator capsule circulated measured clouds of the bacteria. The rules for human experimentation formulated by the Nuremberg Tribunal were to "be considered individually as they arise."
File W/1497-Secret (1953), Entry 1B, Box 257, RG 175, NA

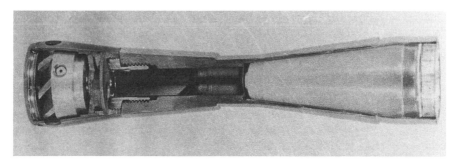

This E61 aerosol bomblet is designed to spread a cloud of anthrax spores.
File 1326-Secret (1953), Entry 1B, Box 256, RG 175, NA

Preparing to test a balloon launch of biological weapons at Dugway Proving Ground, Utah.
File 1284-Secret (1953), Entry 1B, Box 256, RG 175, NA

Brigadier General William Creasy
Commander, Chemical Corps, Research and Engineering Command
SC442969, Box 265, RG 111, NA

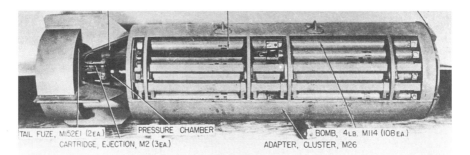

TAIL FUZE, M152E1 (2 EA)
CARTRIDGE, EJECTION, M2 (3 EA.)
PRESSURE CHAMBER
BOMB, 4 LB. M114 (108 EA.)
ADAPTER, CLUSTER, M26

CLUSTER, BIOLOGICAL BOMB, 500-LB. M33

Armed with bacteria causing brucellosis, this bomb was standardized as part of the overt biological warfare program in case of war against the Soviet Union.
File 1329-Secret (1953), Entry 1B, Box 256, RG 175, NA

South Korean civilian workers load leaflets into a 500-lb.-size leaflet bomb (M16) to be used by the Psychological Warfare Section, 1 Sept. 1952.
USAF, Korean War Series, Box 3048, RG 342, NA

The U.S. biological warfare program used the same 500-lb. "leaflet bomb" filled with feathers or other suitable materials as carriers of germ agents. When filled with feathers, it was called the E73R or M115 bomb.
File 1280-Secret (1953), Entry 1B, Box 256, RG 175, NA

New China News Agency Reporting on U.S. Bacteriological Warfare

"Germ-bomb M 105, dropped by U.S. bacteriological war criminals. The markings in English are plainly visible."
People's China, 1 Apr. 1952

"A type of bomb dropped by the U.S. invasion forces that splits into two parts when it hits the ground, releasing its load of germ-carrying insects."
NCNA

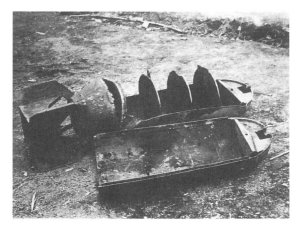

"A mass of infected flies dropped by the U.S. invasion forces. They can creep but not fly when they fall on the ground."
NCNA

"A micro-photo of one of the plague-infected fleas, *Pulex irritans* (f), dropped from the air by American aircraft in Cherwon district, Kanvon Province in February 1952."
NCNA

"Germ-laden feathers dropped in Chinese territory at Kuandian by the aggressors' planes in March 1952."
NCNA

The U.S. Way of Death A Cartoon by Chow Lu-shih from the *People's Daily*
People's China, 16 Apr. 1952

Premier Zhou Enlai
Zhou made it known in March 1952 that members of the U.S. Air Force who invaded China's territorial airspace and used germ weapons would be dealt with on capture as war criminals.

Madame Li Dequan
As minister of health, Li led a commission of inquiry to northeast China and Korea in March 1952 to collect evidence on germ warfare.

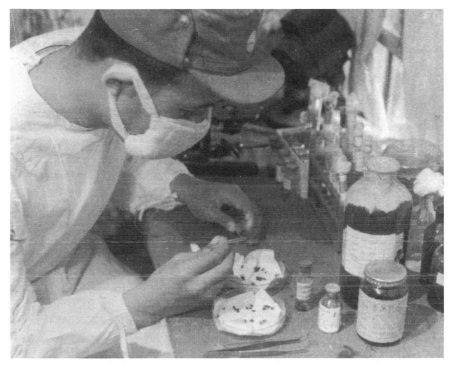

"Kim In-hwan, Medical Officer of the Korean People's Army, examines the germ-laden insects in his laboratory."
NCNA

"Germ-laden insect of the hylemya type, dropped by the American invaders in Munshon district, Kanwon Province, in February 1952."
NCNA

CAMP DETRICK

PRINCIPAL LINES OF CONTACT WITH OTHER AGENCIES IN 1949

From "Report of the Biological Department, Chemical Corps, to the panel on the program of the Committee on Biological Warfare, Research and Development Board," 1 Oct. 1949, Appendix No. 1. Records of the Chemical Corps, Dugway Proving Ground, Utah, computerized keyword index.

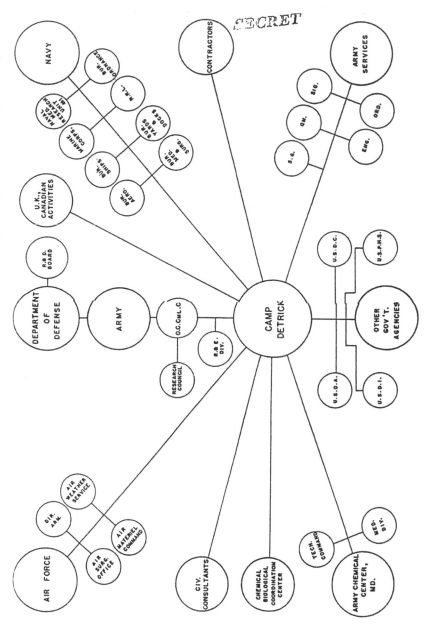

5 Research and Development, 1945–1953

Biological warfare is essentially public health and preventive medicine in reverse.
—Brigadier General William M. Creasy,
U.S. Army, January 1952

In the early Cold War years, the chief responsibility for developing the U.S. unconventional weapons program in biological and chemical warfare lay with Major General Egbert F. Bullene. He undertook this task as chief chemical officer and head of the Chemical Corps of the U.S. Army. In February 1952, General Bullene stood before a large audience at Hunter College in downtown New York City to publicize the work of his organization in the Korean War and to urge greater preparedness for using "toxic warfare." It was an attentive audience made up of the leading technicians and manufacturers of the U.S. chemical industry, many of whom already had contracts with Bullene's department.

Bullene assured his listeners that units of the Chemical Corps had arrived in Korea within two weeks of the beginning of that war, and that its strength there had been growing ever since. Napalm was proving to be "a top all-purpose weapon" in Korea; an average of 70,000 gallons were being employed each day against enemy personnel and supply lines. Flame throwers, white phosphorus bombs, and smoke bombs were also making their mark. He did not mention by name the poisonous gases that his organization had on hand—mustard, phosgene, and sarin—nor progress in the development of nerve gases, but he urged that "the present apathy about gas warfare" be rapidly overcome. He called upon everyone to dissipate the "exaggerated notions and fears of a small minority" and to "help lift the fog of ignorance" about toxicological warfare. The chemical industry had grown to "the number one spot" on the nation's industrial ladder, and in Bullene's opinion, the United States should be prepared to take full advantage of its greatest offensive weapon: "the scientific and industrial genius" embodied in its people.[1]

Also on the campaign trail was the handsome, square-jawed brigadier general William M. Creasy, head of the Research and Engineering Command of the Chemical Corps, and responsible for its biological warfare program. December 1951 found him on the campus of the nearby University of Maryland, joking to students that it was difficult "to sell a closed package." He nevertheless planned to help dispel the highly inaccurate, misleading, and sensational impression created by the large number of popular articles on biological warfare in recent years.

The possibilities of biological warfare were great, Creasy stressed, and "they are frightening only if we give way to panic or we fail to insure that we are ahead of any other nation in knowledge and preparedness." He defined biological warfare as "public health and preventive medicine in reverse," or more precisely as "the intentional use of living disease agents or their toxic products for the purpose of producing disease or death in man, animals, or crops." An advantage of this type of warfare, he commented, was that unlike blast weapons—such as the atomic bomb—it did not "destroy buildings and machines"; it was "essentially anti-personnel in nature . . . directed at man himself or his food supply." The mandate of the program in which Creasy invited his young listeners to seek a career was to study and investigate, to supervise the training of the Army, and "to develop, manufacture, procure, and supply material and equipment" for biological warfare.[2]

By now Fort Detrick (formerly Camp Detrick) contained a vast complex of buildings that housed "modern chemical, physical, pathological, plant, statistical, and bacteriological laboratories,"[3] a "cloud chamber" forty feet in diameter where munitions could be exploded and aerosols tested on animals and humans,[4] greenhouses, an animal breeding farm, machine shops, small production plants, and test grids, all protected by a high chain-link and barbed-wire fence. Also within this complex was the Special Operations Division, composed of research units responsible for paramilitary and covert biological warfare activities, with links to the Central Intelligence Agency. Apart from Fort Detrick, there were career opportunities at the weapons test site at the Dugway Proving Ground in Utah, a 250-square-mile complex containing 22 miles of surfaced roads, an airplane landing strip, living quarters, sewers, septic tanks, power plants, and electricity, steam, and water distribution systems.[5]

Creasy and Bullene were on friendly ground. The alliance that was pushing hardest to give bacteriological warfare a prominent place in post-war strategy included the Chemical Corps, the corporate, scientific, academic, and government interests who had originally helped found the program in 1942. After 1949, this coalition found a voice and representation in the Defense Department's Research and Development Board,[6] and the Chemical Corps sought the ear of the Defense Department through the board, its Committee on Biological Warfare, and its ad hoc committees. When it came Creasy's turn to brief the Stevenson Committee on the potential and readiness of biological warfare, he knew that he had a sympathetic audience.

The case presented by Creasy was carefully argued. Constricted by postwar cuts, the biological warfare program had been forced to consolidate its efforts in an attempt to develop a broad range of promising agents and munitions while conserving advanced work from the wartime program. A Navy research and development program, which was working in cooperation with the Army's Chemical Corps, complemented the work done at Fort Detrick.[7]

Although testing and production sites in the United States—at Horn Island and at Vigo, Indiana—had been closed down or placed on standby, some facilities were still available, and the United States and Britain continued to use the large Canadian testing ground in Suffield, Alberta, as well. Private medical facilities and the Brookhaven National Laboratory helped compensate for the constriction of Defense Department facilities.[8]

The Army Medical Center of the Chemical Corps began an indoctrination in biological warfare defense in 1947, with some knowledge transferable between defensive and offensive preparation. Selected officers from the services and from the reserves took basic and advanced classes.[9]

The Chemical Corps had reason to be optimistic about its deadly bacteriological warfare program as it looked to the future in the wake of its accomplishments during World War II. Its plans called for continuing studies on anthrax, botulinus toxin, brucellosis, tularemia, and "other agents." In addition, more attention was to be given to developing the potential of agents that had received only limited attention during World War II, such as dysentery, rickettsias, and viruses, and "diseases uncommon in different geographical areas." Also emphasized was a series of planned studies on insect vectors.

The projects mandated in 1949 included screening bacteria, viruses, fungi, and protozoan and helminth parasites for use as potential biological warfare agents; study of arthropods (insects and spiders) as bacteriological warfare vectors, with separate reference to a series of studies on insect vectors; and development in the laboratory of selected agents, with studies in the production and processing of selected agents. Munitions projects included the standardization of cluster bomblets; the development of aerosols, surface-contaminating munitions, guided missiles, and small arms; methods for filling bacteriological weapons; surveillance studies; and tactical and covert employment of such weapons.[10] The intensity of the research activity is reflected in the publication of more than two hundred papers and the presentation of approximately another one hundred papers by Detrick scientists working on the bacteriological warfare program in 1949, as well as by the extensive list of research contracts to universities.[11]

In February 1950, Creasy told the Stevenson Committee that the Chemical Corps could provide an offensive bacteriological capability "in case of emergency" with three months' notice. By bringing the Vigo plant on line and by using Detrick's facilities, the Chemical Corps could produce enough anti-personnel agents for the M33 cluster bomb to place an effective dosage over 90 square miles every four days. When a proposed new plant came into production within a year, this capability would increase to 500 square miles every four days.[12]

Creasy also took advantage of his appearance before the Stevenson Committee to promote the strategic, tactical, and covert applications of his biological weapons, a reminder to the services that the leaders of the Chemical Corps were soldiers as well as scientists. In a military atmosphere dominated by the concept of strategic bombing, the Creasy Report hammered home the arguments in favor of biological over atomic weapons, while diplomatically acknowledging that biological weapons were not an alternative but a complement to existing weapons systems. The report was not so diplomatic as not to exploit the controversial conclusions of the World War II strategic bombing survey, arguing that bacteriological warfare would be more effective in the areas of alleged failure, namely in the impact on enemy morale and production. Creasy also played on the comparative advantages of bacteriological warfare as a weapon that would not destroy buildings and other material infrastructures. He supported these arguments by pointing out the relative cost-effectiveness of a bacteriological warfare program. In an environment dominated by the search for inexpensive strategic solutions, it was an argument that could appeal to strategic bombing advocates who were not tied to the A-bomb as the superweapon of choice. And the message for advocates of conventional bombing was that bacteriological weapons provided a flexibility not offered by explosive and incendiary bombing. The arguments were difficult for strategic planners to ignore.[13]

In formulating his strategic outlook, Creasy inadvertently caught the sense of how biological weapons would extend the emotional impact of total warfare. While speaking of the psychological effect of bacteriological warfare, he emphasized the fear that this unknown weapon would instill, even in populations hardened to modern total war:

> There is no doubt that bacteriological warfare offers a unique psychological hazard. . . . Present knowledge of human reactions to the threat of, or actual attack with bacteriological warfare, is incomplete, but the characteristics of the weapon stimulate fear in an uninformed public. Man's dread of disease is universal. The mysteriousness and invisibility of bacteriological warfare agents, the knowledge that they strike via the simplest and most basic sources of man's security—food, drink, and the air he breathes—and a feeling of helplessness in dealing with the unknown, all add to the psychological potential. A combination of psychological effects and reduced rations would be expected to diminish a nation's will and ability to fight.[14]

Creasy tried to reach those interested in military doctrine on tactical and covert warfare as well. He emphasized botulinus toxin as "the agent of choice" for tactical operations at this time because of its lethal effect on an enemy and the ability to immunize friendly troops against it. He saw the tactical role of bacteriological warfare expanding with the development of immunization methods. The report also emphasized the potential of spraying defoliants to expose a hidden enemy.[15]

Pushed on by the Korean War, the threat of general war, and the Defense Department's endorsement of the Chemical Corps' vision, the program expanded: between October 1950 and July 1951, germ agents were ranked in an order of priority, and schedules were adopted to bring them into service. The emphasis was on anti-personnel bacteria that could spread communicable diseases. As early as February 1950, Creasy told the Defense Department that three agents had been successfully tested in field trials with the most advanced munition, the E48R2 4-pound biological bomb, and that the storage and logistical problems for making the weapons available to a theater of operations were surmountable.[16]

By October 1950, five anti-personnel and two anti-crop agents were deemed feasible and could be produced in established or proposed facilities:[17]

- *Bacillus anthracis*, code name N, which causes anthrax in people and animals. This bacteria is spread by dry spores (or in wet fill) that are almost indestructible. If it enters through the respiratory system, and if it is not treated with antibiotics, it is almost 100 percent fatal within two to three days.

• *Brucella suis*, code US, which causes undulant fever in people—an incapacitating disease with a mortality rate of 3 percent. It is mainly a disease of animals, but can cause acute and chronic illness in humans; its distribution is worldwide. Flies, mosquitoes, ticks, and other insects can be infected and transmit the disease by biting animals or people. Brucella can be inhaled, or it can enter the body through the digestive tract or through skin infections. The patient suffers from aches and pains, drenching sweats, rapid swings of temperature, and a loss of appetite, and complains of great weakness and fatigue. Severe depression, anxiety, irritability, restlessness, and apathy are typical of the illness. Since these symptoms are characteristic of other diseases, "undulant fever caused by a biological warfare attack would be difficult to diagnose." Adequate therapy did not exist, and it was difficult to prevent by immunization procedures.[18] In some cases there is "thrombosis of cerebral vessels . . . meningo-encephalitis or meningitis."[19] The most virulent of several strains of the brucella bacteria, "US," was the most advanced, and the only standardized agent fill by the end of 1950.

• *Bacterium tularense*, code UL, causes rabbit fever in people, a debilitating disease that is fatal in 5 to 10 percent of cases. It resembles plague, causing a cough, fever, aches, chest pain, and difficulty breathing. Some strains are resistant to antibiotics. The disease is a parasite of mammals and is carried by insect vectors such as ticks, deer flies, mosquitoes, fleas, and mites. It can also be contracted by breathing contaminated fine dust in aerosols.[20]

• *Bacillus (Pasteurella) pestis*, code LE, causes either bubonic or pneumonic plague in people, a lethal, moderately epidemic disease. The former is spread by rat fleas and the latter through the respiratory tract via aerosols. In the latter case the progress of the disease is rapid, with breathing distress, vomiting of blood, high temperature, and shock, followed by death in about three days.[21] The Navy laboratories had an essential role in the development of *Pasteurella pestis* as a biological warfare agent.[22]

• Botulinus toxin, code X, is a lethal toxic derivative of a bacterium that is highly effective against humans, attacking the neurological system. Blurring of vision, speech difficulty, inability to swallow, and other symptoms appear, and unless expertly treated, those heavily exposed die within a matter of hours.[23]

• Cereal rust spore is a wind-blown agent that is produced by a fungus and kills cereal crops.
• Chemical growth regulators, such as 2,4-D, stunt growth and subsequently kill specific food, oil, or fiber crops. One of the most advanced bacteriological warfare productions at the time of the Creasy Report was the plant growth regulator 2,4-D, which was widely produced commercially and could easily be diverted to military use.[24]

On 5 December 1950, the Committee on Biological Warfare issued its Guidance Report for 1951, recommending some adjustments:

> a) Postponement of work on typhus and anthrax for offensive purposes.
> b) The completion of the development for end-items of brucella melitensis and botulinus toxin.
> c) Intensification of the program for the causative agents of Q fever [*Coxiella brunetii*], tularemia [*Bacterium tularense*], and plague [*Pasteurella pestis* for pneumonic plague], so that they could be considered for end-item development.
> d) Expansion of the program for the causative agents of coccidioidomycosis and psittacosis.[25]

No anti-animal agent was as yet in the developmental stage, though at the time of the Creasy Report, rinderpest and foot-and-mouth disease were considered the most promising agents.[26]

By the summer of 1951, the Chemical Corps' biology department and the services, despite the usual frictions that accompany the development of a novel weapon, had a clear idea of where they were going with testing and production schedules for *Brucella suis, Brucella melitensis, Bacillus anthracis,* and botulinus toxin and other anti-personnel agents:

> Brucella suis and psittacosis in production by 11 September 1951; brucella melitensis was in pilot plant phases with completion expected by October; botulinus toxin was in pilot plant phase with tests nearly complete; pilot tests were complete for tularense; brunetti was in pilot plant phase with completion by September 1951; and pasteurella pestis was approaching readiness for pilot plant tests with a January 1953 completion date.[27]

These priorities and schedules were part of the long-term plan to put a standardized doctrine for bacteriological warfare in place for a general war beginning July 1954. At the same time, this process improved the emergency operational capability already available by the beginning of the Korean War.

The number of agents under development for covert operations and sabotage would add to this list. The creation of biological weapons for covert use started early, with indications of substantial results. Since covert operations are necessarily kept secret, the details are scarce. But in 1950 the Committee on Biological Warfare commended Detrick's Special Operations Division on "the originality, imagination and aggressiveness it has displayed in devising means and mechanisms for the covert dissemination of bacteriological warfare agents."[28] The capacity for covert and sabotage operations was most readily available within the existing state of research and development, and it was considered the form of bacteriological warfare most difficult for an enemy to distinguish from natural outbreaks of disease.[29] Cholera, dysentery, and typhoid were emphasized for use against people in addition to botulinus toxin. Sabotage against animals went beyond anthrax, rinderpest, and foot-and-mouth disease to include the virus causing wart hog disease, fowl plague, Newcastle disease, and fowl malaria. The latter could be spread rapidly with mosquito vectors. The small quantities needed and the consequent ease of production and concealment made biological weapons ideal for sabotage work.[30] In December 1950, the Biological Warfare Committee recommended "that the Special Operations Program be supported and actively encouraged to the fullest possible extent."[31]

The Chemical Corps focused on agents that could be disseminated from airplanes and, depending upon their nature, agents that could be loaded into bombs (either as dry powder or in liquid suspension), dusted on feathers, or dispersed in batches of infected insects, or on infected rodents or other hosts. After "a great deal of experimentation . . . with both man and experimental animals," the scientists and medical professionals of the Army Medical Corps at Fort Detrick concluded that the respiratory tract was the most effective target for the dissemination of human diseases,[32] and therefore the main focus of their work was the discovery of disease agents that could be dispersed in clouds of aerosol by suitable munitions. In elaborating for the military leadership the value of their main field-tested biological weapon—the M33 cluster containing 108 of the M114 four-pound aerosol bomblets armed with *Brucella suis*—the scientists and engineers of Fort Detrick made several points about its advantages and drawbacks.

The aerosol bomb would be most advantageous for strategic use—that is to say, against population centers, factories, complex transportation systems, and other such installations in rear areas:

• The purpose of this weapon was to debilitate and demoralize. If a factory were attacked, the scientists said, "the infection wouldn't kill [the factory worker] in all probability, but he and his fellow workers would be sick men for a considerable period. Even though driven from sickbed to the factory the production of these workers would be markedly reduced."[33]

• Coverage tests indicated "an excellent dispersion pattern on the ground." As the cluster bomb neared the earth from an initial height of 35,000 feet, it would use a "nose injection principle" to free the bomblets; they would spread out in an elliptical pattern and explode to disperse the agent over a target area 800 feet wide and half a mile long.[34]

• Effectiveness would be greatest if biological weapons were launched in conjunction with high-explosive or incendiary bombing; normal health and sanitary facilities would be disrupted, which would render the defense more difficult.[35]

• Surprise was an important consideration. All plans for a biological warfare attack would have to be "very carefully concealed" so that the enemy had no ready defense, and so that maximum psychological effects could be obtained. Surprise would be enhanced by both "the insidious nature of the attack as regards detection and the period of incubation before symptoms appear."[36]

• Bacteriological attacks would need to be conducted on a massive scale in an effort to saturate enemy medical facilities. This was especially true of initial attacks.

• Since the munitions conformed generally "to size and shape configuration of other standard munitions," they could be handled "quite readily with normal bomb handling equipment."[37]

The bombs could be dropped either from the bomb bays of bombardment aircraft or from the external attachments of fighter bombers. By August 1952, the Air Force had requisitioned 23,900 of the M33 clusters.[38]

Certain disadvantages of the aerosol bomb were also apparent:

• Because the disease agents (other than anthrax bacilli) required rather rapid handling, they were best used within thirty days from the time of manufacture and therefore would require air delivery from the production plant to the strike aircraft bases.[39]

• Tactical use near the front lines would be a problem: "high infectivity, persistency and epidemicity in an agent" were a potential hazard to advancing forces. Scouts and patrols would be endangered; infection could spread from captured enemy personnel.[40]

• The weather—wind speed and direction, gustiness, range of humidity, and other meteorological factors—would have a determining influence on the ability of a cloud of aerosol spray to hit a predetermined target.[41]

For these reasons, the Detrick scientists were cautious in their assessments of the aerosol bomb. While they believed that biological warfare could be waged successfully, they said that its effectiveness could not be evaluated until it had been used against a human population. It was not in itself a decisive weapon. It was supplementary and complementary to other forms of warfare.

Although the M33 bomb was not efficient, it gave the Air Force what it needed at the time: "Operational plans were written, logistic equipment was developed and incorporated in procedural documents. The Air Force had a continuing emergency capability with this munition."[42] In an attempt to overcome some of the deficiencies of the M33 bomb, a smaller, improved half-pound aerosol bomblet, the E61, suitable for "medium high altitude, clusterable, anti-personnel and anti-animal" action, was developed and tested in January 1951; it became part of "the new bomb family 750-pound cluster," the E133, a bomb that was suitable for external carriage by fighter-bomber aircraft and, using anthrax spores, could be filled and clustered at overseas locations.[43]

The most successful biological weapon was a surface-contaminating munition, the existing M16-A1 propaganda leaflet bomb, which had the size and shape of a 500-pound bomb. It had several shelves or compartments and was adapted as the E73RA biological feather bomb. The feather bomb employed the agent in dry form, dusted on feathers or other suitable carriers. The Committee on Biological Warfare urged "special attention" to the leaflet-type bomb "using feathers or other suitable materials as carriers of agents."[44] Feathers acted "like a sponge" and were easily windborne, so "random dissemination could be easily accomplished." The Air Force had approximately 70,000 of these M16 leaflet cluster bombs in its storage hangars by 1950. The Special Operations Division, set up for covert and sabotage work at Camp Detrick, produced the initial feather bomb for the dissemination of anti-crop agents.[45] There also is an indication that feathers were considered covert or tactical carriers capable of contaminating the "supplies and equipment" of the military supply system of enemy troops.[46]

By 1951 the Air Force was restless with the progress in munitions development, and it moved directly into weapons work. As Air Force historian Dorothy Miller notes, this made the most of the diverse if overlapping talents of the Air Force and the Chemical Corps: the former knew more about aerodynamic principles, and consequently the suitability of weapon designs for particular aircraft; the Chemical Corps knew more about agents, and it was a storehouse of technical information as well as the repository of previous experience in field testing.[47] This expansion of the research and development program in part reflected the flood of money into the program as a result of the Korean War. Nowhere was it more conspicuous than in the proliferation of contracts with businesses, public-service sectors, and universities and medical schools. The available list of participants in the Air Force's bacteriological warfare munitions development alone includes Stanford University, George Washington University, the Boeing Aircraft Corporation, Arthur D. Little, Inc., the Ralph M. Parsons Company, the General Mills Corporation, the Wenzen Research Company, the EDO Corporation, the Hayes Aircraft Corporation, East Coast Aeronautics, Inc., Aero Projects, Inc., the Aircraft Armament Corporation, the Summer Gyroscope Corporation, the Rheem Corporation, the Electro-Film Corporation, the Standard Container Company, Brown Trailer, Inc., the Steelcraft Manufacturing Company, and the Baker Raulang Company.[48] The University of Pennsylvania was engaged in munitions work under contract to the Air Force with such high priority that the project had not only its own code name, "Big Ben," but its own box in the Air Force table of organization for bacteriological warfare.[49] The Chemical Corps laboratories had let out more than two hundred research contracts, and had "enlisted many of the outstanding biological experts and facilities in educational and industrial organization."[50] By the end of 1951, bacteriological warfare was a major growth industry.

The Navy, which, according to Dorothy Miller, was deeply involved in bacteriological warfare before any other service, proportionately spent more and was the first to have an operational capability. The Navy was quick to define its operational goals, and by January 1952 had "almost completed a draft of BW–CW doctrine for the Navy and Marines."[51] Part of its munitions work was restricted to Navy needs, whereas some had broader application and was developed in cooperation with the Chemical Corps (Army) and the Air Force.[52]

The Naval Ordnance Laboratory developed a submarine-launched biological mine. It also successfully tested a portable aerosol generator.[53] This weapon was designed for covert uses and sabotage, but it had potential for tactical use as well. To quote a 1951 Defense Department report,

> The Navy in conjunction with the Army's Chemical Corps, conducted a large-scale simulated attack on the City of San Francisco [in September 1950] and demonstrated the potentialities of bacteriological warfare attack against a harbor and its installations. Navy underwater demolition teams, using a portable aerosol generator, were able to produce significant aerosols over a wide area.

Immediately following this account, the same report notes that "tests using aerosol bacteriological warfare generators showed that an airbase could be effectively contaminated," and that "secondary aerosols were created by the passage of normal vehicular traffic over a contaminated section of road."[54]

Perhaps the major Navy munitions project was to develop an all-purpose spray tank for the Marine Air Wing and for the Air Force. This was the EDO Corporation's low-altitude spray tank project. It was developed in cooperation with Stanford University and Arthur D. Little, Inc., the Cambridge consulting firm of which Earl Stevenson of the Stevenson Report was president.

The EDO tank was slow to materialize, and in the meantime the U.S. Air Force undertook its own aerosol spray tank program. The development and procurement of the tank was an urgent project.[55] There were problems, but testing indicated that spraying was feasible from up to 2,500 feet with B29, B50, and C119 aircraft. This gave the Air Force an immediate capacity with available anti-crop regulators and the future ability to attack specific broadleaf crops when suitable pathogens were developed. Other anticipated uses of the spray tank were for tactical and strategic purposes. One of the objectives was to employ it against animals and people through low-altitude spraying to contaminate "surfaces such as roads, streets, freight yards, docks, structures, stockyards, forage and crops."[56] The Air Force initiated procurement of its spray tank in October 1952, and the project was completed 1 April 1953.[57]

Another element in the U.S. program was the use of insect vectors. In view of the claim by the Chinese and North Koreans that U.S. armed forces had used insects to spread diseases, and the subsequent American disclaimers, this is an important question, requiring an investigation of whether it was theoretically and practically possible for the United States to use insect vectors to wage biological warfare in the Korean War.

The first statement to be confronted is that of Dale W. Jenkins, former chief of the entomology division at Fort Detrick. In a symposium on biological warfare sponsored by *Military Medicine* in 1963, he stated that prior to 1953 and the "false charges" being spread by the Chinese and North Koreans, "the United States had never investigated the potential of using arthropods for BW."[58] This categorical statement is demonstrably not true. A revised "Research and Development Project Listing" of the Chemical Corps, dated 30 October 1951, reveals that $160,000 was earmarked over three years for research into "arthropod dissemination" in biological warfare.[59] Another Detrick project (No. 411-02-041), a study of mosquito vectors and encephalomyelitis viruses as agents for biological warfare, conducted with Johns Hopkins University, spent $147,905 in 1951 and had a budget through 1953 of over $380,000.[60]

Detrick scientists also worked closely with the developments in the use of insect vectors of the Canadian biological warfare program, where Dr. G. B. Reed, a pioneer in this sector, remained in charge of the Defense Research Laboratory at Queen's University in Kingston, Ontario, through the Korean War era. Reed continued his World War II work on mosquito vectors; like the U.S. researchers, he was conducting extensive work on mosquito vectors and encephalomyelitis, a project in which Canadian records indicate that there was close cooperation between the two programs. Reed also continued his work on the mass production of mosquito colonies, which he was sharing with the Americans as a joint project.[61]

But Reed's research at this time extended to all biting flies, and to plague-infected rats and fleas.[62] During World War II, his Kingston laboratories had a "media unit" for infecting a variety of insect vectors (including houseflies, fruit flies, biting flies, mosquitoes, chiggers, ticks, and fleas) with tularemia, botulinus, anthrax, plague, plague combined with murine typhus, Rocky Mountain spotted fever, salmonella, and shigella dysentery. He was a pioneer in the technique of dispersing infected insect bait over targeted territory as a means of sustaining infected insect colonies. The Canadian program experimented with a 500 pound bomb that could carry 200,000 flies, using canned salmon as infected bait. It also tested the use of urea-formaldehyde cardboard containers to transmit insect vectors. After the war, the Suffield Experimental Station in Alberta continued to breed houseflies "in an extension of the insect vector program."[63]

When he resumed his work after the war, Reed turned again to the development of baits and insect bombs. By the end of 1947 he was working on two methods of dissemination. One was the use of housefly baits "containing attractants for the flies and bacteria of the typhoid-dysentery group." The baits were dropped in clusters of glass jar bombs, which shattered and left pads of the attractant for the flies. Tests showed that flies visited the baits and transferred the organism to human foods. Reed also continued to work on a World War II bomb designed to distribute masses of already infected flies. As he had done with mosquitoes, he developed a means of mass-producing flies and having them feed on cultures of bacteria.[64]

Apart from his own staff at Queen's University, who assisted him in the revived Canadian program, Reed could draw on the Defense Research Board's entomology section of seven scientists, the Suffield Experimental Station staff, and the Arctic Institute of North America, based in Montreal, which cooperated in an entomological survey of the north.[65] The Defense Research Board at the end of 1948 instructed its Entomological Research Panel to closely coordinate with its Biological Warfare Panel. This instruction was wedged between recommendations to begin a survey of the animal and plant hosts of biting flies, and a survey of the external parasites of birds and mammals in the north.

Early in 1949, elaborate plans were made for an entomological survey of the north, with special attention to a study of biting insects. The Research Board set up an infrastructure that included the Arctic Institute of North America and contract work "with foreign parties undertaking entomological research in Canada." U.S. participation included the Naval and Medical Center and the aforementioned Detrick entomologist Dr. Dale W. Jenkins. In April 1949 the United States released Jenkins, at Canada's request and Canada's expense, to work on the survey of biting insects in the Canadian North.[66]

By early December 1951, a Canadian Joint Staff member informed the chairman of the Defense Research Board that "the USAF is giving serious consideration to probable use of special weapons," and that it was looking to use Canadian test facilities at Cold Lake and Suffield. Canada offered cooperation and expanded its facilities in the spirit of the World War II joint programs. The tripartite standardization of biological weapons research between the United States, Canada, and Great Britain was back in place by 1947, and by 1949 there had been joint field trials with agents and munitions at the Suffield Experimental Station in Alberta.[67] Reed's laboratories and the Suffield station were both expanded from 1950 through 1952, though detail is lacking, and Reed's laboratories were actively involved in joint tests with the United States at Suffield by at least the summer of 1951.[68]

At the Medical Section laboratories in Fort Detrick, Dr. Jenkins conducted four projects on mosquitoes and one on chiggers between 1947 and 1951.[69] As previously established, Detrick's Medical Section coordinated its research with Detrick's Biological Laboratories, which worked on offensive biological warfare. Their nominal separation was established upon founding by the creation of two separate committees on offensive and defensive biological warfare research work, which in reality were one. In fact, the mission of the Medical Laboratories, as presented in its 1953 report, lifted the veil of discretion to state, "The overall mission of the Chemical Corps Medical Laboratories . . . is to conduct basic pathological, physiological, biochemical, neurological, and toxicological research and clinical investigation essential to maximum effectiveness in defensive and offensive chemical warfare."[70]

Biological warfare is excluded from this mission statement, but evidence from one project provides a vivid example both that chemical warfare was in fact inclusive of biological warfare, and that the Medical

Laboratories consciously did double-edged defensive and offensive work on insect vectors. The evidence comes from the description of project No. 465-20-001, "Mechanism of Entry and Action of Insecticidal Compounds and Insect Repellents":

> Application to BW: $25,000 (35% of $72,000).
>
> Information on the mechanism of action of insecticides is applicable directly to problems involved in both the offensive application of and protection against insect dissemination of biological agents. Under project 465–20-001, insect strains resistant to insecticides are being developed. These represent a potentially more effective vehicle for the offensive use in BW of insect borne pathogens. . . .
>
> Thus, particularly in the work on insecticides resistance and on factors concerned in insect behavior (i.e. response to chemical attractants, as used for example in baits for dissemination of BW agents), research under this project provides results directly in support of Project 411-04-004, which is financed entirely by Biological Laboratories.[71]

The Medical Laboratory at Fort Detrick had an entire field of research devoted to "the biological action of insecticides and rodenticides."[72] As could be expected, a major activity of the Medical Laboratories would be insect control, both against biological warfare and, more mundanely, to protect troops in infested areas. But project No. 465-20-001 on insecticides confirms the obvious, which officially was denied—namely, that related medical, agent, and munitions development work was closely coordinated.[73] Project No. 465-20-001 also confirms for the first time that the U.S. was following up on or cooperating with the Canadian work on insect baits in biological warfare. The description of the U.S. project on dissemination of biological warfare agents by arthropods is not included in the many project descriptions among more than a thousand pages of declassified materials released to us by the Chemical Corps from its Dugway Proving Ground records center.

Until very recent declassification, U.S. and Canadian work on insect vectors, in the spirit of Jenkins's denial in the early 1960s, had been carefully concealed. And still we have only glimpses. For instance, we have no context for a February 1949 classified supplement to a monthly newsletter distributed to all Chemical Corps officers of the Far East Command indicating that the "Research and Development Board is expected to advocate the spread of plague by lice," and that the budget for this program in 1949 was expected to be twice that for the previous year.[74] We have the record of Canadian work, and we know that Dr. Theodor Rosebury, who became the technical director of the Research and Development Department at Fort Detrick, was interested in spreading plague by lice, as well as by other means.

Rosebury, who later resigned his post and introduced a rare moral note by calling upon scientists to weigh the consequences of their work, was an early advocate of insect vector work. In 1947, while at Fort Detrick, he and his co-author, Elvin A. Kabat, published a lengthy report they had written in 1942 in an advisory capacity, just prior to signing on with Detrick. They rated insect vectors highly. They considered lice and fleas the most promising vectors for disseminating bubonic plague, emphasizing that success would be limited to "relatively few areas on earth where plague conditions are present but plague itself is absent." Indicating that they were aware of rumors of Japanese work, they noted, "The Japanese may have selected such areas in China for their alleged attempt to disseminate infected fleas." Rosebury's lengthy and detailed report went on to recommend mosquito and tick vectors for several agents. Tularemia was singled out as being transmissible by a wide range of vectors, and bacillary dysentery could be spread by flies.

For munitions, Rosebury and his co-author recommended "pasteboard or other light containers," consistent with the means of delivery reported by the North Koreans and Chinese. We have little record of how this work was followed up at Fort Detrick from 1942 to 1946. That it was is indicated by Rosebury and Kabat's comment that "certain portions of the paper are outdated by developments of recent years," and that "technical developments discussed as possibilities of this paper have already become realities."[75]

We know that Ishii's Japanese program had done extensive work with fleas and lice as carriers of plague, as well as with porcelain bombs to disseminate them; that the U.S. military evaluated this work as excellent; and that they integrated Japanese research and development into their own program.[76] The shadowy pictures of research and development in insect vectors at Fort Detrick are complemented by the Army Medical Corps' extensive knowledge of insect vectors and rodent hosts for disease from research in the Medical Section of the Far East Command.

There is little doubt that the Chemical Corps used every facility at its disposal by the autumn of 1951. With the assignment of a priority rating of "A" to both agent development and dissemination, the Research and Development Board turned on the pressure. By late October 1951, the Chemical Corps indicated that it was making optimum use of Defense Department facilities, as well as contracted laboratories and personnel, to implement the expanded program of projects for 1951–53.[77] Among these facilities was the extended use of military and civilian medical and biological laboratories called for by the Special Projects Division as part of the first policy initiative of the postwar bacteriological warfare program in 1945.[78] The best facility for the expansion of research work in insect vectors was the 406 Medical General Laboratory of the Medical Section of the Far East Command in Japan, which is the subject of a later chapter.

The Joint Strategic Plans Committee of the Pentagon summed up the position of research and development by August 1953, saying that the usefulness of biological warfare had received the "attention of many of the best scientific minds in the United States" and had been "the subject of applied research with the attendant expenditure of considerable sums of money."[79] The effort from 1951 to 1953 had cost almost $350 million.

Driving this enormous expenditure was a crash program by the U.S. Air Force in 1952 to incorporate the capability for germ warfare into military missions and plans.

6 Plans and Missions, 1945–1953

Bacteriological warfare had a strong emotional appeal. It was new. It seemed to offer fabulous possibilities.
—Dorothy L. Miller, U.S. Air Force Historian, 1957

By at least 1949, the U.S. Joint Chiefs of Staff and their military services had built a capability for bacteriological warfare into emergency operations plans[1] for a general war with the Soviet Union. With the threat of war surrounding the Berlin Blockade in 1948, preparations had been made for ready implementation. These plans were so secret that they were presented orally to Secretary of Defense James V. Forrestal and Secretary of State George Marshall. The Joint Chiefs of Staff recommended that in the interests of secrecy, the National Security Council be bypassed in favor of agreement on implementation reached directly through the secretary of state.

The issue of who should be consulted on the bacteriological warfare cover and deception plan surfaced again in early 1952, when the Joint Chiefs of Staff discussed whether the secretary of state should be notified prior to implementation; it was decided that only the secretary of defense would be consulted. In light of the 1949 decision to communicate orally, one is left to speculate on whether the 1952 decision meant what it said, or whether this was a discussion of who was to be informed on paper and who was to be informed only orally to protect one or both of the secretaries under the "plausible denial" doctrine.[2]

By 1950 the U.S. Air Force was developing a "BW Annex to the USAF Intermediate Range War Plans." It provided a phased plan for a general war beginning 1 July 1954, the same date that the Joint Chiefs of Staff would select shortly thereafter as the time for bacteriological warfare readiness—a forward revision from the original target of 1956 or 1957.

Phase I of the plan called for the Strategic Air Command to carry, in the same aircraft, bacteriological clusters and atomic bombs. Phase II would continue to combine biological and atomic strikes at enemy defenses and military and industrial personnel. Phase III and succeeding phases would combine the Strategic Air Command, the U.S. Air Force Europe, and the Far East Air Force in separate bacteriological strikes, with the pace determined by the availability of suitable targets and "the exigencies of the situation."[3] An indication of what the Air Force intended to do in China if the Korean War escalated is contained in a telegram of 3 July 1951 from the Air Force vice chief of staff, General Nathan Twining, to General Weyland, commander of the Far East Air Force: "I would like your assurance that you have plans to attack priority strategic targets and airdromes in Manchuria, the Shantung Peninsula, and North China to be implemented when necessary."[4]

There also was a specific targeting of Chinese crops with a schedule of readiness as part of a general biological warfare campaign against Soviet and Chinese food resources. The plan in preparation for the USSR, code-named STEELYARD, was aimed at the Soviet winter wheat crop, and had available the adapted leaflet bomb standardized as the M16 biological bomb. And though no code name is available for the plan against China, it is noted that "the Target Folders should contain the same types of detailed material as . . . for Project 'STEELYARD.'"[5]

In addition, there was a biological and chemical warfare tactical plan against the Soviet armies slated for phased implementation, combining the standardized M33/M144 munition with *Brucella suis* while waiting for a more lethal agent to be standardized. *Brucella suis* was to be combined with nerve gas, which, it is noted, was acquired from the Germans after World War II. This plan appears to have grown out of the emergency plan to use bacteriological weapons if the crisis surrounding the Berlin Blockade escalated to general war, and it was rapidly accelerated, as the plan notes, by General Twining in January 1952.

The tactical plan included the medium bomb wing of the Strategic Air Command in England, and the light bomb wing and four fighter bomber wings on the Continent. It provided unit assignments, with associated supply organizations, to defeat the Soviet armies in detail. The only specifics in available documents at the time of writing are that the medium bomb wing stationed in England would use 52 percent of its sorties to carry *Brucella suis* and 48 percent to carry nerve gas. The planners estimated that the operation would inflict 30 percent random casualties to approximately half the seventy divisions expected in a Soviet offensive, sufficient to render these divisions ineffective.

The tactical plan held priority over the strategic plan because of the limited amount and suitability of standardized munitions, and because the first priority was to hold Soviet field forces. The schedule of implementation called for all Tactical Air Command bomber and fighter bomber wings (including the F-86 Sabrejet in its capacity as a fighter bomber) to be trained and equipped for bacteriological and chemical warfare by 1 January 1953. That these unconventional weapons could be adapted to meet an immediate emergency was indicated by the plan to use bacteriological weapons if the Berlin Blockade escalated into general war.

Documents currently available do not reveal tactical plans for biological warfare in the Far East, but it is noted that the European theatre plan was to be a guide for all operational plans, and its schedule of implementation was extended to the entire Tactical Air Command.[6]

Despite Air Force criticism and the prod from Secretary of Defense Lovett in December 1951 to move more quickly to operational readiness, the Joint Chiefs of Staff had actually been busy. The tone of their response to Lovett's push was predictably cautious in stating that they could not be held responsible for any failure arising from a crash program in biological warfare. At the same time, they indicated that they would do what was possible to accelerate readiness.[7]

Long before the Lovett memo, the Joint Strategic Plans Committee of the Joint Chiefs of Staff had signaled for increased activity in bacteriological warfare. Responding to the Korean War and to the Stevenson Committee, but also to its own vision, it called in February 1951 for further development of bacteriological warfare readiness with respect to "strategic, operational and emergency plans," and for "the development to the extent feasible of doctrine, including tactics and techniques, for the employment of chemical and biological warfare."[8]

There was no more enthusiastic endorsement of the potential of biological warfare than a September 1951 memorandum from its Joint Advanced Study Committee to the Joint Chiefs of Staff. The Chiefs of Staff accepted its recommendations with only minor changes on 26 February 1952.[9] The language of the memorandum is even stronger than that in the Creasy and Stevenson reports, reinforcing the early inclination among the U.S. elite to see bacteriological weapons as potential super-weapons that required rapid development in a period of crisis.

The memorandum followed the logic of the preceding reports in dismissing moral arguments and advocating an offensive strategy because the Soviets would do likewise. Although intelligence information on the Soviets' capacity for biological warfare was acknowledged to be fuzzy at best, the United States acted on the presumption that such a capacity existed and was built into the Soviet operational plans.[10] The memorandum emphasized the critical need for "large-scale realistic trials under warlike conditions."[11] It concluded that bacteriological weapons were more flexible and could inflict more casualties with less tonnage than conventional high explosives or chemical and atomic weapons. The recommendations came close to an argument for bacteriological warfare as a complete weapons system, though the committee pulled back to conclude that it should be considered a complement to other weapons, detailing the ways that it could assist atomic warfare in particular.[12]

The memorandum endorsed the covert potential of bacteriological warfare, and made specific recommendations on tactical use that were conspicuous for their pertinence to the Korean War. It outlined the tactical potential of biological weapons for isolating the battlefield, for weakening the morale of enemy troops in the battle area, and for interdiction "when enemy troops are in assembly and concentration areas or on the move to the front over limited, congested road nets." It recommended the use of such weapons "in a stabilized tactical situation" as a means of attrition against buildup, to make assembly areas uninhabitable, and to soften up the enemy prior to an offensive. It also stressed the value of bacteriological warfare in fluid tactical situations where friendly troops could be immunized, or where agents were laid down in advance of operations.[13]

The recommendations and their adoption coincided with an easing of security restrictions on bacteriological warfare information within the services. Heavy secrecy regulations had hampered indoctrination of personnel and discouraged the endorsement of bacteriological warfare as a favorable career move for young officers. The lack of an indoctrinated officer corps, in turn, had made it difficult to coordinate operational plans with research and development.[14]

Even before the Joint Chiefs of Staff adopted the strategic planning memorandum in February 1952, General Twining, the person directly responsible for operational planning for bacteriological warfare, set up an organizational structure to coordinate the Air Force program. Responding to an inspector general's report in April 1951 criticizing the Air Force bacteriological warfare program for a lack of specific programs and a central coordinating agency, Twining established a special division in the Office of Atomic Energy at Air Force headquarters to organize and manage the bacteriological and chemical warfare programs. He directed that bacteriological and chemical warfare should have the same priority with the same principles, concepts, and operational procedures, as the atomic energy program.[15]

His structure in place, Twining turned to making an operational plan, which became known as the "Twining Directive" of 15 January 1952. It was a phased plan to achieve full operational readiness in bacteriological warfare by 1 July 1954. In what may have been a revision of the May 1950

"BW Annex to the USAF Intermediate Range War Plans," the first phase, to be completed by 31 December 1952, called for one wing of Strategic Air Command medium bombers to be operational with specific standardized anti-personnel, anti-crop, and anti-animal agents and munitions. Three wings of medium bombers were to be added by December 1953, with additional standardized agents and munitions. All Strategic Air Command units were to be operational by 31 December 1954. This directive was amended, at a date not revealed, to include all Tactical Air Command and Far East Air Force units.[16]

The official history of Air Force participation in the biological weapons program notes that the first indication of an *actual* bacteriological warfare capability within this plan came much earlier, when the "USAF Operating Program for Special Weapons," published in March 1952, assigned a specific capacity to Air Force units.[17]

The operational plan included tactical targets in support of ground forces. Bacteriological warfare bombs were initially designed to be dropped from the bomb bays of bomber aircraft, but at an unspecified date they were adapted for external carriage by fighter bombers for close tactical work. The fact that this decision was made while awaiting fighter bomber adaptation for external carriage indicates that it was made early in the Korean War.[18] This extension of tactical readiness for bacteriological warfare was clearly related to Joint Chiefs of Staff specifications in early 1951 "that a real requirement existed for agents for tactical employment, and . . . high priority should be given to the development of such agents."[19]

Responsibility for developing logistical support for the employment of bacteriological weapons fell to the Air Materiel Command (AMC), with headquarters at Wright Patterson Air Force Base in Ohio. The Air Materiel Command's initial guidance was based on the relatively simple concept that munitions would be stored in the continental United States, to be filled and airlifted where needed. This plan assumed only a strategic role for bacteriological warfare, and called for a limited number of bombs per target. The M33/*Brucella suis* combination was developed and standardized within these assumptions.

But by 1951, research indicated that the efficiency of what they had on the shelf was not living up to expectations. Tests suggested that it would require 17,000 of the M33 bombs to cover thirty target areas consisting of thirty square miles each. Such an assignment would require 1,221 C54 transport aircraft or equivalents! The Twining Directive required the Air Materiel Command to come up with a better plan to address this problem and to meet the deadline for a full operational capacity for bacteriological warfare by 1 July 1954. The plan, "AMC Operational Plan 13-53," was to be revised each year in response to improved munitions. There were problems, but emergency logistical plans appear to have been in place no later than April 1952.[20]

The logistical plan (AMC Operational Plan 13-53) considered several options. The most efficient options from a logistical point of view were to store munitions overseas, to be filled when necessary, and either to produce and store the agent fills overseas or to transport them overseas when needed. But the relatively short shelf life of *Brucella suis* reduced the attraction of overseas storage, as did the political problems of permission and international public opinion if storage became known. The option apparently chosen was to make the best of the possibilities of moving assembled agent/munition combinations assembled on a crash basis from the United States overseas. The records available refer only to an early logistical plan for the standardized *Brucella suis*/M33 combination.

This plan was built around the development of a refrigerated trailer that could preserve the agent during shipment, and a mobile surveillance laboratory that could monitor the potency of the agents. Within this technical capacity, the plan called for emergency implementation after the president authorized the use of bacteriological warfare in combat.

Dorothy Miller's official history notes that the plan was in place before the equipment was available. The refrigerated trailers were not delivered until August 1952, and the laboratory was still being built. However, Miller draws a distinction between fully operational and immediately operational plans. She notes that normal "availability" means that the equipment has been standardized, catalogued, stock numbered, and given to a prime air materiel command. This support equipment was not available in that sense. But, she says, "the operational plan could have been used if necessary."[21] The Air Materiel Command's plan provided a means to move limited quantities of biological agents for covert or experimental use, as did the original plan for direct movement of loaded munitions. The Air Force also developed an elaborate organization to implement operational plans for bacteriological warfare, complete with a covert air arm, but this story is more suitably deferred to a separate chapter concerned with participants in the program during the Korean War.

In late summer 1953, the famous Twining Directive and crash program fell victim to its critics. Enthusiasm for the bacteriological warfare program abruptly turned to caution and skepticism as the Korean War ground to its conclusion and the threat of general war eased. The program had its critics from the beginning, especially from the atomic weapons enthusiasts, and heavy-handed implementation by General Twining and his staff won few converts. The types of complaints that began to circulate within military organizations are reflected in Dorothy Miller's appraisal. Those working on the program, she writes, came to feel that the directive "had been rammed down their throats" in an "emotional atmosphere" that did not allow for calm appraisal of the potential of biological warfare. It had tried to put biological weapons "into the operating commands before their development was far enough along to assure reasonable success." The biological warfare division at U.S. Air Force Headquarters in Washington, D.C., had been "overly zealous in directing its implementation."[22]

Specific complaints were that the M33 biological cluster bomb had been "extremely disappointing" to the Air Force, requiring too much logistical support. Realistic "operational planning" was impossible because planners had insufficient testing data to know how many people the bomb could kill or incapacitate. As a result, the Air Force intelligence section had been "unable to determine potential target areas," and "almost nothing" was known of the effects that biological attacks would have on an enemy's economy. Coordination between the developing, logistics, and using agencies had "left much to be desired." This was normal griping in response to the friction of putting a new weapons system in place in time of crisis.

There was some reappraisal of the schedule for all tactical units to be operational by early 1953. A guidance report of 9 January 1953, while retaining the existing emphasis on biological weapons for strategic targets, deemphasized their tactical use in the emergency war plan. Current chemical weapons were proving to be quicker-acting against concentrations of battlefield troops, the dominant concern of European strategy. Biological weapons were, however, retained for "other targets where immediacy of effect was not paramount."[23]

But as Dorothy Miller notes, amid this friction related to getting biological weapons developed and in place, the crash program achieved, in a remarkably short time, what was requested—an emergency capability at a time of crisis:

> The pressure of world unrest called for positive action; the services could not indulge in watchful waiting for something to turn up. Even those who later were to criticize the aggressive policies of the program's leadership would not have been entirely satisfied with policies that were largely negative.
>
> Moreover, the over-optimism was not limited to any one individual or group of individuals. Bacteriological warfare had a strong emotional appeal. It was new. It seemed to offer fabulous possibilities. . . . The Air Force learned the hard way that enthusiasm

could not replace the need for cold calculation. . . . However, by early 1953 it was painfully clear that the entire biological warfare program needed an overhauling.[24]

In response to an inquiry from the new secretary of defense, Charles Wilson, concerning the lack of activity in the biological warfare program, the Joint Strategic Plans Committee, in a long appraisal dated 31 August 1953, signed off the crash program. Six weeks after the end of the Korean War, the chairman of the Joint Chiefs of Staff, Admiral Arthur Radford, endorsed that decision. In a still partly sanitized letter to the secretary of defense, Radford wrote that "the events of the past two years" had demonstrated that the "BW program has suffered from over-optimism and consequent attempts to get a job done quickly."[25] In spite of all their efforts, the U.S. Air Force informed Canadian and British colleagues in September 1952 that they had as yet been unable to achieve a "highly lethal, stable, viable, easily disseminated, low cost, epidemic-producing, BW agent."[26]

Nowhere in the documents pertaining to the change of direction is there any acknowledgment that the crash program was a response to the threat that the Korean War would expand to general war. By contrast, Radford applauded a similar leap of faith in the nerve gas program. This may reflect a feeling on his and others' part that jumping on the nerve gas bandwagon would provide the quickest return, whereas biological weapons were still under tactical development. There is a sense that by mid-1953, disappointment with the admittedly forced results of the biological warfare crash program, reduced world tensions, and a changing of the political and military guard in the United States gave the upper hand to advocates of other weapons systems. But while eased international political tensions allowed more measured development, the biological warfare program was continued and its emergency capability kept in place. As the report of the Joint Strategic Plans Committee summed it up, "Action entails the assumption of an acceptable risk of delay in achieving BW readiness. . . . The most promising BW agent–munition combinations . . . are expected to be developed by 1956." But within this redirection, the services were to maintain "the existing capability in the operational use of biological agents."[27]

7 Korea: A Limited War?

We burned down just about every city in North and South Korea both. . . . We killed over a million Koreans and drove several million more from their homes"[1]
—U.S. General Curtis LeMay in 1965

The Korean War of 1950–53 has often been described as the classic example of a limited war. Even though all the great powers of the world were directly or indirectly involved, it is true that the fighting was mainly confined to the Korean peninsula; the United States did not openly violate the Manchurian sanctuary, nor did China make hostile moves against U.S. bases in Japan or even against the crowded port of Pusan in South Korea. It is true as well that both sides came to focus on restoring the status quo that had existed before the war. It is also a fact that the most destructive munitions known to history—atomic weapons—were not used in this war. There were some limits.

And yet Korea was pulverized. It is not easy to find words to describe the carnage. In a territory smaller than the state of Oregon, two and a half million combatants fought on the battle lines for three seemingly endless years; shells and bombs rained down in unmerciful torrents from naval vessels along the coasts and from aircraft overhead, setting new records for destruction.

When the U.S. Army was in retreat in North Korea in the autumn of 1950, General Douglas MacArthur ordered his air force to destroy "every means of communication, every installation, factory, city and village" from the Yalu River south to the battle line.[2] Mass fire raids using napalm left scorched cities and smoking ruins. This "limited war" became, in reality, another total war.

As it had been in World War II, strategic bombing was extended to the mass destruction of civilian populations; and as in World War II, the reservations that the United States had had about the saturation bombing of Europeans in that earlier war were not extended to Asians. In the ambiguity between wanton destruction and legitimate military objectives raised by the Nuremberg Charter of 1945, American military culture accepted the World War II standpoint that the mass destruction of civilians was a legitimate military target in an expanded war of attrition.[3]

The question is, Why was it that, in this small corner of northeast Asia, a conflict so often described as "limited'" became a fearsome war of massive destruction?

Korea is a country with a rich culture and a long history. More than two thousand years ago, even longer according to ancient legends, the forebears of the Korean people settled there and united into a distinct group with their own physical and cultural attributes, their own language and traditions. Through various invasions and temporary occupations from China over the centuries, the Koreans came to adopt Confucian principles for governing their country. Buddhism was also assimilated from the Chinese, resulting in the construction of many temples and monasteries, while scholars and artisans created an abundant literature and folk art.

The land is generally mountainous in the north and along the east coast, while the western and southern parts of the country contain rolling hills and valleys suited to farming. Like the rest of eastern Asia, Korea developed rice-growing techniques, creating an economy that was able to support a large population. By the middle of the twentieth century, the population was 29 million.

The Koreans were one people, not two. As U.S. scholar George McCune has written of the growth and indivisible unity of the Korean people, "The long historical continuity, during which Korean cultural and social patterns became firmly fixed, has left a unique heritage to the Koreans. They became a nation of one race, one language, one culture, and one proud past. The homogeneity of the Korean people is a significant factor in an evaluation of Korean political problems." After Western capitalist nations came to eastern Asia seeking trade and colonial outports in the late nineteenth century, Korea quickly became a source of acute contention and a focus of international rivalry. The United States, then Britain, France, Russia, and even Belgium and Italy took part in a scramble for economic concessions. "The first modern mines, the first electric lighting, the first modern office building, the first gas plant, the first street railroad, were all American."[4] However, the Western presence was short-lived. Japan, less than one hundred miles away across the Straits of Tsushima, claimed a pre-eminent position in the development of Korea. By 1910, Japan had stamped out the armed resistance of the Korean people and formally annexed the country as a colony. Other nations were excluded except as they served Japanese interests. The hated, often brutal, Japanese colonial administration exploited Korea for thirty-five years, until Japan itself was defeated at the end of World War II.

Meanwhile the struggle for national independence became the central spiritual force in the life of the Korean people. A reservoir of patriotism, including a militant group of Communists active in northeastern Korea, "was built up under Japanese rule and was consequently ready to be tapped at the moment of liberation."[5]

When the liberation of Korea came in 1945, however, it resulted not in the emergence of an independent country, but in a nation divided into two zones at the 38th Parallel, where the liberating Soviet and American armies met each other face to face. Although the wartime allies had agreed in principle to help the Koreans establish a single national government, the understanding was never realized, because the Americans and Russians could not agree on which Koreans should staff the provisional government. Instead, as in divided postwar Germany, each of the great powers began to encourage the growth of an economy and political institutions in its own image: land reform and socialism for the north, a market economy and capitalism in the south.

For the Korean people, freed from years of harsh Japanese colonial rule, the division of their country into two parts was a bitter disappointment. It was artificial, unnatural, and inconvenient, separating families and dislocating the economy. They looked forward to early reunification. Meanwhile, separate governments were established. Backed by the Soviet Union, Kim Il Sung headed North Korea from its capital, Pyongyang, and South Korea was led by Syngman Rhee from Seoul, backed by the United States. Each claimed to represent the interests of a united Korea, and proceeded to organize political and military support for that purpose. Civil war was the result. The protagonists created guerrilla units in rear areas, and their armed forces crossed the imaginary dividing line on the map almost at will, whenever there was an advantage to be gained.[6]

The United Nations Organization, founded by the Allied Powers in San Francisco in 1945, appointed a commission to supervise the affairs of Korea. But since U.S. influence dominated the UNO at that time, the commission was not given access to North Korea, and it was unable to function as a peacemaker.

Elsewhere in East Asia, especially in Japan, the United States had a strong presence. Under the terms of surrender in September 1945, General Douglas MacArthur held the post of supreme commander of the Allied Powers, and he wielded absolute rule over Japan for six years. This gave the United States a strong base, "an unsinkable aircraft carrier," from which to wage the forthcoming war in Korea. The terms of the peace settlement with Japan in April 1952 provided for the continuation of U.S. military bases in that country.

On the other side of Korea, in China, a social upheaval of rare proportions was in progress. Revolutionary forces, supported by the peasantry and led by Mao Zedong and the Chinese Communist Party, had achieved national power by 1949. China's success in overthrowing foreign interventions and in carrying out land reform was an encouragement to many Asian peoples, including the Korean Communists. The U.S. leadership, on the other hand, assumed that the revolution in China represented an unwelcome extension of the power of Soviet Communism in East Asia. Ignoring the advice of its own seasoned diplomatic and military observers in China, the U.S. government scorned overtures from the Chinese Communists for a meeting. Instead, the United States continued to support the Nationalist government of Chiang Kai-shek, who was now living in exile on the island province of Taiwan. The U.S. government and most of its allies refused diplomatic recognition or representation in the UNO to the newly founded People's Republic of China, which had its capital in Beijing. Instead, the United States would try to contain the revolutionary tides beginning to wash over Asia from Korea to Vietnam and beyond.

To understand the fury of the coming war in Korea—where an internal civil war would be transformed into an international confrontation, and a war of mass destruction—one other piece of the puzzle needs to be added. The success of the revolution in China had had a catalytic effect on domestic politics in the United States. A time of witch hunts began in Washington; civil liberties in the United States all but vanished for a time. In its quest for office, the Republican Party, led by its right wing, demanded to know why the United States had "lost" China. Who was responsible for this debacle? Senator Joseph McCarthy wanted answers. McCarthy orchestrated a hue and cry, claiming that the Democrats were "soft on Communism" and were harboring traitors in the State Department. Public servants began signing loyalty oaths; politicians from all corners of the land vied to demonstrate their patriotism, their Americanism; Hollywood created a blacklist of movie producers and actors. In this boiling atmosphere, distrust of the Union of Soviet Socialist Republics grew apace. It was thought that Russian spies were everywhere. Anti-Communist sentiment soon emerged as a full-blown Cold War, a condition most frequently described in the U.S. media and by many academic scholars as a struggle between freedom and slavery, between democracy and dictatorship, between God and Beelzebub.

It was in this concatenation of circumstances that Kim Il Sung, the

North Korean leader, decided once again—in the spring of 1950—to make military preparations for an attempt to end the division of Korea. He very nearly succeeded. Hostilities between North and South Korean forces erupted in the last week of June 1950. Whether they were provoked by South Korea, as some suggest might be the case,[7] or otherwise, within a month the North Korean army had swept down the peninsula, taking everything except a small bridgehead around the city of Pusan in the southeast corner of the country. American writer Robert Simmons sums up the origins and first stage of the Korean War:

> There were constant and sizeable armed clashes and border incursions between the North and South for over a year before the final crisis [in June 1950]. . . . Koreans were accustomed to the fighting and the possibility of war; each side believed that an early reunification was worth a war. While the Seoul regime enjoyed little popular support, it had announced its intention to invade the North and appeared to be preparing to do so. . . . The subsequent rapid North Korean victory was caused not by the size of its invading force, but rather a combination of superior firepower (tanks, artillery and planes), surprise, higher morale, and the support of a significant part of South Korea's population.[8]

However, Kim Il Sung had made several serious miscalculations. He overestimated the speed with which his army could complete the unification of Korea, and he underestimated the determination of U.S. president Harry Truman not to "lose Korea" as he had been accused of "losing China," and to resist unification of Korea except under U.S. terms. He did not foresee that Truman would be able to get the backing of the United Nations Organization for his stand.[9] In addition, Kim Il Sung took the risk of proceeding without any direct commitment from the Soviet Union in case the United States intervened.[10]

South Korean and U.S. forces held on to the Pusan perimeter, and U.S. Navy, Marine, and Army units, fighting under a United Nations banner, made a successful amphibious landing at Inchon in the rear of the North Korean army in the middle of September 1950. The fortunes of war changed rapidly, and Kim Il Sung's army disappeared into the hills to regroup.

The majority of countries in the United Nations General Assembly supported General MacArthur's determination to cross the 38th Parallel and push north to the frontier shared with China. They believed that the

"Korean problem" would soon be satisfactorily settled. Repeated warnings from China's premier Zhou Enlai that the Chinese people would not "tolerate foreign aggression, nor will they supinely tolerate seeing their neighbours being savagely invaded by imperialists," were ignored.[11] There were large hydroelectric installations along the Yalu River that supplied power to both North Korean and Chinese industries—a vital national interest for China. In addition, and perhaps more important, the Chinese felt an obligation to aid their comrades, since so many Koreans had sacrificed themselves in China during the Chinese revolution and in the war of resistance to Japan.[12] In October 1950, MacArthur, already aware that China had sent a substantial expeditionary force across the Yalu River,[13] led his forces over the 38th Parallel, bent upon eliminating the Korean Democratic People's Republic.

It was now General MacArthur's turn, however, to suffer the consequences of both political and military miscalculation, which would lead to his downfall within six months, sending U.S. domestic politics into further turmoil.

Vanguards of the Chinese People's Volunteer Army, under the command of General Peng Dehuai, crossed the Yalu River at dusk on 18 October. Two days later, Peng, considered to be one of the ablest and boldest of China's military commanders, led his troops about fifty miles south of the Yalu and established headquarters in an old mine near the village of Dayudong. Almost immediately, and unexpectedly from Peng's point of view, they had encounters with the enemy. There was a U.S. napalm strike on his headquarters, which killed Mao Anying, the eldest son of Mao Zedong; and there was fighting near the town of Pukjin. In this "first phase offensive," the Chinese army managed to repulse several enemy units and pushed the UN forces into temporary retreat.[14]

Then there was a sudden calm on the battlefront while the Chinese army broke off contact, camouflaged its positions, built up its numbers to about 150,000 in the northwest of Korea, and waited for the enemy to advance to predetermined locations. Peng Dehuai ordered his army to give the enemy the impression that "we are being intimidated into retreat."[15]

General MacArthur slighted all efforts to reach a political settlement, including the arrival of a high-level Chinese delegation at the UN headquarters at Lake Success, New York. Unaware of the size of the Chinese force that faced him, he personally flew to the front in northwest Korea on 24 November to spur on the U.S. Eighth Army. Directing his pilot to fly low over the boundary with China, he described the scene below:

> At this height we could observe in detail the entire area of international No-Man's Land. . . . All that spread before our eyes was an endless expanse of utterly barren countryside, jagged hills, yawning crevices, and the black waters of the Yalu locked in the silent death grip of snow and ice. It was a merciless wasteland. If a large force or massive supply train had passed over the border, the imprints had already been well-covered by the intermittent snowstorms of the Yalu Valley.[16]

In a message to Washington the next day, MacArthur sought to persuade the Joint Chiefs of Staff that any failure on the part of the United States to carry the military campaign through to the "oft repeated objective of destroying all enemy forces south of Korea's northern boundary" would be fraught with most disastrous consequences and would be regarded by the Korean people as "a betrayal of their sovereign and territorial integrity and of the solemn undertaking entered into on their behalf." He stated that "the justice of our course and promise of early completion of our mission" was reflected in the high morale of both troops and commanders.[17] MacArthur had launched 250,000 men—Americans, South Koreans, and a small number of British Commonwealth and Turkish soldiers—toward the Yalu River, which lay but seventy miles distant. Promising quick victory, he confidently told reporters the men would be "home by Christmas."[18]

The role of feelings against Japanese and Western imperialism on the part of its historical victims as a motive to fight in Korea was captured in an editorial by the Chinese supporting the dispatch of their army to Korea:

> As the White terror has moved northwards, mechanised and ruthless, nearer and nearer to the border of their motherland, the wrath of the Chinese people has intensified. Today the mood of the nation is reminiscent of September 18, 1931, when the Japanese imperialists started their fatal "incident" in Northeast China. . . . This is not a warning. The Chinese people have solemnly warned the aggressors on more than one occasion in the past. This is a programme for joint and immediate action to halt the aggressor. . . . After having suffered a century of aggressions launched under all sorts of pretexts by various imperialists, the Chinese people have learned to detect an aggressor, no matter how cunningly he may be camouflaged.[19]

In daily, even hourly, contact by telegram with Mao Zedong in Beijing, Peng Dehuai worked out the strategy for his "second phase offensive." The interlocking hills and valleys and the frozen rivers of North Korea—

even the cold, snow-covered ridges penetrated only by mountain paths—
were favorable terrain for the lightly armed but sturdy country youth
of China, who were already stirred by the revolutionary victories back
home.[20] Lacking heavy armor or air cover, the Chinese would favor night
fighting with hand grenades, encirclement and flanking attacks, and close,
hand-to-hand combat and disguise, always seeking the element of surprise,
always trying to keep the initiative in their hands. They would rely on the
tactics of a "people's war" as outlined by Mao Zedong:

> In order to smash the attack of the stronger enemy in conditions
> where popular support, terrain, and weather are greatly in our
> favour, it is . . . necessary to concentrate [our] main forces . . .
> for a surprise attack on a segment of one flank of the enemy
> while containing his centre and his other flank with guerrillas or
> small detachments, and in this way victory can be won.[21]

The Chinese were encouraged about the possibilities of success because of what they thought to be a fatal weakness in the U.S. Army. A
Chinese intelligence report summarized the experience of the "first phase
offensive" as follows:

> Their infantry men are weak, afraid to die and haven't the cour-
> age to attack or defend. They depend on their planes, tanks,
> and artillery. At the same time, they are afraid of our fire power.
> . . . They must have proper terrain and good weather to trans-
> port their great amount of equipment. They can operate rapidly
> along good highways and flat country; not in hill country. . . .
> They specialize in day fighting. They are not familiar with night
> fighting or hand-to-hand combat. . . . If defeated they have no
> orderly formation. . . . They are afraid when the rear is cut off.
> When transportation comes to a standstill, the infantry loses the
> will to fight. . . . Those surrounded by us will think we are well
> organized and equipped with weapons. In this case, they will
> surrender rather than fight.[22]

No sooner had MacArthur's "home by Christmas" offensive begun to
move forward than the careful planning and well-tested tactics of Mao
Zedong and Peng Dehuai became apparent. The Chinese army descended
from their mountain hideaways to strike at night against the unsuspecting
U.S. and United Nations army. It was as if some "phantom force" had
unnerved the Eighth Army, writes U.S. historian Colonel Roy Appleman,
and "its only desire . . . was to flee the ghastly, dreaded scene. . . . For the
next month it was simply a case of breaking contact with the enemy and

outrunning them southward." In that month "a series of disasters unequaled in our country's history overwhelmed American arms."[23]

The most famous and costly incident of the debacle was the attempt of the U.S. 2nd Division, including six artillery battalions, to escape southward from the town of Kunuri. Mao Zedong and Peng Dehuai had anticipated such an attempt and were determined to block it. To this end they sent two regiments of the 113th Division of their 38th Army on a frenzied forced march, taking shortcuts through gullies and over ridges, practically running all the way, to cut off two southward escape routes: the main highway crossing the Taedong River at Sansouli [Samso-ri], and another secondary dirt road five miles farther west that ran through the villages of Wadong and Longyuanli [Yongwon-ni]. After traveling forty-five miles on foot in fourteen hours, the two regiments arrived in time to make a flanking attack on the retreating U.S.–UN forces. "Although tired, hungry, and thirsty," survivors recalled that "the 113th Division fought a vigorous blocking action."[24]

The official Chinese history of the Korean War has one paragraph on the battle that tore the U.S. 2nd Division apart:

> On the 30th [of November] over one hundred planes and over one hundred tanks made a death-defying effort to support the repeated attempts of the enemy to break through. Our 113th Division undertook the task of intercepting them and indomitably fought back and held our battleground [at Sansouli and Longyuanli]. This was the enemy that was trying to break through; they and their north-supporting army [the British Middlesex Regiment] were less than one kilometer apart; they could see each other, but they were unable to link up. This shattered the attempt of the enemy to retreat through this district. For this action, the 38th Army received from the senior officers of the Volunteer Army an order of commendation.[25]

What is so laconically described by the Chinese historians becomes an entire chapter in Colonel Appleman's U.S. history of the war, a detailed account of the 2nd Division's passage through the six-mile fire block of the Chinese forces on the Kunuri-Sunchon road. It includes the bitter cold, the sound of machine guns and mortars at the narrow pass, enemy snipers at the blown bridge, the dust and smoke from friendly aircraft strafing and napalming the ridges, wrecked and burning vehicles clogging the road or abandoned in the ditches, road shoulders littered with the dead, and the wounded crawling from the ditches hoping that someone would put them on a vehicle as each of seven attack groups—combining tanks, artillery and infantry battalions—groped their way through what was described as "the valley of death."[26] When the retreat from Kunuri was over, the 2nd Division had suffered five thousand casualties and had lost most of its artillery; "it was little more than half strength."[27]

As disaster unfolded around Kunuri during the final days of November, the U.S. military and political leadership looked to the atomic bomb. On 30 November the erstwhile confident MacArthur told the Joint Chiefs of Staff that it was "quite impracticable" to join his Eighth Army and X Corps in a continuous line across the narrow neck of Korea. The length of that line, the numerical weakness of his forces, and logistical problems "due to the mountainous divide which splits such a front north to south" nullified any such possibility.[28] On the same date, but twenty-four hours later on the other side of the Pacific Ocean, President Truman read a somber statement to his press conference and then added that if the United Nations authorized military action against China, General MacArthur might be given the authority to use the atomic bomb at his discretion.[29]

On 4 December, the U.S. Joint Chiefs of Staff supported the president's stand on using the atomic bomb if necessary to avoid defeat. This was in response to a request for advice from the State Department, which was preparing for a meeting between a worried British prime minister, Clement Attlee, and the president:

> The JCS have examined the Dept of State position paper entitled "Use of Atomic Bomb" and perceive no objection thereto from the military point of view subject to the following: situations may arise in the Korean War in which atomic bombs would be the sole weapon readily available to the United States whose employment might materially assist in preventing a major disaster to United States forces.[30]

The language captured the strategic apprehension of decision makers faced with the question of whether to expand the limits of the Korean War. These men were politicians and generals shaped and hardened by the drift of U.S. strategy to the outer limits of total war during World War II. Those who advocated using atomic bombs if they "would be the sole weapon readily available" were also capable of weighing biological weapons in the balance. The Stevenson Report, which had recently been approved by Secretary of Defense George Marshall, expressed enthusiasm for the use of biological warfare, whether by overt or covert means. No U.S. record has come to light showing that it was employed at this time of impending disaster as an alternative to the atomic bomb. But the Chinese prime minister, Zhou Enlai, who could not have been aware of the

Stevenson Report's advocacy of biological warfare, charged that "during the period from December 1950 to January 1951," the U.S. forces "disseminated smallpox viruses in Pyongyang, Kangwon province, South Hamkyong province, Hwanghae province and several other areas while retreating southward across the 38th Parallel."[31]

The second phase offensive of the Chinese army concluded in early December 1950, the army having retaken most of North Korea, including its capital, Pyongyang. According to their own reports, the Chinese had lost 30,700 soldiers (either dead or missing) and had reportedly inflicted 36,000 casualties (including 24,000 American) on the U.S.–UN forces.[32] After a brief rest, in a third phase offensive, the Chinese and the regrouped North Korean army crossed the 38th Parallel and captured Seoul in January 1951. In another two weeks they reached the 37th Parallel, the farthest point of their southward thrust. In what has been described by Colonel Appleman as "a massive retreat, without parallel in U.S. military history,"[33] the Americans kept falling back, following a scorched-earth policy as they went.

With two-thirds of the U.S. Army in Korea facing destruction, and the domestic media clamoring about "superhuman red hordes," Truman had rattled his atomic bombs when speaking to journalists on 30 November. But when European allies protested in unison that to use the atomic bomb in Korea would be to start World War III, Truman backed away.[34]

Soon, and for a short while, U.S. fortunes in the war improved as a new commander for the Eighth Army, General Matthew Ridgway, took charge in January 1951. Ridgway, who came directly from the Pentagon, was determined to restore discipline in the U.S. Army and to start a counterattack. He wanted to have his infantry push the enemy back, ridge by ridge, in a war of attrition. The objective was not territory; it was to wear down, exhaust, and if necessary annihilate the enemy. It was a strategy carried over from World War II, with antecedents in the education and mindset of U.S. officers dating from the Civil War. In an effort to improve morale, he adopted an attitude of moral certitude which invoked historical American values with respect to the "manifest" mission of the United States. In a message to the army on 21 January 1951 called "What Are We Fighting For?" he stated,

> To me the issues are clear. It is not a question of this or that Korean town or village. Real estate is, here, incidental. . . . The real issues are whether the power of Western civilization, as God has permitted it to flower in our own beloved lands, shall defy and defeat Communism; whether the rule of men who shoot their prisoners, enslave their citizens, and deride the dignity of

man shall replace the rule of those to whom the individual and his individual rights are sacred; whether we are to survive with God's hand to guide and lead us, or to perish in the dead existence of a Godless world.[35]

As Ridgway's forces gradually pushed the Chinese and North Korean armies back to the 38th Parallel, inflicting heavy casualties by air and artillery attacks, it became clear that both sides would be prepared to accept a draw. Negotiations for an armistice got underway in July 1951 in Kaesong, just south of the 38th Parallel. These negotiations, however, did not proceed easily or quickly.

General Ridgway's instructions from the U.S. Joint Chiefs of Staff on 10 July 1951 were to use military pressure to influence the settlement by inflicting "maximum personnel and material losses on the forces of North Korea and Communist China."[36] The political motive for this war of attrition was most cogently stated some two years later by John Foster Dulles, secretary of state in General Dwight D. Eisenhower's newly elected Republican administration: "I don't think we can get much out of a Korea settlement until we have shown—before all Asia—our clear superiority by giving the Chinese one hell of a beating."[37]

After six months of sporadic ground fighting and heavy U.S. air attacks, the warring sides reached agreement that the ceasefire line should follow the existing battlefront approximating the 38th Parallel, only to falter on the new U.S. demand that a return of prisoners be based on "voluntary repatriation." Not surprisingly, the Chinese and North Korean negotiators objected under the terms of the Geneva Convention of 1949, which called for all prisoners to be repatriated without delay. But for reasons over which historians continue to battle, the United States insisted, claiming humanitarian concerns for prisoners who would not want to return to Communist control. Said President Truman, "We will not buy an armistice by turning over human beings for slaughter or slavery."[38]

In the fifteen months it took the U.S. and UN forces to win this concession, the costs mounted both at the front and behind the lines. The U.S. Air Force, frustrated by stalemated fighting and by the failure of its interdiction campaign to stop enemy supplies, extended its attacks in June 1952 to hydroelectric plants on the Yalu River bordering China, to population centers in North Korea, and finally, in May 1953, to the irrigation dams of North Korea's rivers—acts of a kind that had recently been judged as war crimes during the trials of Nazi leaders in Nuremberg. Behind the lines, rioting broke out in U.S.-controlled prisoner-of-war camps on Koje Island as pro-repatriation and anti-repatriation factions, the latter incited in part by U.S. activity, struggled for control; many of the prisoners were killed before order was restored. These acts in Korea indicated again that the United States' subscription to laws of war and treatment of prisoners was no check on its political and military leaders' use of whatever methods and weapons were considered necessary to achieve their goals. They also indicated that the real limits of war had been extended by the United States beyond agreed legal attempts to control them.

As the war unfolded on the front lines from 1951 to 1953, conditions increasingly resembled the trench warfare of World War I. The Chinese and North Koreans, operating from almost impregnable fortifications, generally held the upper hand in the stalemated ground war, while the Americans had air superiority. During this period, the U.S.–UN side suffered 125,000 casualties; the U.S. Eighth Army claimed that 250,000 Chinese and North Korean soldiers were killed, wounded, or captured.[39] Several hundred thousand more civilians in North Korea were rendered homeless or annihilated as the result of the U.S. bombing campaign. "Voluntary repatriation" came at a steep price.[40]

In the trench war that developed on the fighting front, both sides dug in, with the Chinese in particular going to great efforts to protect themselves from U.S. bombers and artillery. They dug trenches, caves, and deep tunnels, an "underground Great Wall," as they called it, encompassing 1,250 kilometers of subterranean passages in an area twenty miles wide along the main line of resistance. Here they were virtually immune to bombardment. They could live, cook their meals, tend to their wounded, keep warm in winter, concentrate their forces, and attack the enemy defense line at any point they chose. "Thus our troops won the initiative on the battlefield," wrote General Peng Dehuai. "This tactic . . . created a most favourable condition for conducting positional warfare of a protracted nature."[41]

In the summer and autumn of 1951, the U.S.–UN command, with its mission "to seek out and destroy the enemy" as a way of influencing the truce talks, tried to "elbow forward" to gain dominating terrain. But as "Bloody Ridge" and "Heartbreak Ridge" (the names U.S. soldiers gave some of these battles) indicate, the cost was high. The U.S. I Corps command report for October 1951 contains these telling comments:

> Many positions changed hands three or four times during the course of the day as bitter hand-to-hand fighting marked the intensity of the enemy's resistance. . . . The relentless hammering of artillery, mortar, and tank fire against the formidable bunker system failed to produce a breakthrough. . . . Even air strikes with napalm and 1,000 pound bombs made little impression on

the enemy defenders. . . . The dogged enemy defense—in many cases to the last man—took a heavy toll of 1st Cavalry Division forces and frequently produced a situation in which the American assault forces attained an objective in insufficient strength to resist the fierce enemy counterattacks that followed.[42]

Under these conditions, the U.S. ground operations "sputtered out" in October 1951.[43] The Eighth Army was unwilling to risk high casualties. In order to sustain falling troop morale, it began rotating about 20,000 men out each month, sending them home to the United States. The constant flux made it even harder to maintain battle-hardened teams.[44] If the Americans were going to put pressure on their foes, they would have to starve them out by cutting their supply lines or find some other, unconventional means of penetrating their fortified line.

The Far East Command began "Operation Strangle" in August 1951 to apply maximum pressure from the air against enemy communication and supply lines. During the next eight months, the U.S. air forces (Marines, Navy, and Fifth and Twentieth Air Forces) tried to starve the enemy. They flew more than 90,000 sorties. They claimed 19,000 rail cuts and the destruction of 276 locomotives and 3,820 rail cars, plus 34,211 trucks and other vehicles on the highways. In addition to railroads, bridges, marshaling yards, highways, trains, and trucks, the U.S. pilots targeted their napalm, incendiary, and fragmentation bombs on horse carts, handcarts, and any housing or shelter that might conceivably serve as a storage depot.

In spite of all this technological power, the U.S. high command watched incredulously as enemy ground strength in Korea continued to grow in the year after armistice negotiations began.[45] The bombing program did not interdict ground traffic; the supplies got through.

There were two main reasons why "Operation Strangle" fizzled. The first was the gradual but noticeable buildup of Chinese air defense and air power, including the arrival of some Soviet air units with their MIG-15 jet fighters.[46] As the U.S. Far East Air Force command reported in September 1951, "not only were there more planes but the Communist pilots were more aggressive." The Soviet-built MIG-15 was superior to the American jets in its ability to climb, dive, and accelerate. Although the Chinese MIG-15 pilots were less experienced than the American pilots, by the third week of October 1951, when some of the "greatest air battles of history" were fought over northwestern Korean, "they demonstrated how much they had learned": nine American jet fighters and five B-29 bombers were shot down, and eight more were damaged.[47] This was shocking news. As early as May 1951, the commander of one bomb wing had been relieved in an attempt to check serious morale problems, and by June, the Air Force chief of staff, General Hoyt Vandenberg, was expressing concern over air capability in Korea.[48] As the air war went from bad to worse for the United States, Vandenberg returned to Washington from a quick trip to the Korean front in November 1951 with a gloomy report: "Almost overnight," he said, "Communist China has become one of the major air powers of the world."[49] From then on, American bombers could fly only at night over North Korea. And with the arrival of Soviet-built, radar-controlled anti-aircraft guns, the B-29 and even B-26 bombers had to fly higher, resulting in less accuracy, while losses mounted for lower-flying B-26 light bombers and fighter bombers.

The other reason for the limited success of "Operation Strangle" was the increasing effectiveness of the rear-service system built up by the enemy. At first the Chinese army in Korea had no specialized logistical system, but after the toll exacted by U.S. bombers, and a disastrous flood in North Korea in the summer of 1951, that all changed. The Volunteer Army Logistical Command, with a regular military structure and more than three thousand headquarters staff, was established at Suwon (Suan), thirty miles southeast of Pyongyang and fifty miles from the front line.

Soon this command had 180,000 rear servicemen responsible for transport, for receiving, transferring, storing, and distributing military materials, for taking in wounded soldiers and shipping them home, for repairing bridges and vehicular roads, for protecting communications, for organizing air defense, and for maintaining stability and safety in the rear.[50] In addition, there was a joint Sino-Korean command, consisting of 52,000 people, responsible for railway transport and repairs. General Peng Dehuai also required all combat units behind the front line to share logistical responsibilities such as road-building, digging shelters for trucks along the transportation lines, and sending out more air-watch guards. Along twelve hundred miles of main transport lines, air-watch scouts were posted at every mile. When the scouts heard the approach of U.S. planes, they fired a shot or blew bugles to alert drivers. The trucks would then turn off their headlights and hide in the nearest shelter. In this manner the trucks could cover a hundred miles a night on average, and the damage rate dropped from 40 percent to less than 1 percent.[51]

By December 1951, the midpoint of the Korean War, the United States was stymied. Its superior technology, applied by conventional means in a static war of position, was unable to exert inexorable pressure on the enemy. While the other side had agreed to certain conditions for an armistice agreement, they had not done so from weakness; they were getting stronger daily. Some U.S. military leaders worried that if this trend continued, the Chinese would be able to launch and sustain another general offensive. The front-line fortifications of their army had proved virtually impregnable to ground assault, and their supply system, although often crude, was formidable. Everything the U.S. Air Force poured on them failed to disrupt the combat effectiveness of their main line of resistance.

If, as the Fifth Air Force believed, the Chinese still had 500,000 people working to counter the effects of "Operation Strangle," how could the United States possibly give them "one hell of a beating"? How could the U.S. achieve the victory it wanted?

One answer was to expand the violence of the war against population centers and economic resources. The eleven hydroelectric plants along the Yalu River were bombed in June 1952. In August, Pyongyang was devastated as part of a saturation bombing and burning campaign against seventy-eight North Korean cities and towns. In September, U.S. planes hit the oil refineries at Rashin near the Soviet border. Meanwhile, on the ground there was another failed attempt to "elbow forward" in the battle of Triangle Hill (Sangkumryung Ridge) in the autumn. When China and North Korea failed to break, the United States, in May 1953, started bombing the irrigation dams holding back the numerous river systems in North Korea—an act of war for which the Allies had condemned the Germans as war criminals when they bombed the dikes in Holland in 1945. By this time, as well, President Eisenhower had resurrected Truman's threat to use the atomic bomb if the deadlock at the truce negotiations was not ended. The U.S. Air Force transferred some atomic bombs to Okinawa, and its chief of staff, Hoyt Vandenberg, publicly suggested that Mukden (Shenyang), in northeast China, would be a strategic target to hit.[52]

Did this escalation of the war extend to biological warfare?

It was during this period of increasing U.S. frustration with the course of the war that enthusiasm ran highest for biological weapons. It was the time of the "Twining Directive," which ordered a crash program in the U.S. Air Force for biological warfare. Covert and emergency capabilities were already part of operational war plans. The United States had substantial stocks of biological weapons on hand. Moral qualms about using biological or atomic weapons had been brushed aside by top leaders, and biological warfare might dodge the political bullet of adverse public and world opinion if it were kept secret enough to make plausible a denial of its use. If its use were uncovered, a last resort could be to fall back on the fact that the U.S. had not signed the 1925 Geneva Protocol on biological warfare. Also, by 1952 the United States was well along the road of spending almost half a billion dollars on its biological warfare program. Were the investors inclined to take this extraordinary opportunity to see if it was money well spent? The combination of circumstances and likely motives renders this a reasonable and necessary question to raise.

As for its possible effect on the enemy, the spread of debilitating or deadly diseases could reasonably be expected to create panic among the masses of Chinese and North Koreans engaged in repairing roads, rehabilitating bombed railway bridges, and ferrying rice and ammunition. There would be desertions; the system would be disrupted. Deadly bacteria could penetrate into the front-line tunnels and caves where bombs could not. The energies of combat troops would be drained. U.S. military planners thought that biological warfare offered "fabulous possibilities."[53] When the enemy discovered what was happening and made angry complaints about violations of the Geneva Protocol or about war crimes, the secretary of state—who, it was agreed, was not privy to the biological warfare cover and deception plans—could reassure the United States' allies and officially dismiss the charges as Communist propaganda, placing the blame on poor sanitary conditions and naturally occurring epidemics in China and Korea.

When, in early 1952, Zhou Enlai formally supported the North Korean foreign minister's second charge of biological warfare—with the Chinese claiming that it was used continuously thereafter during the massive air assaults of 1952 and 1953—was it propaganda, as the United States claimed? Or was the outbreak of illness something beyond the normal incidence of disease in a population going through a period of upheaval and war, with which the Chinese already had a generation of continuous experience? The first chapter of this book presents new information indicating that Chinese who were competent to evaluate the situation judged that it was more than naturally occurring disease. They still hold to that view.

Was it a coincidence that the formal charges of germ warfare of early 1952 came shortly after President Truman flew back from his winter house in Florida, a week ahead of schedule, to meet with his top officials over the deteriorating situation in Korea?[54] And that a few days later Secretary of Defense Robert Lovett issued his pivotal, much-quoted, top secret directive of 21 December 1951 ordering the Joint Chiefs of Staff to achieve "actual readiness" in biological warfare "in the earliest practicable time"?

Were certain diseases in North Korea and northeast China induced by germ warfare, as charged by the North Koreans and Chinese, or were they the result of a disease-ridden environment in wartime Korea, as U.S. historians tend to claim?

The United States tried to keep close track of the health of the enemy army through the reports of secret agents. An airdrop of nine U.S.-trained agents behind enemy lines on 13 March 1952 was reported by the Chinese army in Korea:

> Four escaped, but the remaining five were all captured by us. The 39th Army got two, the 67th Army captured two, and the 3rd Branch captured one. This batch of spies were former soldiers of ours who surrendered and were taken prisoner by the enemy and were trained by the American imperialists and then assigned to intelligence work. They can tell each other's names and appearance, and their confessions are generally consistent. They all wear the Volunteer Army uniforms, which were made by the enemy, and the colors are a little too deep. They carried carbon rifles or Soviet rifles, Japanese 14th year brand pistols, binoculars, radios, and instruments to tap telephones. They carry military pigeons, etc. They pretend to be staff officers of our army. . . . Their main task is to know the effect of the bacterial war, the army and civilian epidemic disease situation, how many days it takes for people to die and the number of deaths, the proportion of old and young casualties, which injected medicines were effective, whether there were epidemic diseases in the army, whether there were any dead rats inside the residences, how many fleas and lice, etc.[55]

On the basis of U.S. intelligence reports, the historian of the U.S. Medical Corps in the Korean War, Albert E. Cowdrey, says that in the late winter of 1950 and the early spring of 1951, smallpox and typhus "were reported throughout the country, north and south."[56] On the other hand, Major Converse of the U.S. Army, at a meeting of fourteen allied ambassadors sponsored by the State Department in March 1951, in speaking about the refugees and 100,000 displaced persons in South Korea, stated, "It was notable that there had been no epidemics of any kind in the past eight months."[57] Unfortunately, Chinese and North Korean army records for the incidence of disease in this early period are not yet declassified. In any case, U.S. intelligence sources believed that by late summer of 1951, "the epidemics of the spring had ended" as a result of health and sanitation programs in North Korea.[58] This was six months before the first charges of widespread use of germ warfare were aired. Thus the United States would have known that if disease was to help its war effort in a decisive manner, for the most part it would have to be deliberately induced.

Available Chinese government records indicate that although the pattern of disease was unusual, there were no major epidemics in northeast China or northern Korea in the spring of 1952[59]—a fact that may explain the great disappointment of the U.S. military with the effectiveness of its biological warfare development program, which was subsequently curtailed in the autumn of 1953. The localized outbreaks of plague, anthrax, encephalitis, cholera, and other diseases that did occur in North Korea and northeast China, whatever their source, were quickly contained by the public health campaigns of the Chinese army and local government authorities.

There is no way to measure the extent to which the United States' escalating use of mass destruction influenced the Chinese and Korean negotiators at the armistice talks to accept a modified form of "voluntary repatriation" for prisoners of war. But an armistice was signed at Panmunjom by both sides, and the war ended in late July 1953.

The circumstances surrounding the Chinese and North Korean charges that the United States had used biological warfare present much to be considered. The remaining chapters of this book reflect our research on how large-scale field experiments with biological weapons could have been conducted during the Korean conflict. We investigate the convergence of means, motives, and plans with the actions of those who had the capacity to act. Who among the U.S. forces were able to carry out such activities? What evidence is there that they did so? How do the features of the U.S. biological warfare program, its agents and means of delivery, match up with the details of the Chinese allegations?

Unlike the direct, confirmed evidence of the U.S. biological warfare program and the basic facts of the Korean War, what follows will be based, in part, upon incomplete evidence—extensive and carefully considered, but incomplete. After years of searching and countless Freedom of Information Access requests, many of the documents remain inaccessible to historians. Some are in storage warehouses, where they lack finding aids, or are classified and remain under the control of the Pentagon; others are held classified in the national archives of the United States, Canada, and Great Britain. Some have been lost or destroyed. Still, we believe that recent decisions to give greater access to archival resources provide sufficient information—an abundance even—to allow the reader to further test the reliability of our conclusions, our judgment about the United States' engagement in field tests of biological weapons in China and Korea during the Korean War.

Rugged terrain of the main line of battle in Korea from the observation post of the 2nd Chemical Mortar Battery, U.S. Eighth Army in Korea, in 1952.
Book 4364, SC418463, RG 111, NA

A 155mm Long Tom of the 937 Field Artillery, Eighth Army, firing at a Communist position, Kumhwa, 27 Sept. 1952.
Book 4364, SC426125, RG 111, NA

Hill 603, near Kumhwa, still smoking after being strafed and napalmed by U.S. Navy planes, 14 June 1951.
Book 2362, SC371369, RG 111, NA

Korean woman and child in what is left of their home north of Kumhwa, 14 June 1952.
Book 2362, SC371376, RG 111

Company A, 23rd Infantry Regiment, 40th Infantry Division, U.S. Army, assaults bunker positions in Korea, 20 Feb. 1953.
Box 247, SC421205, RG 111, NA

Foxholes on Old Baldy after many battles, 27 July 1952.
Box 234, SC404671, RG 111, NA

General Mark Clark (*right*) in the war room at Kosandong, Korea, with General Robert Soule, CG, U.S. 3rd Infantry Division, 19 Feb. 1952.
Book 2362, SC378541, RG 111, NA

Right to left: General Matthew Ridgway, CG, U.S. Eighth Army, at Taegu airfield, gives General Walter B. Smith, director of the CIA, and General Charles Willoughby, G-2, GHQ, Far East Command, a personal estimate of the situation, 17 Jan. 1951.
Book 2492, SCA356388, RG 111, NA

General James Van Fleet, CG, U.S. Eighth Army (*right*), takes Field Marshal Earl Alexander, British Minister of Defense (*second from left*), on an inspection of the 189th Field Artillery, 45th U.S. Infantry Division, in a frontline bunker near Yonchon, 13 June 1952.
Box 252 SC427047, RG 111, NA

Sample Psychological Warfare Leaflets

Vampire, Web, and B-29 Bomber
This was the official insignia of the Psychological Warfare Unit, Fifth Air Force in Korea.
USAF, Korean War Series, March 1952, Box 3048, RG 342, NA

這是送來補充你們的精兵

"More recruits for your crack troops."

"Heed This Warning"
Designating peasant homes and shelters as military targets, this leaflet urges people to flee before the U.S. bombers attack.
USAF, Korean War Series, 29 Aug. 1952, Box 3048, RG 342, NA

The Chinese People's Volunteer Army crossing the Yalu River in October 1950.
Photo No. 6241, Resist America, Aid Korea War Collection, Museum of Military History, Beijing

Peng Dehuai (*right*) of China and Kim Il Sung (*center*), commanders-in-chief, during the "Resist America, Aid Korea War."
Photo No. 012925, Resist America, Aid Korea War Collection, Museum of Military History, Beijing

"At the sound of the bugle, the soldiers launch an assault."
Photo No. 6245, Resist America, Aid Korea War Collection, Museum of Military History, Beijing

"During the battle . . . around the Kunuri district [28 Nov. 1950], our army charged the enemy position."
Photo No. 5819, Resist America, Aid Korea War Collection, Museum of Military History, Beijing

Regiments of the 38th Army blocking the U.S. 2nd Division's retreat from Kunuri at Baiyunshan.
Photo No. 6026, Resist America, Aid Korea War Collection, Museum of Military History, Beijing

"Fearless of hardship, we must build the 'Underground Great Wall.'"
Photo No. 6374, Resist America, Aid Korea War Collection, Museum of Military History, Beijing

Contemporary Woodcut
From the cover of Ba Jin's *Living amongst Heroes* (1954).
Courtesy of Foreign Languages Press, Beijing

"This is the . . . indestructible steel line of transportation."
Photo No. 6403, Resist America, Aid Korea War Collection, Museum of Military History, Beijing

"Transporting grain and ammunition to the battleground from the rear area" by every method.
Photos No. 6379, 6376, and 6357, Resist America, Aid Korea War Collection, Museum of Military History, Beijing

"The Second Chinese People's Delegation of Greetings and Appreciation at the Korean front in October 1952, bringing great inspiration to the soldiers and officers at the Shangganlin [Triangle Hill] battleground."
Photo No. 6369, Resist America, Aid Korea War Collection, Museum of Military History, Beijing

"Cultural workers of the Chinese People's Volunteers. They sing and perform for the fighters. In the heat of the battle, they can help care for the wounded and sick fighters. Sometimes they shoulder guns to fight, and to guard war prisoners."
From *Women of China,* October 1951

Victims of napalm attack on 17 Jan 1951, at Jemulpo village, North Korea. Maj. General E. F. Bullene, head of the U.S. Chemical Corps, stated that in 1951 the U.S. air forces were using an average of 70,000 gallons of napalm daily in Korea.
Armed Forces Chemical Journal, No. 4 (1952); NCNA

Remains of bombed rural hamlet near Hai Cangchon, North Korea.
NCNA

406TH MEDICAL GENERAL LABORATORY AND FAR EAST MEDICAL RESEARCH UNIT 8003

(ABBREVIATED CHART)

From "Annual Report of
Administrative Activities—1953,"
406th General Medical Laboratory,
AG 391.1, HUMEDS, Box 163,
RG 112, NA

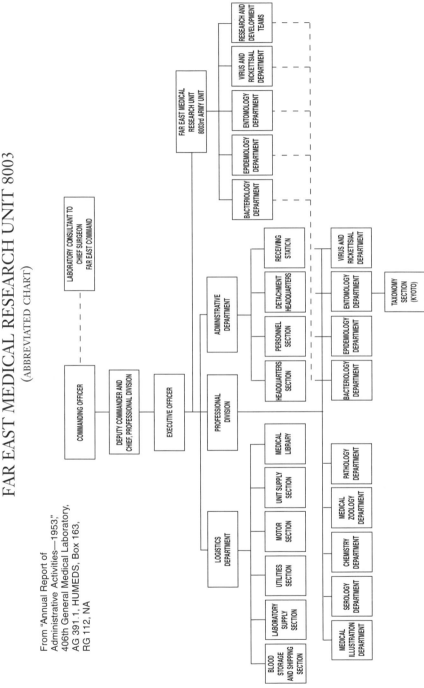

8 Psychological Warfare and Biological Weapons

Well, we've got a helluva problem, particularly with regard to the Far East. . . . Yes. It's got to be disguised. It's a very delicate thing. We can't fool around with that . . . [sanitized]. I don't know how we are going to handle that one. . . . When you get into the Far East problem, you've really got a stinker!"
—Walter Bedell Smith, CIA Director,
at a meeting of the Psychological Strategy Board,
30 October 1952[1]

The Air Force has no responsibility for covert activities in the biological warfare field.   —Colonel Frank Seiler,
Chief of BW–CW Division,
U.S. Air Force, 11 August 1953[2]

The Psychological Warfare Division will direct and supervise covert operations in the scope of unconventional BW (biological warfare) and CW (chemical warfare) operations and programs.   —Major General Robert M. Lee, Director of Plans,
U.S. Air Force, 17 March 1953[3]

The U.S. Air Force staff agency that monitored the Air Force's capabilities in biological and chemical warfare went by the acronym AFOAT–BW. Its chief, Colonel Frank Seiler, reported to the assistant for atomic energy, Major General H. G. Bunker, who in turn reported to the deputy chief of staff for operations, Lt. General T. D. White. In the summer of 1951, Colonel Seiler and his superiors were concerned by the lack of progress, and they decided to set up a new division to increase the speed of development. It was called the USAF BW–CW Division, with Colonel Seiler as chief, reporting to Generals Bunker and White. The task of the BW–CW Division was to establish an overt biological warfare capability.[4]

Recently declassified documents reveal a second chain of command and responsibility for incorporating bacteriological and chemical weapons into war plans. This chain of command also reported to Lt. General White, but it went down through Major General Robert M. Lee, director of plans, and then to Colonel John J. Hutchison, chief of the Psychological Warfare Division. The Psychological Warfare Division was assigned to "integrate capabilities and requirements" for BW and CW into war plans, and to "participate in the determination of munitions requirements for BW and CW to implement approved plans."

The innocuous-sounding rubric "psychological warfare" concealed the fact that this division had a special responsibility "to direct and supervise covert operations in the scope of unconventional BW and CW operations and programs"[5]—warfare that went beyond normal propaganda activities. Psychological warfare included a host of activities aimed at creating delays, confusion, fear, anxiety, and panic among the enemy. It employed a variety of means, including a mandate to use atomic, bacteriological, chemical, and radiological warfare. And—not to be forgotten with respect to the Psychological Warfare Division's responsibility for determining munitions requirements for bacteriological warfare—the most advanced propaganda weapon of psychological warfare units, the leaflet bomb, was adapted as a standard bacteriological munition.

The revelation of the role of the Psychological Warfare Division is the most substantive glimpse we have had into the organization of covert biological warfare operations during the Korean War. This rare document places an operating center in the service with the greatest investment in bacteriological warfare—a service whose chief of staff, General Hoyt Vandenberg, was a founder of the CIA and an enthusiast for unconventional and covert operations. The tasks of this center were set in practical rather than theoretical terms. It directed and supervised covert germ warfare operations and played a part in determining the biological munitions required to implement approved plans. In addition, it had an air arm, the 581st ARC Wing, operating in Asia under the cover of a transportation service, as a means to carry out its mandate. The chief of the Psychological Warfare Division and the deputy commander of the ARC Service were one and the same person: Colonel John J. Hutchison.[6]

According to a knowledgeable CIA insider, it was General Vandenberg's dream to have "a full-sized Psychological Warfare Air Command" to be the equal of the Air Defense Command, the Tactical Air Command, and the Strategic Air Command, but for unconventional, clandestine warfare. He believed that the problems of fighting Communism in the Cold War were such that "they should not be left to the normal forces, but should be dealt with by experts and by highly skilled men who would be in a position . . . to utilize military strength and influence."[7] Selected by President Truman to organize the Central Intelligence Service, the predecessor of the CIA, Vandenberg had many personal connections upon which to build his vision.

The US Air Force, according to Colonel Michael E. Haas, historian of the Air Force Special Operations Command, was inadequately prepared for unconventional and covert operations when the Korean War began in 1950.[8] The most ambitious effort to address this problem was the creation in February 1951 of the Air Resupply and Communications Service (ARCS).

With its headquarters at 3800 Newark Street in northwest Washington, D.C., the ARC was nominally part of the Military Air Transport Service. That was its cover. It actually was under the control of a deputy chief of staff as an operational arm of the Psychological Warfare Division, Directorate of Plans, in the Pentagon.[9] Under Vandenberg's direction, its first commanding officers, Colonels Millard C. Young and John J. Hutchison, had grandiose plans to form four or more air wings, each having a full complement of thirty-five hundred men, with self-sufficient depot facilities including food and medical services. After a few months, this concept was scaled down to two wings of twelve hundred men, who trained at Mountain Home Air Base in Idaho and then moved overseas to work out of existing air base organizations. One wing went to Libya in North Africa for activities over Europe, and the other, the 581st ARC Wing, was posted to Clark Air Force Base in the Philippines to participate in the struggle against China.

A heavily sanitized top secret report to the "President's Committee on International Information Activities" describes the ARC Wing as follows:

> An ARC wing contains a headquarters with its planners, area specialists, idea men, composers, linguists etc., and the following squadrons:
> (1) A reproduction squadron to produce both black and white propaganda material for use in psychological operations. . . . The effort within the small peninsula of Korea is something over three and one half million leaflets per day. . . .
> (2) There is a packaging squadron capable of packing and stor-

ing all of the various items of equipment and supplies to be air-delivered to unconventional warfare forces.

(3) A communications squadron capable of providing communications required in the conduct and direction of unconventional warfare.

(4) A flying squadron to provide support to unconventional warfare forces. I want to note here that there is also a capability within this squadron in the evasion and escape field. The aircraft in these squadrons consist of 12 B-29's, 4 C-119's, 4 H-19 helicopters, and 4 SA-16's amphibious.

(5) A holding and briefing squadron designed to provide secure housekeeping and briefing facilities for indigenous personnel who are to be utilized in unconventional [espionage and guerrilla] warfare.[10]

After the 581st ARC Wing arrived in the Philippines in July 1952, its planes and crews were immediately assigned to units of the Far East Air Force and to the Fifth Air Force in Korea: four of the B-29 bombers went to Yakota Air Base in Japan under the direction of the 91st Strategic Reconnaissance Squadron for "tactical leaflet drops"; four C-119 aircraft went to Ashiya Air Base under the 403rd Troop Carrier Wing for "troop carrier duty"; and the largest contingent, twenty-six officers and ninety-eight airmen—a "composite unit of various elements"—went to places designated by the commanding general of the Fifth Air Force in Korea for work that is described in singularly unenlightening fashion by historians of the 581st ARC Wing as "duty pertaining to the mission of the elements deployed"—and presumably to carry out the mandate of the Psychological Warfare Division.[11]

The commanding officer of the 581st Wing, until he was captured by the Chinese in January 1953 and sentenced to ten years in prison for espionage, was Colonel John K. Arnold. Arnold was, by all accounts, a capable man. A rated senior bomber pilot and a graduate of West Point, he held a master's degree from the California Institute of Technology. At the end of the Pacific War, he had gone to Tokyo as commander of the 43rd Weather Wing, a job that left him thoroughly familiar with the climate and terrain of northeast Asia. And while his 581st Wing was in training in Idaho from April 1951 until June 1952, Arnold made numerous visits to Washington and the Far East, including a month-long tour of Korean battlefronts, where, according to the unit's history, "he studied modern psychological warfare techniques."[12] At his trial in China, Arnold admitted working with the U.S. Central Intelligence Agency to drop special agents into China and the Soviet Union, resupplying and maintaining contact with them on the ground, and trying to evacuate them. There was no admission of or reference to biological warfare activities in the published court record.[13]

The written histories of the 581st ARC Wing, which are available on microfilm in the USAF Historical Research Agency at Maxwell Air Force Base in Alabama, conceal more than they reveal, as might be expected, and are long on vainglory and short on facts. The reader is informed that the "classified paragraphs" of Special Orders have been excluded. The Daily Operations Orders and Daily Mission Reports of the 581st Wing are not included in these histories; nor are the reports of Commanding Officer John Arnold's conferences in Washington, D.C., Tokyo, and Korea. Parading under the banner of the Military Air Transport Service, the histories do not mention that the wing was under the direct control and supervision of the Psychological Warfare Division of the Directorate of Plans, headquarters of the U.S. Air Force in the Pentagon. The result is that the substance of the 581st Wing's mission is absent from these histories, except in the most general terms as a psychological, unconventional warfare unit whose purpose was to "introduce, evacuate and supply guerilla type units in enemy-occupied territory," to package for delivery psychological warfare material—"i.e. leaflets, etc."—and to propagate "the knowledge of truth throughout the world."[14] It is emphasized that the wing was "extremely flexible."

And yet, within these pale histories there remain some clues possibly linking the 581st ARC Wing to the covert biological warfare tasks of its parent command. The first is a reference to a telegram from the Far East Air Force Headquarters to the 581st ARC Wing requesting "the type, model and series of aircraft for installation of chaff dispensers and frequency meters."

Chaff dispensers? Possibly they were for dispensing bundles of tin foil to confuse enemy radar. On the other hand, such equipment would also be ideal for dispersing chopped-up bits of straw, grass, or leaves. What is certain is that as a medium for spreading bacteria, or for conveying insects, chaff is suitable, perhaps even recommended. Chaff was one of several unusual things that the North Koreans and Chinese reported falling on their heads in 1952.[15]

Another clue lies in the miscellaneous equipment that the 581st Wing took when it left the United States. In addition to a folding camp table, a gasoline lantern, and a field desk for each unit, all rather simple items, the movement order to the 581st Wing from the ARCS headquarters in Washington required that the wing take three portable, self-contained walk-in refrigerators, each with a volume of 150 cubic feet.[16] The purpose of these refrigerators, of course, is not stated. The 581st Wing was not responsible for its own commissariat service, and leaflets do not need refrigeration. Perhaps some photographic supplies needed to be kept cool. What is certain is that many bacteria, especially *Brucella suis*, one of the main U.S. bacterial agents, as well as botulism, plague, typhus, and cholera, require cold storage if they are to remain potent until used.

The psychological warfare organizations of the various military services became a competitive hornet's nest for control of covert and unconventional warfare. The U.S. Army Psychological Warfare Division, with atomic, bacteriological, and chemical weapons in its mandate, fought the CIA for control of covert and unconventional warfare in the Far East. Pushed hard by Secretary of the Army Frank Pace, the Psychological Warfare Division ostensibly was concerned with centralized coordination. The Far Eastern participants detected other motives. While giving way on the coordination of propaganda, the Far East Command, the CIA, and the Joint Chiefs of Staff indicated that prevailing ad hoc arrangements favoring CIA control over other aspects of unconventional and covert war suited all parties. The main body responsible for pulling covert psychological warfare operations together was an organization of the Department of Defense known as the Joint Subsidiary Plans Division, which was established in January 1950 and was headed by Rear Admiral Leslie C. Stevens. Its mission was to "coordinate the peacetime development of psychological warfare and covert operations capabilities within the Armed Services, [to] coordinate detailed military plans and other agencies of the government, particularly with Department of State and the Office of Policy Coordination [CIA], and, in wartime, [to] become the means by which the JCS would provide continuous direction and guidance in these specialized fields to commanders under their control."[17]

In early 1951, the White House got involved, ostensibly to coordinate psychological warfare strategy in the Far East Command and the Korean War. And again, those holding the power were wary of the motives of the president and his advisors with respect to operational control. In the light of National Security Council directives in 1947 and 1948 emphasizing covert warfare as a Cold War weapon, everybody sensed that real power was at stake.

Disgusted by the fierce interdepartmental rivalries in this area, President Truman acted in April 1951 to create a top-level Psychological Strategy Board in an attempt to put a White House stamp on unconventional and covert warfare. Although it was an independent entity with direct access to the president, the board was in fact a committee of the top policy officials of the three interested agencies—the Departments of State and

Defense and the CIA. It was headed by a high-profile director, former secretary of defense Gordon Gray, who was appointed by the president. This was a body intended to exercise authority on a level "parallel with, if not equal with," powerful government departments such as State and Defense. Its job was to plan psychological operations, both overt and covert, on the strategic level; to coordinate the implementation of that strategy by the operating agencies; and to evaluate the results of the psychological effort in its fulfillment of national policy.[18] To achieve that end, the board's budget for psychological warfare items alone was $2.5 million in 1952, increasing to $4.5 million for 1953.[19]

The guidance document of the board set as its task, without deliberately incurring grave risk of general war, "to induce a retraction of the Kremlin's control and influence, and to foster the seeds of destruction within the Soviet system."[20] The rhetoric of board proceedings at times exuded a more chilling sense of Cold War mission, such as that espoused at one of its general staff meetings by Dr. Paul M. S. Linebarger, a China expert from Duke University: "Inter-civilizational war is chronic rather than periodic, neither beginning nor ending, with the ultimate choice lying between victory and annihilation. . . . No end to the cold war is visible. Ultimately, the Soviet system must be destroyed. . . . The struggle in southeast Asia will not end. It is part of the oecumenical struggle, and World War III is inevitable."[21]

While acknowledging the strategic authority of the board, the secretary of defense and the Joint Chiefs of Staff early resisted its encroachment on operational jurisdictions concerning the board's first major initiative, Operation Takeoff.[22] The record suggests that the Psychological Strategy Board stayed within its strategic mandate thereafter, though reserving its authority to ensure operational readiness by the agencies involved.[23] The records of the board indicate that it concerned itself with operations of its own making rather than with the range of covert and unconventional warfare activities unfolding under various jurisdictions. The record of its involvement in the Korean War indicates that it was busy.

The Psychological Strategy Board had four contingency plans for the developing situation in Korea. The first, Operation Takeoff (renamed Broadbrim in October 1951), was to deal with a possible breakdown of the armistice negotiations that had begun on 17 July 1951. The second, Operation Hummer (renamed Affiliate in October 1951), was directed primarily to the period *after* a successful ceasefire negotiation, and was a plan to pressure the enemy during the political talks for a peace treaty to end the war. The third, Operation Kumquat, was a plan to bomb Chinese air bases in the event that the Chinese air force shifted from defensive to offensive activities. And finally, there was a sketchy plan for complete withdrawal of U.S. forces from Korea for the defense of Japan in the case of a general war with the USSR. The last three contingencies never did occur, leaving our attention to be focused on Operation Takeoff/Broadbrim.

The negotiations for a ceasefire in Korea showed signs of breaking down shortly after they began, and were in fact suspended from 23 August until 25 October 1951. Operation Takeoff therefore began on an emergency basis, with improvised methods and procedures, the first major initiative after the Psychological Strategy Board was set up. Following several drafts in August and early September 1951, the board hurriedly approved Operation Takeoff on 18 September 1951. Heavily sanitized versions of the plan available to scholars relate to strategic objectives and their coordination; operational details are blanked out (except for references to a leaflet drop over China), as are any indications that the Army, Navy, Air Force, and CIA were all to take part in the covert operation.[24] The Psychological Strategy Board evidently succeeded in imposing its strategic coordination over the projects that it initiated.[25]

There are signs that Operation Takeoff, which Gordon Gray signaled was to be handled on a "need to know" basis, had some highly unusual aspects in support of "the political, economic and military courses of action as planned for this eventuality" that went beyond leaflet drops on China. It ordered that both overt psychological warfare and covert operations "be employed to the limit" in order to increase pressure on "the North Korean and Chinese Communist troops" and on the "Chinese peoples and troops in China." The operational units, according to a paragraph vetted by the Joint Chiefs of Staff, were to "conduct such additional covert operations, including guerrilla activities, as may achieve either the action effects or the psychological effects desired."[26]

Collateral documents show that the plan had fifteen points and seven annexes. One of the latter, Annex G, apparently depended upon "operational feasibility" by relevant departments. The secretary of defense complained that Annex G, "having such military and political implications" and demanding "planning of such magnitude," should be more thoroughly considered by the Psychology Strategy Board before being handed over for action.[27]

At the coordinating committee for what was described as "the covert implementation of 'Takeoff,'" on 3 October 1951, the service personnel were hesitant, even a little suspicious; General John Magruder confessed that he had delayed forwarding the plan to the Joint Chiefs of Staff. Although the documents carried a memo saying that it was an "approved" plan, the representatives of the Pentagon wanted to know why there was no formal indication of this fact on the plan itself. Why was there no box carrying the facsimile signature of the person in authority? Why was there no indication that the plan was "a numbered paper in a series of PSB formal papers"? After receiving assurances, General Magruder indicated to the meeting that he would "probably forward the plan for action tomorrow."[28] An uneasiness, a feeling of reluctance, was clearly evident.

Four days later, in accordance with "an oral directive," three Army colonels left Washington for a "top secret" trip to see General Ridgway, commander-in-chief of the Far East Command in Tokyo.[29] We do not know whether this trip was part of Operation Takeoff. Perhaps it was just a chance event. But in another coincidence, when U.S. Air Force colonel Andrew J. Evans, Jr., who had previously worked in the War Plans Division, was shot down by the Chinese in 1953, he told his captors that planning for the biological warfare campaign in Korea had begun in October 1951. His statement was corroborated by another high-ranking POW, Colonel Frank H. Schwable, U.S. Marine Corps, who added that the Joint Chiefs of Staff had "sent [their] directive by hand" to General Ridgway in October 1951, ordering "the initiation of bacteriological warfare in Korea on an initially small, experimental stage but in expanding proportions."[30]

The three Army colonels, after reporting in person to Ridgway, spent two weeks in Japan and Korea, talking to officers and men not only at all levels in the Army but also in the Far East Air Force—taking "great care," they said, to ensure that no one other than Ridgway and his chief of staff "learned of our true mission in the Theater." At least part of their mission, as revealed in the collateral documents, was to initiate plans and preparations for "the employment of atomic weapons in support of ground operations in the Far East."[31] We know, as discussed in an earlier chapter, that the formal war plans of the United States called for the use of biological weapons in conjunction with atomic weapons; but "covert" matters, especially those on a "need to know" basis, did not get reported in regular channels. Special security regulations applied to activities such as Operation Takeoff because, although it was planned and conducted by the U.S. government, the government had ordered that responsibility for covert operations should not be evident to unauthorized persons; and if such activities were uncovered, the U.S. government could, by deception, plausibly disclaim any responsibility for them.[32]

But the papers of the president's Psychological Strategy Board contain a glimpse of the general intent to consider "novel weapons." As nervous rumblings continued around Operation Takeoff into late November 1951, there was a flap about "statements concerning Novel Weapons," referring to biological, chemical, or radiological weapons.[33] A further clue is found in the overlapping plan Operation Hummer, which was approved 4 October 1951, one day after the mysterious coordinating committee meeting that set Operation Takeoff in motion. The part of Operation Hummer to be implemented during the political negotiations following the ceasefire called for "overt and covert exploitation in Korea of possibility of use of novel weapons of war."[34]

Obvious unease with Operation Takeoff continued, from Secretary of Defense Lovett down through the military staff, but Psychological Strategy Board director Gordon Gray, no doubt with presidential backing, continued to push. The Joint Chiefs of Staff approved the plan 21 December 1951 and reported that "implementing plans have been prepared and are in the hands of operating agencies."[35]

Even though some of the regular military services may have been ill at ease with the directives coming from the presidential office in late 1951, the dominant organization for the implementation of covert operations in the Korean War remained the Central Intelligence Agency, whose head, General Walter Bedell Smith, was on the president's Psychological Strategy Board.

9 The CIA in the Korean War

Covert operations . . . are so planned and conducted that any US Government responsibility for them is not evident to unauthorized persons and that if uncovered the US Government can plausibly disclaim any responsibility.
—U.S. National Security Council Directive, NSC 10/2, Top Secret, June 1948

The secretive nature of intelligence agencies necessarily leaves evidence of their activities incomplete. By definition, intelligence agents are masters of deception that is calculated to cover their clandestine operations. However, as a result of public pressure for "the right to know" and the U.S. Senate's investigation into the Central Intelligence Agency's activities in 1975, there is no need to argue about whether the use of germ warfare fell within the accepted canon of CIA doctrine: it did.[1] The CIA used defoliants classified as biological weapons in Vietnam, and there are accusations that anti-crop and anti-animal agents were used from the 1960s to the 1990s in Cuba, in Jamaica, and elsewhere.[2]

But what of the CIA during the Korean War in the early 1950s?

Colonel Fletcher Prouty, who for many years briefed the U.S. Defense and State departments on the CIA's special operations, confirms that the agency was heavily involved in the Korean War.[3] Predictably, he avoids mentioning operational details. However, he and others provide insights into how the CIA developed a large autonomous presence in Korea through an ad hoc and cooperative relationship with the Far East Command.

The increasing importance of covert operations and the CIA leadership was building as the Korean War broke out. U.S. National Security Council directives in 1947 and 1948 were "without question," as Alfred Paddock, Jr., historian of the Special Forces, observes, "perceived as a significant escalation of US interests in the covert side of the cold war." By early 1950, "it was clear that the responsibility for unconventional warfare . . . was shifting to the CIA," with the center of gravity being the CIA's Office of Policy Coordination. This office was responsible for

1. Political warfare including assistance to underground resistance movements and support of indigenous anti-Communist elements in threatened countries of the free world.
2. Psychological warfare including "black" and "gray" propaganda.
3. Economic warfare.
4. Evacuation, including the paramount responsibility for escape and evasion.
5. Guerrilla and partisan-type warfare.
6. Sabotage and counter-sabotage.
7. Other covert operations (excluding espionage, counterespionage, and cover and deception for military operations).[4]

Thrown into the Korean War, the CIA worked out a complex but largely autonomous operation in cooperation with the Far East Command. Although this arrangement was not without its frictions and inefficiencies, the Joint Chiefs of Staff, the CIA, and (especially after General MacArthur's dismissal) the Far East Command all endorsed it. The most serious critics were Secretary of the Army, Frank Pace, the power behind the Army's Psychological Warfare Division, and its able and aggressive head, Brigadier General Robert McClure. Basing their argument on greater efficiency, Pace and McClure were largely successful in their attempt to coordinate the propaganda aspect of psychological warfare under Army command; but the extent of their failure to make headway with covert and unconventional operations was emphasized when the Joint Subsidiary Plans Division of the Joint Chiefs of Staff, with the backing of the president's Psychological Strategy Board, strongly endorsed the existing ad hoc organization in late 1951. Paddock observes that this endorsement was rooted partly in the fact that the sudden ground swell of high-level political interest in covert warfare caught the services ill-prepared, and they were forced to share the stage with the specialists in the field until they had the time and resources to put their own special forces higher on the agenda.[5]

What the Joint Subsidiary Plans Division endorsed was placing the CIA and covert operations in Korea under the Commander in Chief Far East (CINCFE) and the Combined Command for Reconnaissance Activities, Korea (CCRAK), the latter having been set up by CINCFE to coordinate all behind-the-lines activities. But both CINCFE and the Joint Chiefs of Staff acquiesced in the insistence of the CIA's Far East Command that CIA Korea (operating under cover as the Joint Advisory Commission Korea [JACK] remain an independent organization under the control of CIA Far East. The formal consequence was that CIA Korea did not carry out missions in support of CINCFE without authority from CIA

Far East, which took its direction from CIA Washington. And as CIA insider Fletcher Prouty noted, General Walter Bedell Smith, as head of the CIA and empowered by the growing enthusiasm for "dirty tricks" in the early Cold War, never doubted his authority to run the show in covert warfare. At the same time, he recognized that he had to live with others. The practical result was that when key individuals on both sides were empathetic, the CIA and the military each participated in the other's assignments.[6]

Though there is some difference of opinion as to how much empathy and cooperation there actually was, there is reason to believe that the CIA was a major force in the Korean War. On the skeptical side, Major General John Singlaub, in recollecting his experience while an Army major on CIA assignment as deputy chief of station in Korea in 1952, considered CCRAK a useless and overlapping "hodgepodge" competing for funds Singlaub describes independent CIA assignments deploying military intelligence, espionage, and resistance agents in North Korea. His vehicle was a "small flotilla of fast, heavily armed patrol boats" operating from covert bases on offshore islands, or airdrops. He fails to note whether he used CIA aircraft for his drops.[7]

Prouty, a CIA veteran, saw the grease that turned friction to gain for the organization. He believes that the Korean War saved the CIA not only by giving it the right war at the right time, but also by giving it the resources of other agencies in wartime. As he put it,

> Though the NSC directives state that the CIA could not create an organization to accomplish clandestine activities, and even though the President had said that the CIA must come to the [National Security] Council for any such equipment, the CIA managed to create a huge capability that cost them nothing, and that was ready to do its bidding at the drop of a hat.[8]

Prouty saw the CIA as going into high gear after the removal of MacArthur, who "had always been a foe of the hard-core intelligence class."[9] But even with MacArthur, Prouty observes that the CIA always had allies in high places in the military, most notably in General Vandenberg, and many ranking and rising officers who were enthusiasts for covert war.

> There were many like General Vandenberg . . . who thought that the peacetime military forces should become more proficient in this type of operation. . . . They actively and eagerly supported their CIA counterparts. Many of these men accepted duty assignments with the CIA. These units . . . became the havens for

> a large number of CIA cover-assignment men. These CIA people
> served as military personnel easily in the pseudo-military units.[10]

But the exchange went both ways. CIA people performed regular military assignments, creating a store of personnel who could and did play interchangeable roles with growing ease. Air Force, Army, and Navy special forces were, according to Prouty, "heavily sprinkled with CIA agents, and most of their direction in the field was the operational responsibility of the CIA."[11] But Prouty also paints a picture of regular forces sprinkled with CIA personnel, enhancing capacity for covert assignments across the forces:

> This . . . was a significant departure from the original plans. . . .
> From the beginning a great number of [CIA] jobs, including many
> top-level jobs, were assigned to active duty military personnel,
> and . . . CIA men served in the military by agreement in the war
> planning spaces. But it never had been visualized that hundreds
> of military men would serve with the CIA in its clandestine sec-
> tions in support of such units as the Army Special Forces and
> the Air Force ARC Wings. Nor was it ever envisioned that hun-
> dreds of CIA men would cross over into the military to serve with
> the line military units.[12]

The CIA also had independent means apart from Singlaub's high-speed boats. One of the main vehicles for the agency's operations in Korea was an airline that flew the Chinese Nationalist flag and operated under a Taiwan charter; it was known as Civil Air Transport (CAT). CAT had been directed by General Claire Chennault, leader of the famous U.S. Flying Tigers, who fought the Japanese from air bases in southern China during World War II. After the war, Chennault kept his rough-and-tough band of flyers together by forming CAT as a private American enterprise. Its small fleet of C-46 aircraft helped Nationalist leader Chiang Kai-shek in his civil war with the Chinese Communists. With Chiang having lost the civil war and fled to Taiwan, Chennault and his anti-Communist partners moved there also, but faced bankruptcy for lack of employment. The CIA came along in 1949 and offered to buy CAT. A year later, with Chennault remaining as a highly visible chairman of the board in Taipei, and in close touch with Chiang Kai-shek, the new manager, Alfred T. Cox, propelled the "Chinese Nationalist" airline into the Korean conflict. He was also head of the CIA's covert activities in East Asia.[13] CAT was a perfect cover for activities that would be considered illegal under international law. If something went wrong and a plane was shot down over neutral Chinese territory, the American government could deny any responsibility for mercenary pilots or any connection with a foreign airline.

At first MacArthur tried to keep what he considered the hard-core CIA operators out of the area, and to keep paramilitary operations more under his direct control.[14] However, the exigencies of the war and shortages of air transport soon led to CAT's becoming established at the sprawling Tachikawa air base near Tokyo, under contract to the U.S. Far East Air Materiel Command.

According to Captain Annis G. Thompson, historian of the Combat Cargo Command, the twin-engine C-46 Douglas aircraft of CAT acted as a military squadron, executing the same tasks and taking the same risks as Air Force transport units. They carried "all types of cargo to practically every airstrip in Korea capable of landing a C-46." Ammunition airlifts "included bombs, machine gun and small arms bullets, artillery shells, and napalm, tanks and mix."[15] CAT also made two or three daily multi-stop scheduled flights for the Combat Cargo Command, making the rounds of a dozen or so U.S. military bases in Korea with "a variety of cargo." Captain Thompson fails to mention CAT's link to the CIA, and apologizes for "security limitations" that have "wiped out some very fascinating chapters"[16] in the history of the Cargo Command.

Another historian, William M. Leary, has written on the same subject and provides a fuller picture of CAT's activities. He states that while CAT's airlift contributions to the Far East Air Force Cargo Command were important, they could not compare with its crucial support to the CIA Office of Policy Coordination's operations in Japan and Korea.[17]

The Office of Policy Coordination (OPC), as noted, was a section of the CIA established by President Truman's National Security Council in 1948 and charged with responsibility for covert, unconventional, and psychological warfare. It was a critical strategic meeting point for the CIA and the psychological warfare organization. In the intelligence community, the OPC was known as the "dirty tricks department." The dirty tricks agenda, as shown in the previous chapter, included everything from supplying and evacuating espionage agents, issuing "black" and "gray" propaganda, and organizing sabotage, to "use of unconventional weapons," including biological weapons, "for psychological purposes."[18]

The Office of Policy Coordination grew rapidly during the Korean War. From a small nucleus of 302 people and a budget of $4.7 million in 1949, it became an organization with 2,812 employees and a budget of $82 million in 1952. In explaining this growth, CIA director William E. Colby stated, "Under the impetus of the Korean War, at a time of fierce anti-Communist and anti-Soviet sentiment and rhetoric, covert paramilitary and political action was the name of the intelligence game."[19]

From the start, OPC's operations were structured around the idea of deniability. The most important distinction that set the office apart from the rest of the national military establishment, according to its first head, was that its covert operations had to be conducted in a manner such that "official United States interest or responsibility is not permitted to appear and if such interest should inadvertently appear, it can be plausibly disclaimed by this government."[20] Later, under questioning, Colby described "plausible denial" as meaning that "if the United States could deny something and not be clearly demonstrated as having said something falsely, then the United States could do so. . . . Plausible denial was so our Nation could deny something and not be tagged with it."[21] Official U.S. denials of germ warfare could quite easily fall within this code of conduct. And the U.S. Joint Chiefs of Staff may have had something like this in mind in 1952 when they discussed whether the secretaries of state and defense should be excluded from the decision to implement the "BW Cover and Deception Plan."[22]

The covert airborne activities of the CIA in the Korean War began in July 1950, within a month of the start of the war. At that time intelligence sources arranged for three CIA aircraft to operate between Japan and Korea in something called Operation AD. Based at Tachikawa air base near Tokyo and on twenty-four-hour call, the aircraft transported "sensitive personnel and performed other urgent missions." According to Leary, "Wider use of CAT in support of covert projects followed."[23]

The head of CIA-OPC covert operations in Japan and Korea in 1950–51 was Hans V. Tofte, a veteran of World War II with extensive experience in paramilitary activities. In the 1930s, Tofte had worked in Manchuria for the Danish East Asiatic Company, and during his vacations he had taken long big game hunting excursions in the border region. "Able to identify vital border crossings along the little-known northern frontier," according to Leary, Tofte "could place his units in position to cause maximum damage."[24] Tofte organized the infrastructure for OPC's activities by setting up six CIA stations in Japan. The largest base was in the Yokohama district, an hour's drive south of Tokyo, at the sprawling Atsugi Naval Air Station of the U.S. Navy. Here the CIA had fifty acres in an isolated area along the Sagami River between Atsugi and the factory town of Chigasaki on Sagami Bay. Tofte trained saboteurs and agents to assist downed American pilots in North Korea. By the end of 1950, OPC had more than a thousand men in training in Japan, and a year later it claimed to have twelve hundred guerrillas in North Korea ambushing truck convoys and sabotaging trains, interrupting the flow of supplies from Manchuria and eastern Siberia. In supporting this work CAT, according to Tofte, was "absolutely invaluable."[25]

CIA air support was not restricted to CAT. It also drew on the 581st ARC Wing when the wing was introduced into the Korean War in the summer of 1952. One of the principal responsibilities of the ARC Wing of the Air Force Psychological Warfare Division was supporting CIA special missions.[26] In the creation of the wings, the Air Force resurrected its World War II connections with the Office of Strategic Services (OSS). It drew leaders and flight crews from members of the 492nd Bombardment Group, the "Carpetbaggers," who had performed clandestine missions for the OSS over Europe.[27] In light of the covert nature of the missions conducted by the CIA and the Air Force Psychological Warfare Division, a close relationship could be expected.

Fleeting glimpses into joint ARC Wing and CIA operations are found in three documents that prompt attention. The first is a telex message from the Department of the Air Force to the commanding general of the Far East Air Force indicating the responsibility of the newly formed 581st ARC Wing to support CIA missions. This "Top Secret" message is stamped "personal" and further classified as "OPTIC," which we understand to be a classification above top secret. It is the only optic message we have encountered.[28] One is left to speculate about why this message had such a high security classification. One possibility is that the Air Force was nervous about public disclosure of the company it was keeping, though the heavy involvement of the Air Force in CIA activity makes this unlikely. More significant is the line of authority disclosed in the telex for the command of the ARC Wing when supporting CIA missions: "JCS policy directs that the Chief of Staff, USAF, will act as executive agent of the JCS in exercising operational control over specific missions." Vandenberg's role in directing CIA operations within the Air Force is made explicit. Had the role of the U.S. Air Force Psychological Warfare Division in covert bacteriological warfare been disclosed amid the North Korean and Chinese charges of germ warfare at this time, the additional disclosure of the organizational loop between Vandenberg, the ARC Wing, and the CIA certainly would have been an embarrassing setback to concerted U.S. efforts to refute the charges.

The first CIA operation in cooperation with the ARC Wing may have taken place in September or October 1952, following the wing's arrival at Clark Air Force Base in the Philippines at the end of July. A telex message from CINCFE General Mark Clark to Department of the Army, Washington, D.C., for the Joint Chiefs of Staff indicated that he considered an upcoming mission "to be an excellent opportunity to evaluate ARC Wing concept under combat conditions of limited scope."[29] An accompanying document from General Clark to the commanding general of the Far East Air Force, dated October 1952 (with the exact date seemingly coded), lays out the elaborate line of consultation or authority that Clark put in place for CIA operations with the ARC Wing. He ran the lines of authority through CINCFE, CGFEAF, the Chief Psychological Warfare Section Far East Command, the Far East Command G-2 (Intelligence), and the CIA. This confirms that although the ARC Wing with headquarters in the Philippines was located outside FECOM jurisdiction, and CIA Korea had a sphere of independent authority, there was still at least the appearance of a line of command.

But there is a written comment on the copy of the document in our possession which suggests that this line of authority had a more specific application than day-to-day operations. The comment reads simply "Emergency War Plan," suggesting that Clark may have been setting out the necessary line of authority for the role of the ARC Wing in the plan for general war. In this respect it should be noted again that operational planning for any U.S. Air Force bacteriological warfare annexes to the emergency war plan for the Far East, including covert use, were the responsibility of the U.S. Air Force Psychological Warfare Division, and that the 581st ARC Wing was its only direct operational arm.[30] Perhaps coincidentally, the Japanese journalist Masa Ota of the Kyoto News Agency found this document among declassified Joint Chiefs of Staff records on the bacteriological warfare program.

The ARC Wing also had an H-19 helicopter unit, the 2157th Air Rescue Squadron, that suited CIA needs. Operating through CCRAK, in one six-month period of operations this squadron logged more than eleven hundred hours of combat time, flying in more than three hundred intelligence and rescue missions. It flew missions only at night, mostly from Cho-do Island, ten miles off the Korean coast and sixty miles behind North Korea's front lines. It made deep penetrations into North Korea; one mission was within sixteen miles of China and ten minutes' flying time from Antung.[31]

Air Force Special Forces provided another source of CIA air support. As Prouty notes, Special Forces contained and were frequently under the operational command of CIA personnel. Michael Haas's history of the Air Force Special Forces contains a telling photograph of a CCRAK group planning a special mission. It pictures personnel from the Air Force and Army Special Forces, Navy Frogmen, British Royal Marines, South Korean irregulars, and the CIA.[32]

Air Force Special Forces, also known as the Air Commandos, worked closely with the psychological warfare units, which, if they were involved in covert work, would have come under CIA direction. The official history leaves the impression that there was little contact between the Air Commandos and the 581st ARC Wing, but a declassified Air Force internal history of irregular units suggests that there was active cooperation with the ARC Wing's H-19 helicopters and other aircraft.[33] Another client of the Air Commandos was Far East Command Technical Intelligence, where the CIA might have had some involvement. Technical intelligence included medical intelligence, and would have had to be part of any monitoring mechanism for biological warfare operational plans.[34] Most of the records of the Air Commandos in Korea have not survived, so the full story of their involvements and missions will not be told from their archives, nor from those of CCRAK.[35] We get a revealing glimpse into the very active operational history and the far-sweeping organizational structure of irregular, including covert, units, including the Air Commandos, in the USAF's "Guerrilla Warfare and Airpower in Korea, 1950–1953." One frequent operational objective was rail communications, an area of activity in which the Chinese suspected enemy agents of spreading diseased insects.

The air unit with which the Air Commandos mostly serviced their clients was the 21st Troop Carrier Squadron of the 315th Air Division of the Cargo Command, which came to be known as the "Kyushu Gypsies" because of its early nomadic life operating from whatever airstrips could be found in Japan.[36] After September 1950 it operated from Seoul's Kimpo Airport. The Kyushu Gypsies flew an inordinate number of hours compared to other squadrons in the Cargo Command and, according to Air Force historians, stood out "like a giant among Korean Airlift outfits."[37] There was "nothing too fantastic for the Gypsies to fly. . . . The Gypsies were the only outfit of their kind in the U.S. Air Force. Their status was and is unique."[38]

Within the Kyushu Gypsies was a clandestine Special Air Missions (SAM) unit known simply as Detachment 2. Under the command of Captain Henry Aderholt, Detachment 2 is described by the author of *Air Commando*, Colonel Michael Haas, as numbering from six to eight C-47 aircraft and operating through CCRAK, which in turn operated under cover of Far East Command Liaison Detachment 9.[39] It was deeply buried, open only to those with a need to know. In the autumn of 1951, Aderholt's Detachment 2 received a new assignment, running "psychological warfare operations" under a Fifth Air Force unit based near the front lines. Apart from propaganda missions with leaflets and loudspeakers, the daredevil SAM detachment, according to Captain Annis G. Thompson, historian of the Cargo Command, had "special classified airlift missions."[40] These included reconnaissance and dropping spies, called "rabbits," behind enemy lines.[41] Biological warfare activity is not mentioned, but then records of several "highly classified" projects between January and June 1952 remain unavailable to the public.[42] Haas tells us that the Air Commandos ran special missions from the Fifth Air Force light attack bomber operations desk located at Forward Deployed Headquarters, Seoul. Though he gives no detail on these missions, if they were covert, the CIA was in charge.[43]

The declassified "Guerrilla Warfare and Airpower in Korea, 1950–1953" provides lengthy coverage of a Detachment 2 that it identifies as belonging to the 6004 Air Intelligence Service Squadron. This may be the same Detachment 2; if not, it coincidentally played a major role in irregular warfare. This study goes beyond Haas in describing how, by 1952, Detachment 2 became the hub for a network of subdetachments which ran, supplied, and maintained irregular units with a growing flotilla of boats, as well as by air. The ARC Wing supported it with its H-19 helicopters, and in the spring of 1953 made available two of its SA-16 aircraft, enabling Detachment 2 to reach its more remote field units.[44]

The CIA's "Operation TROPIC" in the spring of 1952 is a dramatic example of an operation inside China. The capture and trial by the Chinese of two CIA agents involved and interviews with participants by William Leary provide rich details about this operation and give an indelible impression of the energy that the United States invested in establishing agents and collecting information from the enemy's back yard.[45]

As part of the U.S. secret war against mainland China, Operation TROPIC was a "third force" project aimed at introducing new agents into China who were unconnected to Chiang Kai-shek and were directly linked to American intelligence. After training in basic skills such as parachuting, use of small arms, explosives, and radio operation, the agents were formed into small teams and taught how to establish secure bases, how to mark out drop zones, and how to organize communication networks. Once on the mainland, they would "recruit local dissidents, collect and transmit intelligence and weather information, and rescue any downed American airmen."[46]

Confirmation of this activity comes from the government of the People's Republic of China, which reported that 212 native Chinese—equipped with weapons, radio sets, secret codes, invisible ink, fake passes, and gold bars—were parachuted onto the Chinese mainland between 1951 and 1953. Of these, 101 were killed and 111 captured.[47]

The focus of Operation TROPIC was the northeastern Chinese provinces of Liaoning and Kirin. These provinces border Korea along the Yalu River and contained China's largest industrial base. This is precisely the area where the Chinese often complained of intrusions by U.S. aircraft, and it was, according to Chinese accounts, the location of most germ warfare attacks on China. It was a prime location for U.S. intelligence gathering about the Chinese war effort and the effects of germ weapons.

Three CAT aircraft, painted drab olive and equipped with flame suppressors to make them less visible from the ground at night, were commissioned for Operation TROPIC. The crews were based at the CIA station in Atsugi, Japan.[48] They routinely flew over to Pusan or Seoul, where the cargo door was removed to make airdrops easier. At dusk the plane would head east over the Sea of Japan, to avoid detection by U.S. Air Force radar, and then turn north. Careful to avoid big cities lest the noise betray their presence to the Chinese, the crew located the drop zone and brought the aircraft in at a low altitude; at a signal from the navigator, the CIA agents on board pushed the supplies or the people out the door. The crew then returned to Atsugi for debriefing.

The leader of Operation TROPIC was John T. Downey, the son of a Connecticut judge, who joined the CIA in 1951 in his senior year at Yale, after hearing a recruiter describe the glamour of parachuting behind enemy lines and developing resistance networks. He interviewed and trained two four man teams of Chinese who were local to Kirin province but had been recruited in Hong Kong or Taiwan, and dropped them into their native area. After several months, he dropped another man in to see how the others were doing.

It was difficult enough to deliver people to the designated target; it was another matter trying to bring them out. In this case, as described by a former intelligence officer, the CIA-OPC group devised a novel method:

> Two poles were set in the ground and a wire strung between them. Attached to the wire was a line leading to a harness in which the person to be picked up was strapped. Approaching slightly above stall speed (at about sixty miles per hour), the aircraft hooked onto the wire and jerked the man up to flying speed, then reeled him into the aircraft. One could only marvel at the courage of those intrepid individuals who agreed to sit impassively in harnesses, awaiting possible decapitation, whiplash, or other serious injury.[49]

After this method was well-practiced, the first real pickup attempt took place on 29 November 1952, but it ended in calamity. The agent who had been dropped in to observe the others had radioed that he was ready to come out. Downey, together with Richard Fecteau, another intelligence officer, and flight crew members Robert Snoddy and Norman Schwartz, approached the rendezvous spot three hours after taking off from Seoul. "Everything appeared normal as they neared the pickup wire," writes William Leary. "A minute later Snoddy and Schwartz were dead, shot down by Communist gunfire. Downey and Fecteau survived the crash and were captured."[50] The "third force" team had been penetrated by counter-espionage police.

After two years of silence on the matter, Peking Radio revealed that thirteen Americans had been sentenced to prison for espionage, including Downey and Fecteau, who received sentences of life and twenty years, respectively. The U.S. State Department, insisting that the two were civilian employees of the Army, denied the spy story and demanded their release immediately. The Department of Defense added that the men had been on a "routine" flight between Seoul and Japan, and that their convictions on spy charges illustrated once again the "bad faith, insincerity and amorality which have characterized that regime's conduct in its international relations." The charge of "spying" was "all too reminiscent," according to U.S. defense headquarters, "of numerous other false charges previously made against the United Nations command." Some American congressmen worked themselves into a fury against the hated Chinese, who supposedly were able to brainwash their captives into making false confessions.[51]

The North Asia Command of the Central Intelligence Agency knew better but kept quiet; it assumed that Downey and Fecteau had told their captors everything. "When they were released many years later," wrote E. Howard Hunt of Watergate fame, who served with the North Asia Command in 1955, "the assumption proved to have been correct."[52]

Another aspect of the CIA Office of Policy Coordination's activity came under the heading of psychological warfare. The National Security Council gave the CIA responsibility for covert psychological warfare in directives during 1947 and 1948, and the agency somewhat ironically spent much of its time and money in propaganda activities to refute enemy claims and in covering up traces of U.S. covert activities so as to avoid scrutiny by the American people and allies abroad. The CIA had to make good the government's demand for plausible deniability of questionable or illegal acts such as using biological warfare.

To accomplish its propaganda objectives, the CIA infiltrated news agencies, established radio networks, gave money to journalists, financed student organizations, subsidized academic journals, and influenced publishers. All this was done through a web of fictitious corporate structures, sham cultural foundations, and financial arrangements that cost up to $200 million annually by 1953.[53] The head of Praeger Publishers, for example, admitted that beginning in the 1950s his company published "15 to 16" books (later he increased it to "20 to 25 volumes") on "Communist-bloc countries" at the CIA's suggestion. Asked by press correspondents if the CIA had financed a book venture in whole or in part, Frederick Praeger stated, "I have no comment."[54]

Although there is no proof that it is one of the CIA-sponsored books published by Praeger, a study worthy of note as supporting CIA objectives, whether consciously or otherwise, is John Clews, *The Communists' New Weapon: Germ Warfare*, published in London in 1953 by Lincolns-Prager Publishers, with a foreword by Professor A. V. Hill, president of the British Association for the Advancement of Science.[55] An expanded edition of the book, with a preface by G. F. Hudson of St. Anthony's College, Oxford, appeared later under the Praeger New York imprint. The Clews book gives the appearance of having the support of unimpeachable academic authority; it suggests reliable historical documentation, a perfect vehicle through which to funnel "black" or "gray" propaganda to Western audiences.

Once a book with respectable credentials is launched into the public arena, it takes on a life of its own. Clews, who treats the possibility of U. S. biological warfare as laughable nonsense, not to be taken seriously, is cited positively by Walter G. Hermes, official historian of the U.S. Army in the Korean War. Hermes calls it an "interesting discussion" of the allegations of Chinese germ warfare.[56]

An enterprising young student, John Clews had been vice president for international affairs of the British National Union of Students in 1950–51 and was a participant in the International Student Conference, an organization set up "to fight international communism." He traveled to Eastern Europe, the Soviet Union, and China. Probably unbeknownst to him, the International Student Conference was initiated and heavily financed by the CIA acting through the international department of the U.S. National Students Association, which it had successfully infiltrated.[57] While Clews may not have known of the CIA's presence, the CIA agents would have been well aware of him, and in a position to assess his capabilities and political inclinations as a potential author. All the necessary connections were present.

In backing up Clews's entry into the publishing world, his Oxford mentor, G. F. Hudson, who himself was advisory editor of a British academic journal then being funded by the CIA,[58] wrote that the Chinese accusation of germ warfare—brought first against the Japanese, "though without any serious attempt to prove actual belligerent use of bacterial weapons," and then as a full-blown atrocity story against the Americans—was "fabricated from start to finish." Clews, said Professor Hudson, showed that the charge "cannot, and never could, stand up to political analysis."[59]

Walter Hermes, unlike Clews and Hudson, had access to the U.S. government's classified records. But in writing his study, either he neglected to introduce or his superiors censored documents, now declassified, showing that the United States had indeed acquired the Japanese germ war techniques that were perfected on Chinese targets in World War II. Hermes fails to mention that the United States was in fact creating a strong offensive bacteriological warfare capacity, and that U.S. Air Force Chief of Staff Vandenberg reported to the Chiefs of Staff in February 1952, after returning from a visit to the U.S. Fifth Air Force in Korea, that there was great progress in biological warfare with "certain offensive capabilities . . . rapidly materializing."[60]

Instead of biting the bullet, Hermes or his censors chose to gloss over the question. Faced with the evidence to which "the public" now has access, one can scarcely escape the conclusion that the official history became part of the cover-up. Given the constraints often placed upon official historians, perhaps this is not too surprising. Apart from citing the secretary of state's indignant denials about biological warfare, Hermes refers the reader to that handy little 32-page booklet written by our student journalist John Clews—a booklet with all the earmarks of official propaganda.

Much has been written about the macho commando psychology that took hold in the CIA at this time, about daring and largely unsuccessful CIA covert operations in North Korea and China aimed at creating civil unrest, engaging in sabotage, or rescuing spies, but little has been said about the agency's role in bacterial warfare.

Congressional hearings into the activities of the CIA, held in the wake of the Watergate scandal that disgraced President Nixon, did something to lift the veil of secrecy. The Washington hearings revealed that the CIA had stockpiled substances that cause tuberculosis, anthrax, encephalitis, Rift Valley fever, salmonella, botulism, and smallpox.[61] In addition, CIA director William E. Colby told the congressional hearing that the agency had records of its biological warfare activities going back to 1952, but now "the records are very incomplete," because some documents were destroyed in 1972–73. In response to further questioning, he hedged, stating that he was "very unsure" of the total destroyed since the agency did not keep an inventory of it.[62]

Though some documents have been shredded, others have been inadvertently lost or destroyed, and others are not expected to be opened in the foreseeable future, there is nevertheless a trail of documented circumstantial evidence that the CIA was closely involved in operational planning for the covert use of biological weapons during the Korean War, and that it had access to an extensive covert structure to implement these plans.

10 Insect Vectors in Occupied Japan: Unit 406

Infectious material of plague, cholera, anthrax, undulant fever and tularemia will be transported only by a courier who is aware of the precautions necessary for his own safety and the safety of others. —Standing Order, 406 Medical General Laboratory, Tokyo, Annual Historical Report 1947

Because of the many reports of their biting humans and their great potentiality as vectors of disease the emphasis was placed upon the study of the black flies. —Taxonomic Entomology Section, 406 Medical General Medical Laboratory, Tokyo, Annual Report 1953

The cessation of the Korean War brought to completion our studies concerning the ectoparasite fauna of small mammals and birds. —Department of Entomology, 406 Medical General Laboratory, Tokyo, Annual Historical Report 1953

Work of a classified nature, for security reasons, is reported elsewhere. —406 Medical General Laboratory, Tokyo, Monthly Technical Report, August 1951

As the pressure for biological warfare research and development heated up following the start of the Korean War, the Far East Medical Section's 406 Medical General Laboratory became a storehouse for the growing research on insect vectors.

Unit 406 began operations in a warehouse near the Atsugi air base in Yokohama in 1946. Later it established its headquarters in the Mitsubishi

Higashi Building in the Maranouchi district of downtown Tokyo, and added a branch in Kyoto. During the Korean War, Unit 406 was involved in supplying and supporting laboratory personnel for the combat zone.[1] Its original purpose was to provide health services—diagnostic testing, a blood bank, and vaccines—to the U.S. soldiers stationed in Japan and Korea, and secondarily to help General MacArthur's occupying power deal with the numerous public health problems of the civilian population.

Unit 406 was activated largely on the initiative of Brigadier General James S. Simmons, chief of the Preventive Medicine Section of the Surgeon General's Office. Simmons had been the driving force behind the founding of the U.S. biological warfare program some ten years earlier and will be remembered as the principal architect of the subterfuge that enabled the Army Medical Corps to participate in offensive bacteriological warfare research. It was perhaps less coincidental that the first commandant of Unit 406, Lt. Colonel W. D. Tigertt, M.D., a distinguished researcher on insect vectors relating to Japanese B encephalitis, moved from Japan in 1949 to assume a series of high-level research posts in the United States, including a five-year stint as commander of the Army Medical Unit at Fort Detrick.[2] Considering their relevance, it could be expected that research reports from the 406 Laboratory would be routinely forwarded to Fort Detrick.[3]

The annual reports of Unit 406 show the laboratory growing from humble beginnings until it included full-scale departments of epidemiology, bacteriology, entomology, and viral and rickettsial diseases. By 1949 and through the Korean War period, the activities of Unit 406 required huge quantities of small animals—twenty thousand white mice monthly, guinea pigs, even frogs—for the testing and manufacture of biologicals. Some of these animals were supplied by former associates of General Ishii.[4] That Unit 406 worked with a wider network in Japan, the Far East, or the United States itself is suggested by a standing order called "Special Provision," which stated that "infectious material of plague, cholera, anthrax, undulant fever and tularemia will be transported only by a courier who is aware of the precautions necessary for his own safety and the safety of others."[5] The 406 Laboratory let out some work to the National Institute of Health in Japan, where former Lt. General Yujiro Wakamatsu—commander of Unit 100, which conducted biological warfare experiments in China during World War II, and the most important person in the Japanese bacteriological warfare program after Ishii and Kitano— turned up as a research scientist, and where other Japanese bacteriological warfare scientists headed various divisions.[6]

After World War II, the leaders of the Japanese bacteriological warfare units found jobs in Japan's public and private health institutions, including medical schools, pharmaceutical companies, and the Japan Blood Bank, later named the Green Cross Company.[7] These people were in a position to mobilize the many faceless scientists and technicians who had worked for Ishii in the far-flung system of military, university, and public health laboratories in Japan, China, and other parts of occupied Asia.[8] The U.S. Army acknowledges that the help of former "Ishii scientists" was sought in one emergency, and this "Ishii infrastructure" certainly had the potential to support the research and development of biological materials and, if called upon, to assist the United States in adapting them to biological warfare.

In 1951, Colonel Richard P. Mason, MC, Commanding Officer of Unit 406, required all enlisted personnel to complete a twelve hour course in chemical, bacteriological, and radiological warfare. In addition, the personnel of every department had four hours of training each week. Topics of study for these sessions included biological warfare, mosquito-trapping methods, mosquito-borne diseases, mosquitoes in relation to equine encephalomyelitis and Japanese B encephalitis, flea identification, fleas in relation to plague, fleas in relation to typhus, tick biology, ticks in relation to viral diseases, and ticks in relation to rickettsial diseases.[9]

The 406 Laboratory conducted a broad range of experimentation in Japan, Korea, and Okinawa, and even observed what was happening in Beijing prior to the victory of Mao Zedong's Communist forces in 1949.[10]

The largest body of reported work at Unit 406 relates to insect and especially to mosquito vectors. From the unit's creation in 1946, a major continuing concern was the spread of Japanese B encephalitis by mosquitoes, particularly overwintering mosquitoes.[11] This insect vector work, which drew on previous work by Japanese scientists, intensified in the summer of 1951, when the entomology department of Unit 406 set up an ecology section.[12] Encephalitis was also a major concern of the department of viral and rickettsial diseases.[13]

Before the Korean War, major projects included a study of fleas, flies, and mites as vectors for malaria, dengue, filariasis, and equine encephalitis; a Tokyo rat survey; and considerable work on diphtheria. During the Korean War, in 1951, mites and fleas of Japan and Korea became the subject for "a special group" at the branch of Unit 406 in Kyoto.[14] In 1951 there also was a major survey of birds as carriers of Japanese B encephalitis; a rodent survey; a study of salmonella in Korea, chiefly involving North Korean prisoners of war; a study of a smallpox outbreak among U.S. troops in Korea; the expansion of insect vector studies from mosquitoes, mites, and fleas to include chiggers, lice, and flies; and a study of rodent reservoirs.

In 1952, in close cooperation with "the leading Japanese authorities in these fields," Unit 406 started a special program to research the geographic distribution, biology, and breeding and biting habits of the black flies and biting midges of Japan and Korea. The emphasis placed upon this study was a result of the many reports of these insects' having bitten humans, and "their great potentiality as vectors of disease."[15] There also were studies of fleas as vectors for plague and murine typhus, which will be remembered to have been of special interest both to Theodor Rosebury at Detrick and to Dr. G. B. Reed's program in Canada. Plague carried by fleas was a high-priority project for Ishii, and the results of his experiments were appreciated by U.S. scientists at Detrick. Unit 406 also studied ticks in relation to viral and rickettsial diseases.

Other diseases studied during the period 1947–53 included anthrax, undulant fever, tularemia, typhoid, paratyphoid, dysentery, tularensis, and schistosomiasis (snail fever). There was a continuing cholera project, which in 1953 developed a successful vaccine.[16]

An increasingly important addition to the 406 Laboratory was the 8003 Far East Medical Research Laboratory, founded in Tokyo in the spring of 1952—at the same time, coincidentally, as the U.S. Air Force crash program to develop biological weapons. This unit has been a shadowy presence for historians. Its structure paralleled that of Unit 406, with departments of bacteriology, epidemiology, entomology, and viral and rickettsial diseases, and teams for research and development, yet it shared common laboratory facilities with the older unit. The fog surrounding 8003, at least in the records of the Far East Medical Section, begins with when it was established and who pushed for it. Various founding dates are cited between the end of January and the end of March 1952. The unit appears to have been established 10 March 1952 by order of the Japan Logistical Command, after having been planned much earlier to supplement the Ecology Section of the Entomology Department of Unit 406 by extending its work on insect vectors of Japanese B encephalitis. Its stated mission was to carry out such activity as "directed or approved by appropriate authority," a description so general as to encompass anything. The need for the duplication involved in the overlap of departments with Unit 406 is not made clear in available reports.[17]

What is clear is that in conjunction with Unit 406, it attracted a heavy flow of scientists from the stateside military, public, and private health establishments. By the end of the year, a major transfer of knowledge was taking place.[18]

Whether the 406 Medical General Laboratory and the 8003 Far East Medical Unit were involved in the U.S. biological warfare program is a subject of conjecture. Though few links have been substantiated, some of the harder questions should be raised. The one established connection is the transfer of data from these units in Japan to the Medical Unit at Fort Detrick, Maryland, and, where relevant, to research work on germ weapons by Detrick's biological laboratories. Canadian sources also refer to work in Japan relevant to joint work by the Canadian and U.S. biological warfare programs on vaccines.[19]

The rumors that have attracted the most attention concern the integration of scientists from Ishii's germ warfare unit into the U.S. program via a cover provided by the 406 Laboratory. The charge received much public play in Japan through the trilogy *The Devil's Gluttony*, by well-known novelist Sei-ichi Morimura. Morimura portrays the U.S. Far East Command's G-2 intelligence section as introducing Ishii people into a secret biological warfare unit with the code name J2C-406, sharing facilities with the 406 Medical General Laboratory in the Mitsubishi Building in central Tokyo. Investigative work by Ishii watchers Kei-ichi Tsuneishi, Sheldon Harris, Peter Williams, and David Wallace, as well as our own work, has failed to establish concrete links, but some of the circumstantial evidence warrants repeat scrutiny until the question can be answered satisfactorily.

Morimura's fictional account of how Ishii people may have become part of the U.S. biological warfare program through Unit 406 is based on the speculation that Ishii's group was infiltrated by members of the Japanese Communist Party. It was through a memorandum from the Japanese Communist Party to U.S. authorities in 1945, according to U.S. military intelligence records, that the United States first learned details of General Ishii's germ war program in Manchuria.[20] U.S. author Sheldon Harris says that this information "was on the whole so reliable that the people lodging the complaints must at one time have been intimately involved in BW work."[21] It could be expected that the Communists would have remained in place with the Ishii group once it became obvious that Ishii was striking a deal with the United States. We were unsuccessful in our attempt to obtain information on this conjecture through our correspondence with the current leadership of the Japanese Communist Party, who indicated that contacts with members from the era who might be helpful had been lost.

According to its own records, Unit 406 had 309 personnel, including 107 Japanese nationals, by 1951.[22] Japanese nationals help positions ranging from professional scientists to lab technicians and assistants, drivers, animal caretakers, interpreters, mechanics, and janitorial and custodial staff. There was a relatively rapid turnover of disaffected or unsatisfactory Japanese staff members—one year as much as 50 percent. While most of the

Japanese workers understood a certain amount of English, the commanding officer of Unit 406 complained that "their inability to understand orders is given regularly as an excuse for non-compliance."[23] This was an ideal situation for the Communist Party to plant people in Unit 406 who opposed the war in Korea. A pamphlet produced by the Japan Peace Council in 1952, entitled "American Bacteriological Base Is Located in the Center of Tokyo," reported that "closely wrapped packets of insects laden with germs of infectious diseases such as plague, cholera, scarlet fever, dysentery and meningitis, are being regularly transported there along with instructions for experiment from Deterric [*sic*] Research Center of the United States. Then Detachment 406 immediately begins work of mass cultivation."[24]

An example of possible infiltration brought to our attention from another source involves Shinkichi Taguchi, a Communist Party member who worked on MacArthur's staff until the Red Purge of 1947. Afterwards he lived in Saitama prefecture, where most of the experimental animal production for Unit 406 took place. He deliberately got involved in guinea pig production and joined the Producers' Association. He also established a hospital there, in which the chief doctor was from Ishii's Unit 731.[25] Morimura's novel has the Japanese Experimental Animal Laboratories in this prefecture supplying an undercover biological warfare operation within Unit 406 with rodents for the testing and cultivation of bacteria for weapons.

Scientists from the Japanese biological warfare program did assist U.S. Army doctors from Unit 406 and Unit 8003 during an outbreak of hemorrhagic fever in Korea. The first reported case of this unusual disease was in April 1951, and then a year later, in May and June of 1952, a major epidemic occurred among U.S. troops. The contagion followed the main line of contact with the enemy north of the 38th Parallel, an area that U.S. troops had passed through on their way north in 1950, had fought over in the spring of 1951, and were occupying at the time of the outbreak in 1952. U.S. Army doctors were eventually successful in treating the disease, but they could neither identify its nature nor isolate its vectors and hosts. Some evidence suggested that it was a virus, and that chiggers carried by rodents were the most likely route of infection, but testing done on several possible animals failed to confirm correlations of occurrences in the field.

More significantly, written reports from Unit 406 indicate that its scientists were already working on hemorrhagic fever in 1951, before the general outbreak among U.S. troops in the spring of 1952, and that "the initial attempts at recovery of the etiologic agent were in part a reduplication of the experience of Japanese investigators," among whom was cited Shiro Kasahara. Kasahara was a member of Ishii's Unit 731 and had been debriefed by the Americans on his work, which included inducing hemorrhagic fever "in a volunteer" after inoculation.[26]

What was the rationale for the early work on hemorrhagic fever that began in 1951? Apparently Captain John Craig, preventive medicine officer of the U.S. X Corps, and an epidemiologist who was assigned to Unit 406 in 1951, became aware at that early date "of the possibility of encountering the disease in Korea."[27] There was no history of hemorrhagic fever in Korea.[28] But one of the two places in the world where hemorrhagic fever had been confirmed was a small area of Manchuria, a territory of China which Japan had controlled for fifteen years until 1945. This raised the possibility that either migrant populations or enemy armies had carried the disease south. How likely this possibility was remains a question, but there is no question that it was the duty of Army epidemiologists to cover the range of possibilities. As it turned out, Craig's caution paid off. Confirmation of his prediction is registered in the monthly technical report of the 406 Laboratory for August 1951, which states, "New activities relate to studies of a disease heretofore considered Leptospirosis, but resembling that described by Japanese as Epidemic Hemorrhagic Fever." This statement is preceded by a tantalizing sentence: "Work of a classified nature, for security reasons, is reported elsewhere."[29] "Elsewhere," if it still exists, has not become available to historical researchers.

An obvious question is whether this link between leptospirosis and hemorrhagic fever was made as the result of Ishii scientists' working closely with the 406 Medical General Laboratory on bacteriological research in 1951, either within the unit or externally affiliated with it. One is also tempted to ask a further question: Was the awareness of this disease heightened as a result of U.S. biological warfare researchers' pursuit of earlier Japanese work on hemorrhagic fever? As yet there is no evidence from Chemical Corps records for confirmation. In any case, the work on hemorrhagic fever quickly got under way. Following the diagnosis of a single fatal case in April 1951, Unit 406 established a department of epidemiology with this disease as its main concern.[30] In response to Captain Craig's request that Unit 406 gather information from Japanese sources, the Medical Section of GHQ Far East Command interviewed Kitano, Kasahara, pathologist Tachiomaru Ishikawa, and Takeo Tamiya, a researcher, all of whom had been associated with Ishii's biological warfare Unit 731.[31] Unit 406 scientists also made use of the work of Dr. Yasuo Tokoro, who discovered the disease. The literature indicates that Ishikawa, at least, was taken into a laboratory to review slides. A summary of the above was translated by Captain Ralph Takami of the Medical Section of the Far East Command and published and distributed through the Far East Command in August 1951.[32] It appears that the 8003 Far East Medical Laboratory was put in place at least partly to assist the department of epidemiology in dealing with hemorrhagic fever. Why was there so much concern in response to one reported case? One must ask whether this was not an indication of a systematic consulting process in a laboratory setting to transfer Unit 731 research to the U.S. biological warfare program through Unit 406 and the 8003 Far East Medical Laboratory.

Two incidents raise questions with respect to the involvement of the U.S. Army Medical Corps in biological warfare field research. Both surround Brigadier General Crawford Sams, MacArthur's chief of the Public Health and Welfare Section in Japan. A swashbuckling commander in the image of his friend Douglas MacArthur, Sams was expected to become surgeon general of the Army, but his road was blocked when "MacArthur men" fell after President Truman fired their commander in April 1951.

Sams thrived on action. He led a mission behind enemy lines which has become part of the American lore of the Korean War, and which bears mention with respect to the varied roles of the Medical Corps. The incident occurred one night in March 1951, when Sams and a small party took a naval landing craft equipped as a laboratory into North Korean waters and went ashore. According to Sams's official account, the mission was in response to an agent's report that bubonic plague had broken out among Chinese troops in the Wonsan area. If so, it would have been necessary to organize the immunization of U.S. and UN soldiers, because, according to Albert Cowdrey, the historian of the Medical Corps in Korea, plague inoculations were not given and large stores of vaccine not kept, as immunity lasted only three to four months.[33] Sams's mission was to drug and kidnap a diseased soldier, bring him back to the floating laboratory, and conduct tests. Once ashore, Sams met an agent with a scientific education who gave him information suggesting that the infection was not plague but hemorrhagic smallpox; consequently, the kidnapping never took place.

One wonders why, considering its innocuous content, the report was kept classified for so long. The official explanation for its not being declassified upon earlier request was that Sams's intention to drug and kidnap a diseased enemy soldier would "reflect upon the ethical actions of General Sams as a medical officer. . . . As a result, the Army Medical Service could expect that its reputation would suffer." The denial went on to argue that release of the report would damage the U.S. internationally. "The fact that General Sams planned to administer a drug, unnecessarily, to an unwilling patient, is in itself, probably an unethical action. The fact that General Sams did plan . . . to enter a hospital by force, and abduct, under morphine sedation, a sick patient, is in itself, an apparent intended violation of the Rules of Land Warfare, and of the Geneva Convention. . . . To put it simply, the US had encouraged the commission of a 'War Crime.'" It is indeed curious that the released explanation for the denial of declassification acknowledged everything about which the Army purported to be concerned in giving its reasons for refusal to declassify. One can only wonder if there was more behind the report than has been revealed, but there is no available evidence to show that the Sams mission was other than reported.[34]

The other episode also involves Sams's converted naval landing craft laboratory, and leaves unanswered questions about the incentive for biological warfare research on enemy prisoners of war at the giant POW camp on Koje Island in South Korea. Testing done aboard the landing craft was allegedly in the interests of coping with an epidemic of dysentery at the camp. But North Korea and China claimed—a claim that students of the war subsequently raised—that prisoners were actually being used for testing methods of germ war.

In this case, the activities of the laboratory ship were picked up by the U.S. media when the 9 April 1951 issue of *Newsweek* reported on the enemy charges, referring to the "infantry landing vessel with a laboratory installed" on which "numbers of Chinese Reds" were tested as the "Bubonic Plague Ship." The Associated Press also ran a story, reporting on 18 May 1951 that each day, on Landing Craft Infantry No. 1097, about three thousand tests were being made on oral and rectal cultures obtained from patients at Koje Island's sprawling prisoner-of-war camps.

The content of a short scholarly article that appeared later, in the January 1952 issue of the *Journal of Tropical Medicine and Hygiene*, organ of the American Society of Tropical Medicine, also raises some question about what the laboratory ship, identified as the "Fleet Epidemic Disease Control Unit," was doing at Koje Island. The piece is about an unusual epidemic of dysentery among prisoners of war.[35] Though the article avoids mentioning where the outbreak took place, the authors, Doctors Hardy, Mason, and Martin, were members of the "Joint Dysentery Unit," 64 Field Hospital, Far East Command, which was at Koje Island. The dysentery epidemic among the prisoners began in early in 1951 and lasted about a year. We know (from other media reports) that the landing craft laboratory was at Koje by at least early 1951, and the Army doctors indicate that it was already there when the outbreak started. They state that "the most unusual feature of the epidemic was its size."

> An outbreak of enteric infections, with 161 hospitalized cases with a fatality rate of 9 per cent, and some 800 milder non-hospitalized cases, would be regarded as a major epidemic. In the Korean outbreak an average of this number of cases and deaths occurred each day throughout a four month period. Moreover, the outbreak continued at a lower level for about one year. There were, in other words, some 150 major epidemics compressed into one.

In a four-month period, there were an astonishing 19,320 hospitalized cases and just under 100,000 milder non-hospitalized cases, with a mortality rate of 9 percent. The Army doctors observe that in ordinary epidemics, the norm is for a single pathogen to appear; but this situation was markedly different. "Each day . . . there would be an admixture of cases of amebic dysentery, bacillary dysentery due to several types of *Shigella*." Moreover, the dysenteries "differed widely" from the form found in the United States, which usually consists of a simple diarrhea. The description of cases indicated that the manifestation in the prisoner-of-war camp was a highly virulent strain of bacteria. Noting the comparatively simple laboratory procedure for identifying *shigellosis* in adults in the United States, the authors said that the cultures in Korea, in contrast, "had the widest variety of suspicious colonies." The usual media for cultivating salmonella were found to be ineffective.

The Army doctors describe an elaborate and widespread testing program over a six-month period, in which the "uniformity of conditions and type of case provided unusually favorable conditions for comparative studies," and they comment that the outbreak demonstrated once again that "an epidemic situation provides an opportunity to accumulate valuable scientific data very rapidly." They also observed that the "Fleet Epidemic Disease Control Unit with its well-equipped floating laboratory . . . was already there, and permitted the immediate initiation of indicated studies at the site of the epidemic." Perhaps the floating laboratory had a double role, both testing and infecting, which may not have been known to the authors of the article.

With modern medical facilities on hand and antibiotic drugs, and with an elaborate, large-scale medical program in place, the most obvious questions are, Why was there such a high mortality rate? Why did the epidemic grow to such proportions and linger for such an abnormally long period as a year? Did Unit 406 and the Far East Medical Section not have sufficient knowledge of tropical dysentery to bring this epidemic under control, and could they not have done so without the need for such an elaborate testing program? Also suspicious was the fact that the raging epidemic, as the article noted, "had been in progress four months before its occurrence was made known to responsible officers in Washington."

The above must be weighed in the light of the 5 December 1950 guidance directive by the Department of Defense Committee on Biological Warfare, which urged that "the armed forces program for the search of evidence of immunity against diseases of BW importance in enemy deserters and prisoners of war be activated."[36] This, in turn, must be placed in the context of the interest in dysentery transmitted by insect vectors expressed by Dr. Theodor Rosebury, Fort Detrick's one time technical director of research and development, and by Dr. G. B. Reed, head of the Canadian biological warfare laboratories, whose first post–World War II project with insect vectors and insect baits was with typhoid–dysentery–type bacteria. In 1947, Reed had indicated that he was doing research with certain dysentery organisms that had possibilities of circumventing current means of immunization against dysentery; his report appears among the information that was transmitted to the U.S. biological warfare program in 1949.[37]

There is no question that the U.S. Army Medical Corps in the Far East created an infrastructure that, through the laboratories of Units 406 and 8003, provided extensive research on insect vectors and rodent hosts which was integrated into biological warfare development at Fort Detrick. As early as 12 December 1950, in a memo to G-2 (Intelligence), Far East Command, the Army Medical Section assured the Chemical Corps of its cooperation in biological warfare research and specified its role:

> Continued cooperation between the chemical and medical services is, of course, essential in the evaluation of potential biological warfare hazards and activities. It is certain that this cooperation will continue. The Medical Section appreciates fully the desirability of complete epidemiological coverage of all disease occurrence, not only from the biological warfare point of view but also as part of the overall medical service program.[38]

This memo carried the standard qualification that bacteriological warfare planning was for defensive purposes only, but we know from U.S. military policy documents that there was a secret offensive strategy draped in the language of "for defensive purposes," that there was a program for research on and development of biological warfare agents, and that the Medical Corps was involved. The Medical Section's assurance of cooperation was made during the intense period of crisis surrounding the U.S. Eighth

Army's retreat from the Yalu, when General MacArthur was telling the Joint Chiefs that he could not stop the Chinese army, and when the Joint Chiefs and Truman considered using the atomic bomb if it was the only available weapon that could prevent a serious defeat.[39]

The discussion in this chapter demonstrates that, disclaimers to the contrary, the U.S. government had ample theoretical knowledge and sufficient practical means to wage biological warfare with insect vectors if it so chose. The claims of the Chinese and North Koreans were well within the realm of possibility. When captured Air Force colonel Walker M. Mahurin later recanted his confession to the Chinese about the use of insect vectors for biological warfare and assured the American people on his return home that any notion of employing "fleas, flies, and mosquitoes" to spread germ warfare was a complete absurdity and a crude fabrication,[40] it was an Aesop's fable—the thief crying, "Stop, thief!"

11 The Flyers

During the heated period of my confession process, when they had begun to affect my thought processes . . . I blurted out that I had visited the Army camp of Detrick, at Frederick, Maryland. This, of course, was a thing that they wanted, and they pressed me to write the details of my visit. . . . After getting me to break on this information, they began to press me quite heavily to make a total confession.

—Colonel Walker M. Mahurin, Group Commander,
U.S. Air Force, former POW in Korea,
statement after repatriation in 1953

He constantly harangued me with stock questions on what was I thinking, what were my feelings, what was Communism etc., etc. I can't write sensibly about what that does to a person when he can't fight back, because my emotions are too wrapped up in it.

—First Lieutenant John Quinn,
U.S. Air Force pilot, former POW in Korea,
statement after repatriation in 1953

Let me tell you something about the personality of American officers. Over the years, I met many of them. They are very malleable. They don't need a lot of pressure to change their minds. They do that rapidly. The English officers, now they are different. If they don't agree with you, it is not easy to change their opinions.

—Zhu Chun, former political officer,
Prison Camp Division Headquarters,
Chinese Volunteer Army in Korea, interviewed in 1996

The so-called "germ warfare" confessions were not simply a sudden bright idea on the part of the Communists, but were an integral part of a tremendous and calculated campaign of lies.

—Dr. Charles Mayo, U.S. alternate representative
to the United Nations, 26 October 1953

A number of U.S. Air Force officers shot down by the North Korean and Chinese armies during the Korean War wrote confessions stating that they had participated in germ war attacks—some of them starting in late 1951. Chinese military intelligence used this information as confirmation of other evidence they had gathered about the enemy's alleged commencement of biological warfare experiments,[1] and they published twenty-five of these statements. Later, when the officers returned to the United States, they all issued denials, saying that their depositions were false and had been obtained under duress. In this chapter we consider the prisoners' evidence from both the Chinese and Western perspectives, as well as some unexpected records of the U.S. Fifth Air Force.

At a bend in the Yalu River near the town of Pyoktong, the Chinese army had a number of prisoner-of-war camps. One of these, in a little settlement called Pingchangli, was for captured enemy officers—Americans, British, Australians, Turks, and others, all but the South Koreans, who were held elsewhere. These prisoners were from all branches of the military and by the spring of 1952 totaled some three hundred men.

"There was a barbed wire fence, not a very high one, put all around the camp, to help the guard company keep control of the prisoners," recalls Zhu Chun, who was an officer of the Prison Camp Division Headquarters of the General Political Department of the Chinese People's Volunteer Army in Korea between 1951 and 1953.[2]

A man of medium height, with a firm handshake and a relaxed way of speaking, Professor Zhu was seventy-one at the time of this interview in 1996. The deputy general secretary of the China Institute for International Strategic Studies, he stayed healthy by riding his bicycle to work every day. Zhu was one of the interrogators of thirty-six captured U.S. Air Force officers who made depositions about germ warfare in 1952. He welcomed our questions but warned that the passage of forty years might have dimmed his memory. He was certain that he had been the one to interrogate Lieutenants John Quinn and Kenneth Enoch, two of the first to be captured, and after looking at photographs, he thought he might have conducted the interviews with Lieutenants Charles Kerr and George Brooks, but he could not be sure.

As a young man, Zhu studied journalism and English at Fudan University in Shanghai. (He told us that his English was rusty, but it was still quite passable.) He went to work in Chongqing, Sichuan province, for a year and a half after graduation, and then in July 1951, at the age of twenty-six, he arrived in Korea as a member of the Prison Camp Division of the Volunteer Army.

"There was a total of twenty Chinese officers to run the camp at Pingchangli, and a company of guards," he recollected. "Our officers were in two sections: one section looked after the administration of the camp, providing for the material needs of the prisoners; the other section, the larger half, all English speakers, including myself, took care of political matters." The buildings in the camp, he remembered, were "very poor, but livable." It had formerly been a school compound. The courtyards were of typical Korean style—wooden buildings with tiles on top. Out front there was a sports ground for basketball, soccer, and baseball.

The U.S. Air Force officers who they believed had taken part in germ warfare were required to make written statements. In the case of other officers, the Chinese intelligence-gathering was by word of mouth.

Asked if they had gotten confessions of germ warfare from all the U.S. Air Force officers captured after January 1952, Zhu replied in the negative. "It's hard to say now, exactly," he said, "but it was somewhere between ten and twenty percent. We decided on whom to ask after talking with them for a while and finding out some information."

Zhu explained the conditions under which the POWs wrote their depositions:

> When the prisoners first came to our camp, they filled out a form requiring information about themselves, their family, life prior to joining the armed forces, military career, social activities, and political affiliations, if any. This was for the use of our administrative officers. Then after a few days, we in the political section called each one in for an interview. It might last an hour or two, all day, or even a couple of days. In special cases, with those who we believed had participated in germ warfare, we required them to make a written statement. They worked on it right there in our office. When they were finished, they left the paper with us and returned to their barracks. After we read their paper, we called them back in a day or two and had further discussions, asking them to give more details, to provide a fuller account of themselves. This procedure went on until we were satisfied that they had told us everything they knew.

As Zhu listened to portions of statements made by the captured Air Force officers after they returned to the U.S. in 1953 and in later years, his reaction varied from disdain and definite disagreement with certain parts, to head-nodding, even a smile, at others. The former captives were saying that they had given in to Chinese demands for confessions about germ warfare because of bad treatment, poor food, being kept in solitary confinement for months on end, mental cruelty, and in one case physical beatings; they had assured their military superiors and the American public that they gave false confessions: they knew nothing about U.S. use of biological warfare.[3]

"Many of the things these men said are simply not so," Zhu said in response to what he was hearing, disagreeing with some of the accounts of treatment.

> Let me tell you something about the personality of American officers. Over the years, I met many of them. They are very malleable. They don't need a lot of pressure to change their minds. They do that rapidly. The English officers, now they are different. If they don't agree with you, it is not easy to change their opinions. . . . When we discovered that the American Air Force was dropping bacterial bombs in early 1952, we decided to question the officers about this, and we would have those who knew about it give written statements so that we could publicize the facts.

In response to a question, he explained how they got the men to make these written statements:

> We called them into our offices. We talked to them patiently, individually. At first they didn't want to say anything. But we had evidence. It was snowing out, there was snow on the ground, and yet our army was finding poisoned insects on the ground. Yes, there was pressure from us. We let them know about the bombs we found. We let them know the results of this criminal action. We told them they would have to write out all the things they had done, where they had been since joining the Air Force. They would write something and hand it in. It was usually incomplete, vague in places. We asked more questions. They came back and wrote some more.

> We worked on them, and they seemed afraid of us. We reasoned with them, told them of our principles. Explained to them why we had volunteered to come to Korea. Reminded them that Premier Zhou had warned the Americans through the Indian ambassador that if their army approached our borders at the Yalu River, where we share power dams with North Korea, then we would enter the war and defend our interests and our sovereignty. We asked them, "How would you feel and act if a hostile foreign army approached the frontiers of your country?" They

> seemed to understand. They gave in very easily. Afterwards, when they went back among their fellows in the camp, they pretended that they had disobeyed us; they denounced us behind our backs. But we had their written statements. One by one, it was very easy to have them say what they knew.

Zhu was then asked whether they had tried to talk to the prisoners about the difference between capitalism and socialism and the history of foreign imperialism in China.

> Yes, we may have talked about that, especially at first. We had lectures on these topics. But not later. We saw that we couldn't convince them. We left various magazines around and let them read if they wanted to. Most of the time we just let them organize sports and recreational activities. On certain occasions, especially at Christmas or at Easter, we tried to accommodate the cherished traditions of our captives.

As the conversation with Professor Zhu came to an end and he prepared to mount his bicycle, he happened to mention that one of the people he had interrogated, General (formerly Captain) Anthony Farrar-Hockley, had expressed an interest in revisiting China. Zhu had sent the general a message, through a friend, inviting him to be a guest of Zhu's institute during his stay in China. So far he had received no reply.

Prior to writing the official military history of British participation in the Korean War, General Farrar-Hockley wrote a racy account of his experiences as a POW in Korea titled *The Edge of the Sword*. First published in 1954, it overflows with the language and images of the early Cold War, with simple ideological truths of good guys and bad guys, of lies and brutalities meted out at Pingchangli by his captors, whom he variously described as "sallow faced," "frog-eyed," an "evil gnome," "a thorough-going liar," a "sincere communist who believed the ends justified the means," "a nasty little man with an unpronounceable name." The camp commander, Ding San, had eyes that were "narrow even for a Chinese," and that "glittered like a snake's," and his subordinates "hissed" at the luckless listener. Some years later, after the Cold War had abated, Farrar-Hockley attenuated his criticism of his Chinese captors. "There was no great physical brutality inside the camps by the Chinese," he said. "Quite the contrary: the Chinese had a disciplined atmosphere. . . . The whole character of the camps was that we were a lot of 'bad-hats' who had got to be reformed. At times it took the form that we were naughty children, and that nanny was going to punish us, until we fell into line and admitted our mistakes."[4]

The one captor to whom Farrar-Hockley accorded a degree of respect was Zhu:

> Big Chu came into a different category. He was the staff member who undertook affairs of special significance: interrogation, discipline, even propaganda were his fields, providing that some important aspect was involved. Slim, about five feet ten high, he walked with a peculiar bouncing gait. When Big Chu paid a visit to a prisoner to converse in excellent English with a heavy Chinese accent, it usually meant that the Camp Commandant was concerned in his call.[5]

Zhu spoke respectfully of Farrar-Hockley and his fellow officers from the Gloucesters:

> I got to know the officers captured from the British 29th Gloucesters 1st Battalion. I personally contacted them, including Captain Anthony Farrar-Hockley. They were all very well educated, and had extensive knowledge and thorough military training. At the beginning they were proud and aloof, but later, after talking, we got to know each other, and we were able to communicate. We asked about British Army information, but they were stubborn, tough men. Gradually they loosened up.

One could only wish to be an invisible presence should these old adversaries ever meet in Beijing and attempt to reconcile their memories in a world with fewer stereotypes and softer ideological edges.

In Sarasota, Florida, a few months before our interview with Zhu, Howard Hitchens, Jr., recalled his experiences as one of the captured American flyers who had confessed to participating in biological warfare in Korea.[6] A tall, slim man, Hitchens, like Professor Zhu, was seventy-one years old at the time, youthful and fit for his age. Intelligent and articulate, he talked easily of his Korean experience, his long association with the U.S. Air Force, and his formative years in the early Cold War and after.

Following a three-and-a-half-year stint as a young flyer in the Pacific during World War II, Hitchens returned to university in his native Delaware, married, and was completing a master's degree at Columbia University in New York when the Korean War claimed him as a B-26 navigator. Following the war, worn out by his POW experience, married with a child born while he was a POW, and admittedly in love with flying, Hitchens chose to remain in the Air Force.

Because of this decision, his experience as one of the flyers who had confessed to using biological warfare became an important part of his sub-

sequent military career. After a four-year tour of duty as a navigator in-
structor, Hitchens was assigned to the founding faculty of the new Air
Force Academy in Colorado Springs. He remained there, completing his
doctorate in communications from Syracuse University, and heading up
the academy's communications program, until he retired from the Air Force
twelve years later. Hitchens also assumed the responsibility for explaining
to the public and a decade of officer cadets the reasons for his confession
and its implications for military doctrine. Hitchens made endless public
speeches, tailored, he observed bemusedly, for virtually any time slot with
stopwatch precision. More significantly, he developed the lessons of his
experience for the survival and code of ethics courses at the Air Force
Academy.

The lessons that Hitchens drew and taught, and which the Air Force
endorsed through him, mark a point of convergence with both the
reflections of Professor Zhu and a postwar study by the U.S. Army. There
is a possibility that Zhu interrogated Hitchens. Though Zhu could not
remember the names of all of those whom he had interrogated, he thought
after seeing photographs that he might have interrogated George Brooks,
who following interrogation was one of three flyers housed with Hitchens.
Hitchens's description of his principal interrogator as intellectually sophisticated with good English and a cool rational approach is consistent
with the description of Zhu provided by Farrar-Hockley.

Hitchens and Zhu differ over some of the details of treatment and
camp routine. For example, Zhu recalled that the flyers were in a camp
environment, Hitchens that they were isolated; Zhu that the flyers were
taken to the interrogation offices to write their statements, Hitchens that
the interrogators came to them. But they agreed that the American flyers
broke not because of physical abuse but because they lacked the emotional
and intellectual maturity and toughness to deal with their situation.
Hitchens agreed with Zhu that he and the other flyers that he talked with
in the camp and afterwards were not physically abused in the sense that
they were beaten or tortured—though Hitchens, like other flyers, disagreed
with Zhu over the extent of deprivation and physical and mental duress.
But Hitchens was adamant that it was just that, extreme duress and stress.
And he was equally adamant that with greater maturity or the training to
understand what was happening to them, they could and would have resisted. Hitchens said that he, like the others who confessed and with whom
he talked, all agreed at the time that they had confessed just to end the
relentless pressure on them.

In talking about what Zhu and other interrogators encountered when
they met the American flyers, Hitchens reflectively described his own back-

ground as one of naivety and ignorance of the world, politics, and war. He said that the flyers with whom he went to war were pretty much like him. They held their share of patriotic and anti-Communist views, but they had little interest in and less knowledge of politics. Their focus was to get the job done and get home. Along the way, he said, they were thinking mostly about their next beer and plate of eggs, and about getting laid. They thought very little about getting shot down, and even less about what they might confront and what they would do if captured; their Air Force training had not prepared them for that eventuality. It was this void that Hitchens would spend most of his military career addressing. Standing behind the code of conduct that you do not collaborate with or give vital information to the enemy, he sought to teach others not to do what he had done when interrogation falls short of torture or other methods virtually impossible to resist.

The most exhaustive study of the extent of U.S. collaboration in the Korean POW camps, conducted by the U.S. Army, agrees that there was no "brainwashing," and that physical abuse in the sense of beatings and torture was not the cause of the high incidence of collaboration among Army POWs.[7] The cause was a cultural background that had failed to give them the insight and maturity to deal with their experience, and inadequate military training to compensate. While this study deals with a group that might not match up in many respects with the flyers, in balance the conclusions would probably hold. Hitchens's observations and conclusions, which the Air Force incorporated into doctrine, were basically the same as those of the Army study.

Hitchens agreed with Zhu that the interrogators did not provide information for his confession beyond informing him that they knew the name of the wing commander. He further agreed that his interrogators simply kept asking him to provide more information until they were satisfied. Though the Chinese intended to publicize the confessions, Hitchens was of the opinion that his interrogators believed that the Americans were using biological weapons, and that they were using basic intelligence-gathering techniques to collect and collate information. Hitchens told us that he was not involved in biological warfare, and that he concocted a confession that was a mix of fact and fiction. But he expressed surprise when presented with detailed documentation on the extent of the U.S. bacteriological program at the time of the Korean War, and with the match between material in the confessions, including his own, and the realities of that program.

He said that there was no discussion about the possibility of a bacteriological warfare program among those with whom he flew. With the small and intimate crew of a B-26, a scenario in which the pilots were informed and kept the information secret would not have been possible; it would have leaked. He did not discount the possibility that knowledge could have stopped with squadron commanders, nor that personnel secretly assigned to a bomb dump could have substituted bacteriological for explosive or leaflet bombs. But as the person on his crew who inspected the bombs for each mission, he was dubious. While he could not say with certainty that other units were not involved in a bacteriological program, he did not believe that his 17th Bomb Wing was among them.

What did the Chinese learn about biological warfare from their captives? How convincing are the later denials by returning American POWs? To what extent do the available operational records of the U.S. Far East Air Force substantiate or refute the germ war charge? These are the questions that occupy the rest of this chapter.

In all, thirty-six U.S. officers gave the Chinese statements about their participation in biological warfare. Twenty-seven of these statements are available.[8] Most of the depositions are from airmen belonging to the Fifth Air Force—two colonels, two captains, and twenty lieutenants. Seven of them were from bomber wings flying B-26s out of the Kunsan (K-8) and Pusan (K-9) airfields; ten were from fighter-bomber wings flying from bases at Suwon (K-13), Chinhae (K-10), and Taegu (K-2); five were from fighter-interceptor wings flying the latest F-86 Sabrejets out of Kimpo (K-14) and Suwon (K-13); and two were from a tactical reconnaissance group that supplied photographs—twenty-four altogether. The other statements are from the 1st Marine Air Wing—by Colonel Frank H. Schwable, chief of staff, and Major Roy Bley, ordnance officer, who were shot down together in July 1952, and by Lieutenant Thomas Eyres of the 20th Air Force, who was based in Okinawa.

From these officers, the Chinese acquired information about U.S. high command decisions on biological warfare, why the U.S. resorted to this type of warfare, where the germ weapons were manufactured, the type of weapons used, the kinds of diseases spread, how the missions were conducted, the content of lectures given to servicemen on the history and development of and the training for biological warfare, the phases of the U.S. germ war program, security precautions, and the assessment of results of germ warfare by the U.S. military. Whether accurate or not, the Chinese pieced together the following picture:

In December 1950, at the time of heavy U.S. defeats in Korea, the U.S. Joint Chiefs of Staff (JCS) directed their Research and Development section to complete preparations for the use of biological weapons by the end of 1951. The program began in October 1951, when the JCS sent an order by hand to the commanding general of the Far East Command, General Ridgway, directing the initiation of bacteriological warfare in Korea on an initially small, experimental stage, but in expanding proportions. At that time, General Vandenberg, chief of staff of the U.S. Air Force, ordered the shipment of seventy-five of the latest F-86 Sabrejets to Korea to replace older aircraft; according to Major General G. P. Saville, deputy chief of staff for development, they were for use in connection with the germ war program.[9]

Beginning with the B-26s of the 3rd Bomb Wing at Kunsan and the B-29 medium bombers of the 20th Air Force based in Okinawa, experiments started in November. Following the success of these experiments, formal approval was given, and other units began such missions at the end of December 1951. Not long after that, according to Brigadier General Ernest K. Warburton, deputy commanding general of the Fifth Air Force, as related by Colonel Andrew Evans,[10] the Joint Chiefs of Staff made the decision to include germ missions north of the Yalu River into China. These began in January 1952.

The Chinese learned that on or about 24 May 1952, there was a change in the U.S. biological warfare program from experimental to operational use. The command came through General Glen Barcus, the newly appointed commanding officer of the Fifth Air Force. Barcus said this change was a matter of national policy, not just military policy, and was subject to top security regulations: only specially qualified, hand-picked, reliable, and loyal pilots were to be involved. The aim was to establish a contamination belt across the central part of North Korea to interdict the movement of soldiers and supplies from Manchuria southward to the main line of resistance near the 38th Parallel.[11] The reason the United States had begun to employ bacterial weapons, according to the intelligence officer of a fighter bomber wing, was "to shorten the war and save American lives." On the same theme, in a lecture to pilots of F-86 Sabrejets in March 1952, Major James McIntyre, commander of a training squadron at Nellis Air Force Base, Nevada, stated that the main objective was to try to end the war quickly, "as the atomic bomb had done against Japan in the last war." The use of biological weapons would cause epidemics at the front and in the rear. It would cause the morale of the people to drop to the point where they would want to give up the fight. After explaining the types of germs and germ bombs in use, he warned that this was all top secret and that "we were not to discuss it with anyone, not even among ourselves."[12]

Another explanation given for the use of biological warfare was the difficulty of getting at the Chinese enemy, of disrupting his supply system. "It was virtually impossible to rout him out of the mountains and hills, after once lodged there, with ordinary weapons." In addition, it was not possible to paralyze the enemy's transportation system by bombing bridges, roads, railroads, supply areas, and personnel areas. "We were all aware that in spite of our efforts supplies were constantly being built up . . . at night." The efficiency of the Chinese and North Korean repair system was too great. Thus a plan was adopted whereby one flight in each mission "would be equipped with germ bombs in order to delay repairs." Only "drastic measures" could stop a spring offensive, which the enemy was "building up for right now."[13]

Colonel Eppright, deputy chief of staff for materiel for the Fifth Air Force, is quoted as saying that the bomb casings, fuses, and spray tanks were manufactured in the United States and shipped to Korea. The live biological agents, on the other hand, were produced in a factory near Tokyo, packed in containers, and flown in cargo aircraft as needed "to the two germ weapon dumps in Korea, one in Pusan and one in Taegu."[14]

The munitions and germs used varied as the months passed. The most common weapon described was a 500-pound bomb with compartments that could carry infected insects, feathers, or other vectors. Next in importance was a spray tank, of "a 120-gallon size similar in appearance to a fuel tank," which dispensed a liquid or a germ-laden powder. Some types of bombs had parachutes attached.[15] Colonel Robert Rogers, commanding officer of the 49th Fighter Bomber Wing, told his deputy that germ warfare flights were generally integrated into the regular schedule of operations that came daily from Fifth Air Force headquarters in Taegu. Another informant said that for these special missions, the germ bombs were loaded onto the aircraft on the taxi strip just off the end of the runway. After spray attachments were used, chemicals would be run through them to sterilize them.[16]

General Frank Everest, head of the Fifth Air Force, in explaining to Colonel Mahurin that the powers of court-martial would apply in the case of pilots who were reluctant to carry out this type of mission, said that the insects being used as carriers for disease were flies, fleas, and mosquitoes infected with malaria, typhoid, plague, and dysentery. Other flyers reported attending lectures at Maxwell, Turner, Luke, and Nellis air bases in the United States and at Itazuke air base in Japan in which smallpox, yellow fever, cholera, undulant fever, typhus, and encephalitis were also mentioned as possible agents of infection. In these lectures they were told the history of the U.S. biological warfare program, beginning in World War II—that the Japanese had worked on biological warfare, and "we continued and improved on their work."[17]

Commanding officers stressed secrecy about the biological warfare program. The enemy should be deceived by every means possible to prevent his acquiring actual proof that these weapons were being used, and on the friendly side, steps were taken to confine knowledge and control information on the subject. Biological weapons used in conjunction with ordinary bombs or napalm gave the appearance of normal attacks on enemy supply lines. Warnings to pilots stressed that if they were caught discussing the germ bomb, they would be court-martialed and "given maximum punishment under the Air Force regulation covering violations of security." "To relate top secret information in time of war meant death." On their mission summaries, pilots used covering words such as "dud," "suprop" (super-propaganda), or "results unobserved," or notations that it was a Joint Operations Center (JOC) mission or a "flak suppressor mission," to report biological bombs. The reports were sent directly to headquarters via a separate top secret channel.

The U.S. side used every possible means to assess the results of the campaign—employing spies, questioning prisoners of war, watching the nightly truck count, observing public announcements by the North Korean and Chinese authorities. They presumed that no large-scale epidemic could occur without the news leaking out. At the air wing level, no overall assessment was available, but the feeling seemed to be that the results were "not worth a damn." "No one that I know of," Colonel Schwable told his captors, "has indicated that the results are anywhere near commensurate with the effort, danger and dishonesty involved. . . . The sum total of results known to me are that they are disappointing and no good."[18]

On Sunday, 6 September 1953, the Chinese and North Koreans repatriated the last of their American prisoners of war. That morning, as the trucks bearing the prisoners headed south, Peking Radio broadcast the names of twenty-five U.S. Air Force officers who had admitted to participating in biological warfare in Korea. The first jeep to cross the 38th Parallel from Panmunjom carried the three colonels in that category, Andrew Evans, Walker Mahurin, and a nervously smiling Frank Schwable, who were pictured riding together in the *New York Times.* The paper reported most of the officers as "sitting dully in trucks," responding only when their names were called.[19] They were, quite naturally, anxious about what might happen next. The *Times* reported that Colonel Schwable was not available to be interviewed.

What happened next was a rather frantic effort to prevent further impairment of U.S. prestige. All returnees were classed as hospital patients, and according to Colonel Mahurin, "all were kept under close surveillance." There was strong pressure on them to make recantations or else face heavy, perhaps extreme, penalties. U.S. Attorney General Herbert Brownell was on public record as saying, "United States prisoners of war who collaborated with their Communist captors in Korea may face charges of treason," a charge that carried the death penalty. Senator Richard Russell, a ranking member of the Senate Armed Services Committee, wrote a statement that Secretary of Defense Charles Wilson saw fit to release to the press: "My views may be extreme, but I believe that those who collaborated and the signers of false confessions should be immediately separated from the services under conditions other than honorable." Preparations by the Marine Corps to hold a court of inquiry of Colonel Schwable before a board of superior officers in Washington were widely publicized.[20] Colonel Mahurin said he was "beginning to lie awake nights worrying about the future."[21]

It was in this atmosphere that all returnees received a pen and some paper to write retractions to their confessions. They also had a list of leading questions prepared by Major J. J. Kelleher, Jr., of the Office of Special Operations in the Pentagon.[22] Most began by saying that they were doing this under "my own free will," without any monetary inducement, while acknowledging that "this statement or any portion thereof may be used as evidence against me in a trial by court-martial." The completed statements, which took the form of legal documents, were sworn and witnessed according to Article 31 of the code of military justice in front of Summary Court officials, a colonel in the Judge Advocate's Office, or superior officers or agents of the Office of Special Investigations of the Air Force. Even the State Department expressed concern about the public credibility of retractions under such publicly orchestrated pressure.[23]

Six weeks later, Henry Cabot Lodge, Jr., chief U.S. delegate to the UN, put ten of these sworn statements before the Political and Security Committee of the UN General Assembly, triumphantly describing them as revealing "a record of unparalleled and diabolical mendacity" by Chinese Communists against the United States.[24] The statements were from eight of those who had made confessions and two of those who had successfully resisted. Of the eight, only the ones by Lieutenant Paul Kniss and Colonel Andrew Evans cited "severe mental and physical torture" as the reason for their compliance.[25] The others, including Colonels Mahurin and Schwable, spoke of "duress" or "maltreatment," physical deprivation, and mental cruelty. In the latter category, all of them referred to threats that they would be put to death as war criminals as a motivating factor, since interrogators promised leniency if they confessed their "war guilt." (This threat flowed from Premier Zhou Enlai's statement of 8 March 1952 "that members of the American air force who invade China's territorial air and use bacteriological weapons will be dealt with as war criminals on capture.")[26]

Colonel Frank Schwable, the most senior person to give a germ war confession, said on his return to the United States that he had never heard of "a proposal for its use." It was "incredible." He thought the Chinese did not believe it themselves. He said that while held in solitary confinement he was forced to write a "false, fraudulent and in places absurd confession." His captors pursued overlapping steps to degrade and humiliate him, exhaust him, intimidate and threaten him, finally "trying to contaminate my mind with vile slanders against my country, giving me false hopes and promises and trying to instill in me a sense of war guilt that could be eradicated only by 'confessing.'" They wore him down, trying to make him believe "that the type of warfare conducted by United States forces was inhumane." Although he realized that living standards were low in Korea and wartime conditions imposed greater limitations, still he thought "they could have moved me to the rear areas along the Yalu as they did after I broke down, where facilities were a little improved." At the pickup camps Schwable complained that the humane treatment called for by the Geneva Convention was inadequate:

> I was given shelter, inadequate as it was, at all times; I was never starved although the food was miserable, skimpy at times and many times I went without water; I was given heavy winter clothing, quilts and a blanket but . . . I was bitterly cold and partially frost bitten. . . . [As for mental cruelty and having to sit for so long in confined spaces in continuous solitary confinement] I . . . consider that I was subjected to extreme torment in order to force a false confession from me.

This is why he had given his germ war confession.

Perhaps the most poignant statement was that of Lieutenant John Quinn, who declared that, suffering from malnutrition and lack of sleep, he was "coerced by diabolical mental torture, which it would take a poet like Poe to justly describe, into writing Communist propaganda." Quinn said he was in solitary for more than eight months, living with an interrogator, presumably Zhu Chun, "the only man I have ever learned to hate with a passion that borders on insanity":

> He constantly harangued me with stock questions on what was I thinking, what were my feelings, what was Communism, etc., etc. I can't write sensibly about what that does to a person when he can't fight back, because my emotions are too wrapped up in it. . . . I hope others who might have been confused by the things

I was forced to write, say, and do, may get some vague feeling
for what I—and others—have been through. . . . The result is
living dead men, controlled human robots, which willingly, as
long as they are under the spell, do their master's bidding.

Quinn swore that he knew nothing about how bacteriological warfare might
be conducted; he had not attended any lectures on the subject. Much of
his confession, he said, was dictated to him. Much he added which seemed
"fantastic beyond belief" and would make this "germ warfare, hate
America" campaign "ridiculous to any thinking person."

In most of the sworn statements there is a determined denial of any
knowledge about bacteriological warfare, of having attended any lectures
or special training on the subject. This stance reflects the intense pressure
that was on these men to distance themselves from their confessions to the
Chinese, because we already know that the Joint Chiefs of Staff had decided to include biological warfare in their "strategic, operational and
emergency [war] plans" in February 1951 and at the same time ordered
appropriate training for the armed services.[27] These training sessions got
going on an ad hoc basis at different times and places, but the records of
the Office of Special Investigations (OSI) of the Inspector General of the
U.S. Air Force reveal that lectures on germ warfare had taken place in the
3rd Bomb Wing at Kunsan (K-8) air base by the end of 1951, when Quinn
and Enoch served there. It is maintained that these were about defensive
germ warfare. Lieutenant Irwin Rogers, who was named by Quinn as one
of those attending the 18 December 1951 lecture, told an OSI investigator that "he did attend a lecture at Kunsan in approximately December, at
which time biological warfare was discussed to the extent that they should
be prepared in case they were attacked by germ warfare because the Ori-
entals were very adept at the study of virus and bacteria." Another member of the 3rd Bomb Group, Captain Ralph Everett, told the OSI that
"germ warfare was discussed" in a course given under his supervision to all
members of the group.[28]

Further corroborating evidence about training or orientations for germ
warfare appears in James A. MacDonald, Jr.'s, *The Problems of US Marine
Corps Prisoners of War in Korea*, where it is reported that a helicopter pilot
shot down in the spring of 1952 "successfully concealed" from the Chinese "the fact that he had attended certain specialist schools and had fairly
extensive theoretical knowledge of atomic, biological and chemical warfare."[29]

Similarly, Colonel Mahurin's scornful dismissal of "fleas, flies, and
mosquitoes" used as vectors to carry disease must be weighed against what
we now know to have been extensive research and development on these

and other insect vectors dating from World War II—as must his protest that the information he gave to his Chinese captors about activities emanating from Fort Detrick was "completely ridiculous."[30]

Mahurin has chosen or was chosen to be the most visible public spokesman for the flyers who made confessions. Whereas interviews with this group have been relatively hard to come by over the years,[31] Mahurin generally has made himself available, and he published his memoirs of his Korean experience, *Honest John*, in 1962. Circumstances surrounding his Korean experience should be revisited in light of what we now know of the U.S. biological warfare program.

Colonel Mahurin, a 34-year-old fighter pilot in 1952, who had been an air ace during World War II, was a career officer.[32] Before going to Korea, he served at the Washington headquarters of the U.S. Air Force, with top security clearance in such capacities as chief of the Fighter Section, Requirements Division, in the Strategic Air Division, and later as assistant executive to the secretary of the Air Force. In the course of his work he visited Camp Detrick, Maryland, the center of the U.S. biological warfare program, and he also had working contacts with the Central Intelligence Agency.[33]

In December 1951 he was sent to Korea. According to his confession, his task was to brief pilots and help implement the germ warfare program with the new F-86 Sabrejet fighters; in his biography he claims that he requested a temporary posting for reasons of personal rivalry with old World War II friends who were over there fattening their scores by shooting down Russian MIG fighters, and thus pulling ahead of him as air aces.

Secrecy was an important component of Mahurin's task. "It became increasingly difficult to keep other members of the Wing from discovering what we were doing," he wrote in his memoirs. Combat films had to be concealed and burned. "We just couldn't let anything incriminating get away from our base."[34] What was the nature of this secret work? In his confession he said that it was germ missions in North Korea and across the Yalu River into China, as far as the city of Shenyang, to contaminate railroads and disrupt the work of repair crews after bombing. In his later version he said the secrecy was required because he and a few of his friends engaged in "hot pursuit" of enemy planes into the neutral territory of China in violation of UN command standing orders.[35] Yet he also reveals that the U.S. Joint Chiefs of Staff had secretly approved an unwritten policy of "hot pursuit" into China[36] which all pilots would have known, making secrecy at the air base on this score unnecessary.

This point is confirmed by the occurrence of something that bordered on an international incident. A Royal Canadian Air Force pilot, W. G.

Nixon, flying U.S. F-86 Sabrejet aircraft in Korea in the spring of 1952, acknowledged upon questioning by an RCAF group captain about reports of a violation of Chinese airspace that the reports were true. Nixon told his superior that there were deliberate, repeated, organized flights across the Yalu into Manchuria.[37] "Everyone knew the guys were going over the Yalu," he said. "It was a goddamn joke, really."[38] Lester Pearson, minister of external affairs, requested an explanation from Washington. The Canadian ambassador to Washington reported back to Ottawa as follows: "The basic circumstance is the allegation that there has been a very serious violation of discipline, at any rate at wing or squadron levels, by the U.S. Air Force in the Far East. My conversation yesterday was the first intimation received by the State Department that this might be the case."[39] Unwilling to acknowledge to the Americans the source of its information, and having made its point, the Canadian government dropped the inquiry.

The contradictions in Mahurin's story make any intelligent observer deeply suspicious of his attempts to renounce his confession. This suspicion is reinforced by a statement in his recantation that was placed before the United Nations after his return from Korea:

> During the heated period of my confession process, when they had begun to affect my thought processes . . . I blurted out that I had visited the Army camp of Detrick, at Frederick, Maryland. This, of course, was a thing that they wanted, and they pressed me to write the details of my visit. . . . After getting me to break on this information, they began to press me quite heavily to make a total confession.

In his confession, Mahurin had provided the Chinese with details about the Air Force's use of infected insects as disease carriers. But when he returned to American hands and faced Henry R. Petersen, official of the Summary Court, aboard the ship MSTS *Howze* on his way home from Korea, and the possibility of a court-martial, the details that he had provided the Chinese about activities originating from Camp Detrick were dismissed as something absurd, "asinine to anyone who . . . used a little thought."[40] The whole story, Mahurin swore, was "completely ridiculous," but it was accepted by the Chinese.

The true story, however, was apparently closer to what Colonel Mahurin told the not-so-gullible Chinese. As we now know, Camp Detrick, building on the information it had received about earlier Japanese experiments, was heavily engaged in developing insect vectors as a means of conducting germ warfare. The scientists there knew of or had conducted successful field experiments in their use. Thus the "absurd" and the "incredible" in the documents that Henry Cabot Lodge, Jr., presented to an unsuspecting UN General Assembly as diabolical Chinese lies turned out to be entirely workable methods for the U.S. armed forces to use in conducting germ warfare.

The records indicate that air units enacted increased security precautions at the time when Chinese allegations of germ warfare grew more intense in the spring of 1952. The U.S. Marine Aircraft Group-33 located at K-3, Pohang, under Colonel A. F. Binney, was flying a "classified" mission every second day on average, and in March 1952 the colonel ordered the installation of a partition within the quonset hut of the group's intelligence section so that pilots could be briefed and debriefed in privacy. The following month, his successor, Colonel M. A. Severson, wishing to provide even more secrecy, inaugurated a "burn barrel" for the destruction of classified matter. Constructed from salvage materials—an old 45-gallon oil barrel punched full of holes and with a crank handle—this burn barrel proved "very efficient," according to the group's intelligence officer.[41]

The U.S. Air Force was clearly anxious to limit knowledge of some of the activities of the Marine flyers to personnel with "a need to know." And as if to underscore the secrecy of these matters, the U.S. Far East Command, following the war, twice ordered that documents dealing with germ warfare be kept in secret or top secret classifications. The subject matter of the documents to be kept from public view were

> military operational policies, plans, and directives dealing with the offensive employment of BW [biological warfare] against specific targets. . . . The fact that specific living agents or their toxic derivatives, identified by scientific name and/or description had been standardized for offensive military employment. . . . Details of processes and plants involved in the large-scale production of living BW agents.[42]

In spite of the hiding or destruction of classified materials, however, it should not be concluded that the front-line paper trail for this activity was stopped or destroyed at the air bases. The headquarters intelligence staff of the Fifth Air Force in Nagoya, Japan, needed every available scrap of information to help the high command plan the next day's bomb attacks. The reporting and planning procedure was as follows: After flight crews returned from their bombing missions, they went to their squadron's debriefing room, filled out a standard form, and presented it to the local intelligence officer. After an oral interview, this officer passed the handwritten forms to a nearby teletype operator, who immediately transmitted the contents to Nagoya. At Nagoya the staff of the intelligence headquarters tabulated, analyzed, and summarized the information to produce a mimeographed "Daily Operational and Strategic Summary" of about six pages in length. In the course of preparing this summary, the intelligence staff made notations on their copy of the teletype messages, and, working from some other knowledge or list in their possession, they wrote "classified" or stamped "confidential, restricted" on certain mission reports. These yellowing, annotated copies of the teletype messages, whose original sources were so carefully burned at the front-line air bases, continue the paper trail of covert activity. Some of them are in the archives of the Fifth Air Force, while others have been removed and are in such classified envelopes as "B-5" and "D-5," filed in some undisclosed place.[43]

In the early hours of the morning, the "Daily Operational and Strategic Summary" was flown from Nagoya by courier to the Fifth Air Force operations center at Taegu, Korea (K-2), in time for Colonel J. L. Mason, director of operations, and his associates in the high command to review what had been achieved and to plan the next day. The result of this meeting was another mimeographed document called "Operations Order." Fragments of this document ("Frag Orders") then went by courier to the different units, instructing up to eight hundred daily sorties as to their precise tasks and targets for the following twenty-four hours.

Only a few of the "Operations Orders," Nos. 140-52 to 142-52 of 19–21 May 1952 and No. 153-52 of 1 June 1952, have come to light. They are in the archives of the 1st Marine Air Wing, which operated under the direction of the Fifth Air Force in Korea. These rare documents have had certain items "extracted" from them, but the instructions, in particular those to Quinn and Enoch's 3rd Bomb Wing, when taken in context, require the historian to check any circumstantial evidence that the Chinese version of B-26 sorties may be the correct one.[44]

On these dates in May and June, the Operations Order dispatched thirty B-26 aircraft of the 3rd Bomb Wing (each armed with ten or more 500-pound GP [general purpose] bombs) on armed reconnaissance night flights to certain designated areas of western North Korea to hunt and destroy vehicles and rolling stock. From these B-26s, one flight of four bombers was directed to a particular place where a railway bridge or short piece of the railroad had been attacked all day by divebombing fighter bombers. At night the four B-26s added their ten tons of high explosives to ensure the rail cut. The bombs of the last two aircraft in this flight had delayed-action fuses, and the last aircraft dropped *two leaflet bombs* at the very end of the attack. This was the typical pattern.

On 20 May, for example, the Operations Order for the flight of the four B-26s in the 3rd Bomb Wing read as follows:[45]

> (c) 4 acft wkg P-3 w/drop internal bb load at rail cut area F-3 YD 4744 to YD 4846 last 2 acft w/b carrying max 500# GP bbs with 1 to 48 hr delay fuses w/last acft carrying two leaflet bbs. No. 8281 on last two stations.

In expanded and plain English, this order says that four aircraft working the Purple-3 target area northeast of Pyongyang will drop their internal bomb load on a 1.5-mile section of the East-West Pyongyang–to–Wonson Railway. The topographical map coordinates of this section of railway are YD 4744 to YD 4846. The last two aircraft in the flight will be carrying their maximum 500-pound GP bomb load, fused to explode from one to forty-eight hours after landing. The last aircraft also has two leaflet bombs containing something called No. 8281.

This bombing pattern by B-26s fits well with that described by the Chinese following their interrogation of captured pilots Quinn and Enoch and from their own observations.

The Chinese said that germ attacks were carried out by the B-26s as part of regular bombing raids, and that the germ-infected feathers or insects came in 500-pound-size leaflet bombs, which were reported as "duds" or as having "no visual results owing to darkness."[46] The purpose of these attacks was to contaminate the bombed area and disrupt the work of repair crews trying to restore the rail line bringing supplies from China into North Korea. The delayed fuse bombs had the same purpose of disrupting repair efforts.[47]

After the Chinese allegations, other members of the 3rd Bomb Wing were questioned by the adjutant general's office of the U.S. Air Force in the Office of Special Investigations hearings to clear the Air Force of allegations of biological warfare. While denying any biological warfare, several of them confirmed that they had carried mixed bomb loads including leaflet drops (from about 4,000 feet) that warned Koreans "to stay away from damaged railroad tracks and not to attempt to repair them," or offered "safe conduct passes for enemy troops through UN lines." Colonel William G. Moore, commanding officer of the 3rd Bomb Group from January to November 1952, signed a sworn statement declaring that while the allegations of germ warfare were "entirely false," "the group did fly leaflet missions, the purpose of which was to warn non-combatants in the areas adjacent to military targets that those targets were subject to attacks by USAF, thus enabling civilian personnel to avail themselves of an opportunity to escape injury and fatalities."[48] When compared to the actual

Table 4
U.S. Air Force Special Missions in Korea
1–21 March 1952

DATE 1952	"Classified Sorties" By Organization and Type of Aircraft			Psychological Warfare Sorties	Total Sorties All Types
Total classified missions	5th Air Force & associated units	5th Air Force 6167th AB Group "Kyushu Gypsies"*	U.S. Marine Corps Marine Air Group 33 Detachment No 2	"Kyushu Gypsies"* Squadron 21 315th Air Division	
1 March (2)	1 (F4U)		1 (AD-2)	3 (C-47) 1,130,000 leaflets 1 (C-47) Voice broadcast	633
2 March (4)	1 (F4U) 1 (RB26)	1 (C-47)	1 (AD-2)	7 (C-47) 2,455,000 leaflets 1 (C-47) Voice broadcast	671
3 March (3)	1 (RB26)		1 (AD-2) 1 (F4U)	6 (C-47) 2,125,000 leaflets	767
4 March (3)	1 (C-46) 1 (B-26)	1 (C-47)		13 (C-47) 4,680,000 leaflets	806
5 March (4)	1 (F4U) 1 (AD-2)		2 (AD-2)	7 (C-47) 2,920,000 leaflets	653
6 March (3)	1 (F4U) 1 (C-46)		1 (AD-2)	6 (C-47) 2,050,000 leaflets	748
7 March —	records missing		—		—
8 March (2)	1 (RB26) 1 (C-46)			5 (C-47) 705,000 leaflets	109
9 March —				8 (C-47) 1,910,000 leaflets	714
10 March (6)	1 (F4U) 3 (C-46) 1 (RB26)		1 (AD-2)	9 (C-47) 2,590,000 leaflets	835
11 March (2)	1 (B-26) 1 (C-46)			8 (C-47) 3,920,000 leaflets	931
12 March (3)	1 (RB26)	2 (C-47)		6 (C-47) 1,370,000 leaflets 1 (C-47) Voice broadcast	records incomplete
13 March (3)	1 (C-46)	2 (C-47)		1 (C-47) Voice broadcast	records incomplete
14 March —	records missing				—
15/16 March (7)	1 (F4U) 2 (C-46) 1 (B-26)	1 (C-47)	1 (AD-2) 1 (F4U)	1 (C-47) 50,000 leaflets 1 (C-47) Voice broadcast	518
17 March (5)	1 (F4U) 2 (C-46)		1 (AD-2)	1 (C-47) Voice broadcast	804

DATE 1952		"Classified Sorties" By Organization and Type of Aircraft		Psychological Warfare Sorties	Total Sorties All Types
Total classified missions	5th Air Force & associated units	5th Air Force 6167ᵗʰ AB Group "Kyushu Gypsies"* Detachment No 2	U.S. Marine Corps Marine Air Group 33	"Kyushu Gypsies"* Squadron 21 315th Air Division	
18 March (6)	1 (B-26) 2 (F4U) 1 (RB26) 1 (B-26)	1 (C-47)	1 (AD-2)	1 (C-47) Voice broadcast	480
19 March —	bad weather				
					239
20 March (2)		2 (C-47)		3 (C-47) 1,635,000 leaflets	969
21 March (1)	1 (RB26)			7 (C-47) 2,450,000 leaflets 1 (C-47) Voice broadcast	499
Total: (56)				Total: (103)	

Sources: 5th Air Force, Korean War Era, Mission Reports, "Daily Operational Summary and Statistical Summary" for March 1952, RD 3598, Box 7102, RD 3599, Box 7103, RD 3600, Box 7104, RG 342, NA; U.S. Marine Corps, Marine Air Group 33, Historical Diary from 1 Mar. through 31 Mar. 1952 (classified missions are listed as "Miscellaneous Missions" in this month), Acc. No. 65A-4620, Box 58, RG 127, Suitland Records Center; Captain Annis G. Thompson, *The Greatest Airlift: The Story of Combat Cargo* (Tokyo, 1954), pp. 413–417.

*For discussion of the "Kyushu Gypsies," see chap. 9; for their link to the 6167th Air Base Group, see Stephen Pease, *PSYWAR* (New York, 1962), p. 61.

Operations Orders of May 1952 (and for the other days for which Operations Orders are available), these explanations ring hollow. The time for warnings and humanitarian gestures to the Korean villagers in Sainjang and Sinwon in the Purple-3 target area on 20 May—if that is what they were intended to be—would have been before, not after, the descent of 100,000 pounds of fiery explosives from thirty-six F-84 dive-bombers of the 49th and 136th fighter-bomber wings, beginning at 7:15 A.M., and four B-26s of the 3rd Bomb Group late in the evening.[49] If the M-105 leaflet containers did indeed contain biological weapons, then the logic of U.S. planners is discernible: The reason the leaflet containers came last was so that the insect vectors or contaminated feathers would be undamaged by the other bomb explosions; then when the repair crews arrived after the bombing stopped, even if the delayed-action bombs did not get them, they would see these strange, out-of-place objects. And even if only a few of the workers caught fevers or the plague, the Fifth Air Force, determined to stop the large and effective road gangs, hoped that the rest would panic and the work would be disrupted. If, on the other hand, the M–105 bombs contained humanitarian messages or warnings, then there is no logic to their arrival at the end of the attacks.

In passing, it might be noted that the U.S. Air Force did have a propaganda leaflet program. It was a massive effort. It involved the "Kyushu Gypsies" squadron of C-47 Douglas "Skytrain" transport aircraft, which dropped up to 3 million leaflets over North Korea night after night containing humanitarian promises and safe-conduct passes. As a contribution to this propaganda campaign, a couple of leaflet canisters from a fully loaded B-26 bomber could have been only a drop in the bucket.

The May–June 1952 Operations Orders for the other unit flying B-26 bombers, the 17th Bomb Wing (which replaced the 452nd Bomb Wing) covering the more mountainous and less developed eastern half of North Korea, had fewer details than those for the 3rd Bomb Wing. There is nothing noticeable in them that would evoke suspicion of germ warfare. Each evening, thirty-three B-26s were dispatched "to perform maximum destruction of vehicles, rolling stock and maintain continuous night coverage to prevent the enemy from moving" in certain designated areas. On the other hand, the yellowing teletype messages sent to Nagoya from the 17th Bomb Wing at that time, while not confirming every detail, offer much supporting evidence for information contained in the Chinese intelligence records of POW interrogations.

For example, Lieutenant Bobby E. Hammett, a navigator bombardier in the 37th Squadron, was indeed one of his squadron's intelligence officers, as he had told the Chinese, and was involved in debriefing tasks. In the twelve nights from 19 to 31 May 1952, Hammett flew nine sorties, mainly in the company of pilot James Gunnoe, Jr., and shoran operator David E. Penny, with whom he was shot down and captured on 7 June 1952. As stated in their depositions, these airmen flew "pre-briefed" missions arranged by the squadron's project officer. They told the Chinese that these pre-briefed squadron projects were germ missions; in the teletype mission reports to Nagoya, their purpose is not stated. They did bomb near Suan (Green–7, the center of the Chinese Volunteer Army's logistical force) and recorded three "duds," not on 24 or 25 May, as stated in their depositions to the Chinese, but on 28 May.[50]

At this time the Chinese learned from their prisoners that General Glen Barcus had taken command of the Fifth Air Force. Coinciding with his arrival, according to the U.S. Air Force archives, the number of "duds" reported by the 17th Bomb Wing multiplied dramatically—forty-two in the last twelve days of May alone, half of them delivered by a single squadron, the 95th.[51] The words "Confidential," "Restricted," " Security Information" began appearing. They were stamped on the teletype copies of radar-controlled bombing missions called "volleyball" or "tadpole," and sometimes on routine mission summaries; some pilots began to report "unknown bomb" to describe their ordnance.[52]

As General Barcus demanded "increasing vigor and efficiency" on the part of his bombers, the scope and frequency of clandestine missions grew along with the intensity of the air war in the spring and summer of 1952.[53] And if the Chinese military intelligence, fed by the confessions of captured American flyers, is credible, there was ample room within the U.S. air galaxy over North Korea and China to accommodate both covert tactical experimentation and covert special operations aimed at affecting the morale of those countries.

Colonel Frank H. Schwable
Chief of Staff of the U.S. First Marine Air Wing, shot down and taken prisoner in July 1952, shown making a broadcast describing the germ warfare operations of the U.S. Air Force in Korea.
NCNA

"Barrel for Destroying Classified Matter"'
This burn barrel was created by the U.S. Marine Air Group-33 in Korea in March 1952.
Command Diary, April 1952, Appendix 2, Box 58, ACC No. 65A-4620, RG 127

Floor plan of the quonset hut used by intelligence officers at the U.S. Navy's Marine Air Group-33 base, Pohang, Korea. New partitions were installed in April 1952 so that pilots could be briefed and debriefed privately.
MAG-33 Historical Diary, March 1952, ACC No. 65A-4620, Box 58, RG 127, Navy Yard, Washington, D.C.

No. 5 Prisoner-of-War Camp at Pyoktong (Bitong), North Korea.
Photo No. 5832, Resist America, Aid Korea War Collection, Museum of Military History, Beijing

POWs bathing in the Yalu River near Pyoktong.
NCNA

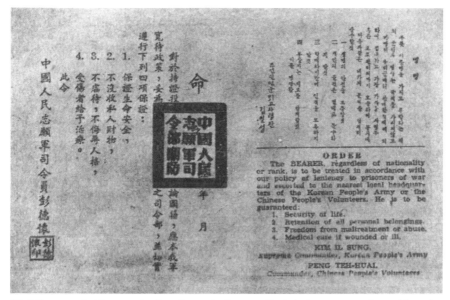

"Soldiers . . . in Korea who lay down their arms find their way to safety with safe-conduct passes such as the one reproduced above."
People's China, 16 Dec. 1951

Professor Zhu Chun
Formerly a political officer of the Prison Camp Division of the Chinese Volunteer Army in Korea between 1951 and 1953.
Photo by S. Endicott

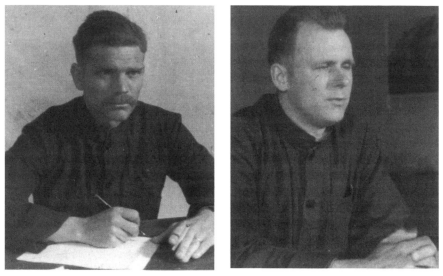

Pilot **John S. Quinn** (*left*) and navigator **Kenneth L. Enoch** of the 3rd Bomb Wing were shot down together on the night of 13 Jan. 1952 and became prisoners of war.
NCNA

Howard B. Hitchens, Jr.
A navigator in the 17th Bomb Wing, Hitchens was shot down 29 Oct. 1952.
NCNA

Walker M. Mahurin
A pilot and the leader of the 4th Fighter Interceptor Group, Mahurin was captured in North Korea on 13 May 1952. On the day of his repatriation, still wearing a POW tag, he takes part in a news conference with Western reporters on his prison camp experiences. September 1953.
USAF, Korean War Series, Box 3048, RG 342, NA

Three colonels who confessed to waging germ warfare in Korea, pictured in the *New York Times* as they were liberated at Panmunjon on 7 Sept. 1953. *Left to right:* Walker Mahurin, Frank Schwable, and Andrew Evans, Jr.

The International Scientific Commission presenting its report on the facts about bacterial warfare in China and Korea to Guo Moro (*center*), president of the Chinese Peace Committee. Joseph Needham is to the left of Guo, with arms folded.
Photo No. 6355, Resist America, Aid Korea War Collection, Museum of Military History, Beijing

A B-26 of the 3rd Bomb Wing, Fifth Air Force, over North Korea, 10 Oct. 1952.
USAF, Korean War Series, Box 3002, RG 342, NA

12 Conclusion

If the accusation were true, the United States would have betrayed the trust to which the United Nations have appointed us in Korea. . . . The two highest responsible men in the United States government—who would have to give the orders to conduct germ warfare—have said on their word of honor that there is no truth of any kind in the charges.
—Walter Lippmann, Washington columnist, in 1952

As for the allegation that the U.S. used germ warfare in the Korean War, I can only say with dismay and some shame that what I dismissed as incredible then seems altogether credible to me now.   —George Wald, Nobel Prize Laureate, letter of 15 March 1979

As the Cold War got under way the U.S. government decided that it needed to expand its biological warfare capabilities, this time with the USSR as its primary target. Citing precedents for total war during World War II, U.S. military strategists were prepared once again to approach the outer limits of war. Some strategists even argued that biological warfare was more humane than many other forms of warfare. The moral compromise involved in using medical science to kill enemies, which had raised a ripple of concern during World War II, was casually dismissed by policy makers and program participants in the atmosphere of the early Cold War. In the heat of the political and military crises surrounding the Berlin Blockade, the fall of Chiang Kai-shek in China, the successful Soviet test of an atomic bomb, and the outbreak of the Korean War, any and all military means were justified toward the end of saving Western civilization.

By 1949, the U.S. Joint Chiefs of Staff had biological warfare built into emergency war plans, and if the Berlin Blockade led to general war, they intended to use it. By 1951, after considerable discussion, a mature policy for first use if militarily advantageous was in place, with the Joint Chiefs placing biological warfare in strategic category number one, with the same priority as atomic warfare.

As far as the Joint Chiefs were concerned, biological weapons could be employed from the outset of war at the discretion of the president. This position was not formalized by the National Security Council until March 1956. However, it is clear that biological warfare had been assimilated by the U.S. military and had become a significant, even central, element in U.S. military thinking and practice by 1952; they expected to have a mature operational plan in place within two years. Lingering doubts pertained mainly to the effectiveness of current methods for delivering available bacterial agents.

Those who maintain that the United States did not employ or experiment with biological weapons during the Korean War follow several lines of argument. One is that the U.S. lacked the technological capacity for bacterial warfare during the Korean War. Available evidence refutes this argument. Another is that the Korean War was intended to be a limited war, and that the use of new, unconventional weapons might have escalated a local conflict into a general war for which the United States was unprepared. Against this argument stands the belief of the U.S. military that a great advantage of biological warfare would be the enemy's difficulty in distinguishing it from naturally occurring diseases; if it was detected, the United States could plausibly blame any outbreaks of disease on poor sanitary conditions in enemy territory.[1] Another doubter's argument is that the United States, faced with many competing demands for rearming its anti-Communist coalition, lacked the funds to make a success of a program employing weapons of unproved worth. This supposition is not supported by the evidence that there was ample funding in the years 1951–53, nor by the continued faith and joint participation in the program by two of the most important allies of the United States—Great Britain and Canada. As well, plans were pending to extend the program to the North Atlantic Treaty Organization. Perhaps the most important argument against our conclusion is that the U.S. biological warfare program was governed by a "no first use policy" throughout the Korean War period, and therefore it could not have happened because the enemy did not use such weapons.[2] This is an untenable position in view of the documentary evidence to the contrary.

In fairness to scholars who advance the "no first use" argument, it must be recognized that some official documents exist in which it is stated that biological warfare was governed by "use in retaliation only" during the Korean War.[3] The debate in the highest circles of the U.S. government and military over a national policy with respect to biological warfare is therefore subject to misunderstanding and is not easily summarized.

Until a "first use" position was officially adopted in 1956,[4] the United States had no formal national policy on the use of biological warfare. There was only doctrine by analogy to two other existing policies: the use of chemical warfare "only in retaliation," adopted by the government on 17 February 1950, and use of the atomic bomb at the discretion of the president.

During the Korean War, the U.S. Joint Chiefs of Staff were of two minds about having a formal national policy for biological warfare. They favored a policy stating that the U.S. would be prepared to use biological weapons "whenever it is militarily advantageous," as this would stimulate interest in the military services and speed up the development of the biological warfare field. They opposed a formal policy because they feared that American and European public opinion would not accept the one they wanted, and anything else would tie their hands. The U.S. military chiefs had a hunch that in the public mind, biological warfare possessed "to an even greater degree" the characteristics that caused chemical warfare (CW) to be placed in a special category. Therefore, a biological warfare policy formally established at this time "could only be similar to, and no less restrictive than the contemporaneous CW policy."[5] Faced with this probability, they thought it more practical and desirable to have no formal policy. They preferred to rely on the second analogy, governing the use of the atomic bomb. On 25 February 1952, following a strong push from Secretary of Defense Robert Lovett, the Joint Chiefs of Staff adopted a position favoring "a strong offensive BW capability without delay" and the development of "all effective means of waging war without regard for precedent as to their use." They directed their staff "to prepare directives to the Services" to implement this as an order.[6] This was their working policy on biological warfare during the remainder of the Korean War. There never was a "no first use" policy to revoke in later years; the military was free to use biological weapons subject only to presidential approval.

As for developments during the Korean War, much of the U.S. documentation on biological warfare at that time has been destroyed,[7] is lost, is still classified, or has been painstakingly and more or less successfully laundered before being provided for public viewing. The details are being treated with a secrecy that one might expect for this particularly aberrant type of death-dealing activity. Perhaps the most telling example of this cover-up is the twice-repeated request of the U.S. Far East Command that its records and documents on biological warfare be kept secret after the Korean War. We have documented that at least nineteen "secret" category communications of 1952 between the Far East Command and the organization within the U.S. responsible for biological warfare were pulled out before the Chemical Corps records were finally turned over to the U.S. National Archives in 1969.[8]

However, the existence of a well-developed covert program for biological warfare as such is no longer a secret. The U.S. Army's Special Operations Division at Fort Detrick produced germ agents and delivery systems, receiving high praise for its ingenuity and success.[9] The U.S. Air Force headquarters had a special division that, among other things, directed and supervised covert biological warfare operations,[10] and it had a specially trained air wing sent to the Far East to carry out its tasks.[11] The planning and supervisory responsibility for this division, which was in place at least by mid-January 1951 and extended to all types of bacteriological warfare activity, also provided a structure to implement tactical experimentation in Korea. By February 1951, the Joint Chiefs of Staff indicated "that a real requirement existed for agents for tactical employment," and they requested that a high priority be placed on their development.[12] In 1952 the division entered into agreements with the CIA to manufacture and test biological weapons for aggressive applications.[13]

There is also partially declassified documentation of a "BW Cover and Deception Plan" on the part of the U.S. Joint Chiefs of Staff. It indicates that while referring to cover and deception in the conventional sense of a plan to create diversion and surprise, it was something more; the U.S. military chiefs were discussing whether the secretaries of defense and state should be informed of the implementation of bacterial warfare. After discussion in which they initially considered excluding both secretaries, they recommended informing the secretary of defense but not the secretary of state, most likely in order to protect the latter under the doctrine of "plausible denial" as discussed by CIA director William Colby before the Church Committee hearings in the U.S. Senate.[14]

Given the foregoing and the Chiefs of Staff directive to use all effective means of waging war without regard for precedent, there was a signal lack of political or practical deterrence to the U.S. military's experimentation with biological weapons under conditions of actual combat—especially in an effort to weaken the North Korean and Chinese forces during the prolonged and rocky negotiations for an armistice.

Clear and identifiable *direct* evidence that the United States experimented with biological weapons in the Korean War is not available in the U.S. archives *as they presently exist* for public scrutiny. However, a wealth of recently declassified materials provide strong corroboration of materials released by the Chinese army and Chinese public health authorities showing that the United States was using insect vectors and other means of conducting biological warfare.

According to Colonel Qi Dexue, Chinese historian of the Korean War, Chinese military documents indicate that the early skepticism of Mao Zedong and Zhou Enlai about the rumors of bacteriological warfare turned to alarm with increasing medical evidence from the Chinese 42nd Army in Korea.[15] So warned, Zhou supported the North Korean charge that U.S. forces were using germ warfare, and alerted and organized public health authorities in areas of China adjacent to the logistical route to Korea.

Derogatory comments have been made in the West about the quality of Chinese and North Korean medicine at the time. There is no question, however, that the Chinese and Korean medical and scientific staff involved in documenting the charges of biological warfare were qualified, even by Western standards. Many of the medical scientists held degrees from major Western medical schools. Others had been educated in Chinese medical schools established by Western missionaries. Under Mao's administration, medical schools did develop a shortened course to provide a cadre of practitioners with practical skills to serve a mass population. There remained, however, a core of highly trained medical scientists and doctors. Though the Chinese Communists distrusted the medical profession as a Westernized and bourgeois segment of society, they continued to cultivate it out of respect for Western medical science, and because it was essential to Mao's plan to free China from epidemic disease.[16]

Some in the West have speculated that Chinese scientists were compelled to participate in a propagandistic fraud. This is not a credible notion, since Chinese scientists who were involved then are still convinced today of what they found. Their conviction stands in this current era when public discourse in China is more open and Chinese medical scientists leave to travel and to work abroad.[17] Could Western scientists have been deceived by those who gathered the specimens? Members of the International Scientific Commission asked themselves this question and decided that the testimonies of the hundreds of witnesses interviewed and interrogated "were too simple, too concordant, and too independent" to be subject to doubt.[18]

Though this commission, headed by Dr. Joseph Needham of Cambridge University, consisted of people sympathetic to the Chinese revolution, only one member was from a Soviet-bloc country, and all had distinguished careers and major reputations to protect in the West.[19] They did their work at a time when there were few neutrals. With the hindsight of history, their 60-page report, with its 605 pages of appendixes, must be treated with more respect in the light of evidence from the Chinese archives and our knowledge of U.S. military activities. There is only one conclusion: The report is a plausible re-creation of equally plausible data from North Korean and Chinese sources that the United States experimented with insect and other vectors of biological warfare during the Korean War.

Similarly, to reach the truth, there is a need to revisit the extensive Western campaigns to debunk the observations of two other visitors who came on the scene in China. Though not scientists, Dr. John Burton, the former head of the Australian Foreign Service, and Dr. James G. Endicott, a Canadian missionary who was born and spent much of his life in China, were trained observers of people and motives. Recently declassified documents on the Canadian bacteriological warfare program indicate that Endicott hit closer to the mark than the Canadian government was willing to acknowledge at the time.

Canadian External Affairs Department files reveal a massive top-level attempt, which extended across the range of External Affairs' diplomatic net, to refute Endicott's charges that the United States, with possible Canadian support, was carrying out bacterial warfare in northeast China.[20] Part of their case was a dismissal of Endicott's conclusions on the grounds that he was an active sympathizer of the revolutionary government in China. But the heart of the refutation was a report submitted by three Canadian scientists, solicited by Canada's External Affairs Department at the suggestion of the U.S. State Department. The Americans made this suggestion in the context of discouraging the Canadian government from its plans to possibly prosecute Endicott for treason. The Canadians had raised the necessity of having U.S. officers from the UN command in Korea testify against the credibility of the evidence that Endicott presented. The Americans were reluctant to participate.[21]

The report of the three Canadian scientists debunked the scientific plausibility of the Chinese reports,[22] and the Canadian government circulated this report throughout the non-Communist world. None of these scientists, the records indicate, had any involvement with, and possibly none had any knowledge of, the Canadian bacteriological warfare program.[23]

However, External Affairs also quietly solicited the opinion of a fourth scientist, Dr. G. B. Reed, a member of the government's biological warfare panel and head of the Defense Research Board's biological weapons research laboratory at Queen's University in Kingston, Ontario. Professor Reed, a scientist of great reputation, had established himself as a pioneer during World War II, and the records show that he was the scientist most involved with insect vector work in the coordinated Canadian, U.S., and

British biological warfare programs. He remained involved in the joint programs with the United States through the Korean War period. Reed, like the other scientists, was asked to comment on the summaries of laboratory reports prepared by the North Korean Army's Medical Corps, serving with the Chinese army. These indicated that U.S. aircraft were using insect vectors to spread disease. Reed concluded that although there were some anomalies, the evidence was feasible. Reed's account is stamped as having been seen by External Affairs minister Lester Pearson.[24] His report went nowhere, remaining secret until its recent declassification. Reed suggested that Pearson avoid getting involved in a public discussion of the scientific aspect of the charges.

As a moral footnote to the era, Reed, whose work on offensive biological warfare was highly secret and deeply buried, was part of the Canadian delegation to the Fourth International Congress of Microbiology in Copenhagen in 1947. Congress delegates carried by acclamation a resolution condemning biological warfare and urging microbiologists throughout the world to do everything in their power to prevent the exploitation of "such barbaric methods."[25]

As late as 1963, the former chief entomologist of the U.S. Army's Biological Laboratories at Fort Detrick, Dr. Dale W. Jenkins, claimed that prior to 1953 and the Chinese charges, "the United States had never investigated the potential of using arthropods for BW."[26] U.S. documents show this not to be the case. Participants in Fort Detrick Project No. 411-04-004, "Dissemination of BW Agents by Insects," spent $34,617 in 1951 and had a budget through 1953 of more than $163,000. Another project, No. 411-02-041, on mosquito vectors and encephalomyelitis viruses as agents for biological warfare, conducted with Johns Hopkins University, spent $147,905 in 1951 and had a budget through 1953 of more than $380,000.[27] In addition, the United States possessed full knowledge of the results of research on insect vectors in the closely coordinated Canadian program conducted by Professor G. B. Reed at Queen's University.

Much was made at the time of the fact that the Chinese refused to accept the U.S. version of neutral observers. Such critics, however, were ignoring the fact that the World Health Organization was an agency of the United Nations, against which China and North Korea were at war. As well, the Swiss International Committee of the Red Cross (ICRC), the dominant member of the International Red Cross, had a dubious history of neutrality from World War II, which included covering up the existence of Hitler's extermination camps in the face of evidence from its representatives. And its president during the Korean War was a member of the ICRC during World War II. In addition, newly released secret documents show that when the United States made an offer for international inspection to counter the Chinese and North Korean charges, the offer was less than candid. The U.S. Defense Department plainly told UN ambassador Benjamin Cohen that a statement saying that "the United States did not intend to use bacteriological warfare—even in Korea—was impossible." General Matthew Ridgway, the U.S. Far East commander, was secretly given permission to deny potential Red Cross inspectors "access to any specific sources of information." Nevertheless, Anbassador Cohen went before the United Nations to proclaim that the U.S. followed a policy of openness—"we make no effort to conceal such matters"—and at the time he cast aspersions on the Communist case. A document in the Canadian External Affairs file on bacteriological warfare confirms suspicions about the neutrality of the International Red Cross, revealing that this body, without any firsthand information, prepared a position paper refuting the Chinese charges.[28]

American professor Paul Cassell, writing in the *Stanford Law Review* in 1983, addressed the problem of how adversarial systems make it difficult to establish violations of international law.[29] He selected the biological warfare charges lodged by China against the United States during the Korean War as a case study. He believed that the Chinese had done what reasonably could be expected of them in seeking bodies composed of politically sympathetic Western scientists of major reputation, backed up by a body of politically sympathetic Western legal experts with major reputations. This is the best support that international law is likely to get during a state of war. Should we simply write off the findings of the International Scientific Commission and the International Association of Democratic Lawyers as propaganda, or should we step back with historical perspective and take a critical look?

Realistically, international justice always falls victim to the passions of war. But by weighing the evidence on both sides long after the battle, legal scholar Cassell concluded (even with the limited information available to him at the time he wrote) that there was mounting circumstantial evidence that the United States was guilty. Such guilt would be but a continuation of the United States' drift to total war when it walked away from the law of war restrictions on strategic bombing during World War II and the Korean War, and then expanded the legitimate scope of strategic bombing in the U.S. Army's 1956 revision of the *Law of Land Warfare* in such a way as to permit easy justification of the unrestricted bombing of civilians.

The data that Dr. Needham's International Scientific Commission passed on from the Chinese and North Koreans to the Western world was consistent with the knowledge that we presently have of the biological warfare program of the United States and its allies, and of the Japanese program of World War II to which the United States had access. The new evidence, as well as a longer historical perspective, has shifted the opinions of some skeptics of the time. Among those who have accorded the Needham Report more respect in retrospect is the late Professor George Wald, Nobel Prize winner in biology and former head of the Biological Laboratories at Harvard University. In a personal communication to us, he wrote,

> I remember the newspaper reports well; and entirely rejected the thought that we were using germ warfare in Korea and over China. Joseph Needham was the only person I knew on the International Commission, and believing him to be biased toward the Communist side . . . I dismissed his testimony in this instance as another evidence of what I took then to be his unworldliness and suggestibility. I say this now with embarrassment: Needham is a great and utterly decent person and a monumental scholar. As for the allegation that the U.S. used germ warfare in the Korean War, I can only say with dismay and some shame that what I dismissed as incredible then seems altogether credible to me now.[30]

Perhaps the most difficult and contentious issue that the International Scientific Commission had to confront was China's complaint that the United States used insects—fleas, flies, mosquitoes, and other arthropods—to disseminate disease, and that the disease-bearing insects appeared following U.S. air attacks in quantities and in circumstances and under meteorological conditions that were often highly unusual and unnatural.[31] Later "plausible denials" on the part of the U.S. ranged from Air Force colonel and POW Walker M. Mahurin's ridicule of the possibility that "fleas, flies, and mosquitoes" were used for spreading germs,[32] to the contrary view of the former head of entomology at Fort Detrick, Dale Jenkins. Jenkins wrote that insects could be employed for such purposes, but he maintained, as noted above, that the United States had never investigated the potential of using arthropods for biological warfare until 1953, as the Korean War wound down.[33] In contradiction to these claims of innocence, subsequently opened U.S. archives clearly demonstrate that as early as 1942 and almost continuously afterwards, the U.S. government and its allies in Canada and Great Britain sponsored projects to develop "fleas, flies, and mosquitoes" for the purpose of biological warfare, and that they were successful in doing so.[34] The Chinese claims about the viability of insects as vectors of disease—claims that were supported by the International Scientific Commission—were *entirely* plausible; the American denials were misleading and false.

Another charge the Chinese made was that infected feathers were dropped from U.S. aircraft to contaminate areas and spread disease.[35] The top secret U.S. Secretary of Defense archives, which the Chinese could not have been privy to in 1952, confirm this possibility. The archives reveal that turkey feathers were a standardized vector in the American biological weapons system, for use against crops and to contaminate the supplies and equipment of the military support system of enemy troops.[36]

There is also considerable overlap between the kinds of diseases that the United States was preparing for its biological warfare program and those which the Chinese claim followed attacks by U.S. aircraft in the spring of 1952. Newly opened Chinese archives show that Chinese medical personnel were uncertain about the diagnosis of some unusual illnesses or sudden deaths. From what they were finding, however, it seemed clear to them that the pathogenic microorganisms used in the U.S. germ war experiments included plague and anthrax bacillii, meningitis, encephalitis, typhus, relapsing fever, cholera, paratyphoid, and salmonella.[37] All of these diseases (and several more) had been studied and considered by U.S. scientists for their potential in biological warfare.[38]

With respect to methods of delivering infected insects, feathers, bacteria, viruses, fungi, and other materials, according to the Chinese and North Koreans' observations, the most important were spraying, non-exploding objects and paper packets, air-bursting leaflet bombs the size of 500-pound general-purpose bombs (with the marking M105),[39] cardboard cylinders with silk parachutes, self-destroying paper containers with paper parachutes, and cylindrical porcelain/eggshell containers.[40]

The U.S. archives show that spray methods and the leaflet bomb were part of the overt biological warfare program during 1952–53. The covert program is less easy to determine, but it also successfully experimented with a wide range of mechanisms. As early as 1942, Dr. Theodor Rosebury, later technical director of Fort Detrick's Research and Development department, was interested in paper-package delivery systems for insect vectors similar to those reported by the North Koreans and Chinese.[41] He reiterated this interest in 1947 when he published the previously classified 1942 study that he had co-authored as a consultant to Detrick, noting that much progress had been made in the development and delivery of insect vectors in the meantime. Photographs of a cylindrical cardboard (or paper) container fitting the description of a parachute paper container bomb for insect vectors and rodent hosts developed by the Japanese can be found in a Korean War–era folder in the U.S. Chemical Corps records. It carries no identification other than "Secret."[42] Chinese publications show Dr. Needham pictured beside a parachute paper container bomb resembling that in the American photograph.[43]

Then there is the information that the U.S. Army learned about dissemination of germs from its connection with General Ishii. Although the U.S. government denied any such connection for many years, the Far East Command top secret documents on Ishii, declassified in 1992, reveal that the U.S. Army interrogated Ishii and twenty members of Japanese Unit 731 who were directly connected with the actual biological warfare experiments on allied prisoners of war. As a result, the United States was "in full possession of all the details of this work." As early as 1947, the U.S. command ordered that "information concerning the activities and whereabouts of ISHII, Shiro was a Top Secret matter, and no information re his whereabouts or activities was to be reported to any outside agency." Ishii and his fellow war criminals were "taken care of" financially by the U.S. government so that their information would go no further.[44]

There is a long circumstantial trail of corroborative evidence that the United States experimented with biological weapons in Korea: the existence of an elaborate U.S. covert operation for conducting biological warfare; the production of disease-bearing insects (United States) and their subsequent discovery in northeast Asia (China and North Korea); the preparation of infected fowl feathers (United States) and their appearance near exploded bombs (China); the overlap between bacteria and viruses cultivated (United States) and diagnosed (China and North Korea); the manufacture of specific weapons such as spray, non-exploding objects, leaflet bombs, cardboard cylinders, etc. (United States) and the discovery of the same in China and North Korea; and finally, the U.S. Army's connection to Japan's biological warfare experts denied (United States), alleged (China), and later confirmed. Underlying all this as well was the affirmed policy of the U.S. high command to have an offensive biological warfare capability and to deploy "all effective means of waging war without regard for precedent as to their use." This was too large and too complex an operation, and was possessed of too much inner logic, to have been concocted by the Communist side for propaganda purposes, as some have suggested.

And there is more. The United States' handling of the returning prisoners of war who had confessed to participating in biological warfare reinforces the impression of guilt. These confessions were a strong corroboration of the Chinese case, and they proved to be a delicate and vexing matter for the United States. The highest levels of the U.S. government tried to develop measures "designed to seize and maintain the initiative" in the propaganda field.[45] The State Department twice asked the Canadian government to supply affidavits from Canadians once held prisoner in China that would describe methods of "physical violence" and "subtler forms of pressure" to extort confessions. But the Canadian government twice declined to comply with this request, because the statements taken from imprisoned missionaries in China did not include complaints about "consistent or deliberate ill-treatment by the Chinese."[46]

The U.S. Psychological Strategy Board's Working Committee on "Planning for Psychological Exploitation of Communist Methods of Indoctrination and Inducing Confessions" adopted the word "brainwashing" for releases to the U.S. media in an effort to put a sinister cast on the Chinese methods of obtaining confessions. (The term "menticide" was thought to be too strong, giving the Chinese too much credit).[47] But when a congressman proposed a "Day of National Dedication for the Korean POWs" in the spring of 1953, the committee urged caution, thinking that it might backfire. Likewise, they cautioned against a proposal that the U.S. POWs who had confessed to dropping bacteriological warfare bombs in Korea be brought before the United Nations to tell their side of the story. The Working Committee had some warnings to offer about this initiative: First, "it is not yet clear . . . how much compulsion the U.S. prisoners of war . . . have undergone at the hands of their captors in order to lead them into such extravagances of confession." Also, "the chances should be carefully weighed that the prisoners of war might appear before the U.N. and speak their piece exactly as they do in the Chinese Communist propaganda films which we have seen."[48] The Working Committee proposed instead a rather lame press release accusing the enemy of "inducing false confessions from our prisoners of war, and again denying bacteriological warfare charges against the U.S."[49] What the government later took before the United Nations were eight recantations secured under threat of court-martial, a move that prompted the Psychological Strategy Board to observe that recantations under these conditions are less than convincing.[50] From then on, the U.S. Department of Defense decided to play down the airmen who had confessed and "play up the boys who held out."[51]

The detailed content of the airmen's confessions weighs more heavily when matched with what we now know about the U.S. biological weapons program. Most captured flyers acknowledged that while they were subject to stress and duress, they were neither physically beaten nor fed information to put into their statements. A massive study by the U.S. Army concluded that brainwashing was not an issue in the high rate of collaboration by U.S. prisoners of war.

When the International Scientific Commission completed its work in China and North Korea, it stated that it had found itself in the presence of a great mass of facts, some of which formed coherent patterns that had turned out to be highly demonstrative. After concentrating its efforts on these, this group of men and women concluded beyond a reasonable doubt that "the peoples of Korea and China had indeed been the objective of bacteriological weapons." The weapons had been employed by units of the U.S. armed forces using a great variety of methods, some of which seemed to be developments of those employed by the Japanese army during World War II.

Dr. Joseph Needham, who authored the final report, stated that the commission had reached its conclusions reluctantly, "because its members had not been disposed to believe that such an inhuman technique could have been put into execution in the face of its universal condemnation by the peoples of the nations." The commission called for all peoples to redouble their efforts "to preserve the world from war and prevent the discoveries of science being used for the destruction of humanity."[52]

The sentiments of the commission reach through history to connect us with continuing concerns of war, policy, and public morality. Half a century after Joseph Needham uttered his appeal, we are beginning to see into the black hole of the United States' biological warfare policy during the early Cold War. Declassified documents reveal how U.S. policy makers casually dismissed moral issues, deftly sidestepped the risk of public accountability, and built biological warfare into offensive military strategy.

Lying just beneath the surface of all the details of the U.S. biological warfare program is the question, Why was it used in the Korean War?

The argument we have put forward is that the U.S. experience of the war in Korea reveals a military culture that allowed an army to resort to scorched-earth tactics, to incendiarism, to a strategy of total warfare within the confines of Korea, even to the condoning of war crimes. Prominent among the factors promoting such a culture was a brand of moral certitude exemplified in General Ridgway's message to his troops called "What Are We Fighting For?" in which he implied that the Almighty was on the side of the U.S. Army. This certitude encouraged ethical blindness and required the utmost secrecy and deception to prevent the American people—with their deeply ingrained democratic culture—from learning about questionable activities that violated the moral consensus. Secondly, the U.S. Army's possession of technology and know-how, which minimized the threat of retaliation in kind (including napalm, atomic and biological weapons, and overwhelming superiority in delivery methods and communications), fostered a willingness to engage in total war, a war without any humanitarian limits. Another factor was a racial bigotry that dehumanized as it laid waste an alien people: Koreans were referred to as "gooks" and the Chinese as "hordes."

Finally, there was fear—fear among the military and political leaders of the United States during a time when the ideological supremacy of Western capitalism itself was being challenged. Unless they were prepared to risk a wider and uncertain conflict, they might lose more than the war if they could not find an effective method to weaken the enemy and, in John Foster Dulles's words, "teach him a lesson." Many in the U.S. expected that events would inexorably lead to a total war that would decide the fate of the world. For a brief interlude, from 1949 to 1953, there was a wide consensus among U.S. policy makers and strategists that biological science could provide a new superweapon, superior in many ways to the atomic bomb, that would give the United States the military advantage in a war to end all wars.

What unravels is the story of how the newly empowered U.S. Defense Department revived and funded a broad coalition of military, private, and public-sector interests from World War II to implement a crash program in biological warfare. Its mission was to achieve emergency operational readiness in the shortest possible time. Support for the program was driven by the mixed motives of ideology, fear, racism, power, profit, and the visceral excitement of an opportunity at the new frontiers of science and war. The inner bureaucratic logic of the program was built on the initial commitment: research and development, strategic concepts, military plans, and operating structures grew together in the search for an ultimate devastating weapon. Pushing the program forward faster and faster was the Korean War, with the possibility that it could lead to general war, and its potential for testing new weapons. The Strategic Air Command built bacteriological weapons into its strategic plans for general war, both the strategic and tactical air commands had a high-priority tactical plan to use them against ground forces, and the Air Force established a planning structure for covert biological warfare, complete with a Far Eastern air wing for covert operations. When these pressures and capabilities are added to the accumulation of circumstantial evidence from the United States, Canada, Australia, Korea, and China, we are led to the conclusion that the United States took the final step and secretly experimented with biological weapons in the Korean War.

The history of the biological warfare program, experimentation in the Korean War, and the continuing evasiveness and secrecy about what happened in those distant days make the Korean War a living part of the continuing debate on public morality and the waging of war. Secrecy still surrounds this period, raising doubts about whether the United States was sincere in finally ratifying an international protocol against biological warfare in 1972. In 1977 hearings on "U.S. Army activity in the U.S. biological warfare programs" before the Senate Subcommittee on Health and Scientific Research, which he chaired, Senator Edward Kennedy made an opening statement calling for less concealment. The Army report to his committee turned out be one of the more notorious pieces of official concealment and historical misinformation on the Korean War period, and has helped to mislead the public, including some historians, who chose to believe that the military establishment would not lie to the U.S. Senate.

Concern continues over the path of the world's greatest military power. As one biological warfare watcher, Professor Richard Falk of Princeton University, warned in 1989, "BW developmental pressure and prospects are increasing at a rapid rate."[53] The need for less concealment remains Greater knowledge and historical perspective can help the public and policy makers join together to prevent what happened in the heat of the early Cold War from happening again. We hope that one day the full story will help prod medical doctors, scientists, and universities to take effective action to ensure that the science of healing will never again be used to build weapons of war. Apart from this, our wish is that the record of deceptions and "plausible denials" from the Korean War era, precedents that continued through much of high policy making in the United States and other nations in the second half of the twentieth century, will alert future generations to more seriously question special pleas about national security that are advanced in times of international tension.

APPENDIX 1

U.S. Joint Chiefs of Staff on Biological Warfare
(See pp. 81–83.)

J.C.S. 1837/26

21 September 1951

MEMORANDUM BY THE JOINT ADVANCED STUDY COMMITTEE
CONCLUSIONS

"3. BW possesses a great potential as a weapon of war.

"4. National security demands that the United States acquire a strong offensive BW capability without delay. A sound military program requires the development of all effective means of waging war without regard for precedent as to their use.

"5. A more vigorous test program including large-scale field tests should be conducted to determine the effectiveness of specific BW agents under operational conditions.

"6. BW is distinctive as a weapon in that it does not destroy structures or property. The use of such a weapon would greatly simplify certain postwar economic rehabilitation problems.

"7. If low production costs of BW agents can be realized, a partial solution may be offered to the acute need of maintaining a strong military posture for long periods without jeopardizing our economic structure. Further, the achievement of a BW capability may not compete with the procurement of our present weapons systems.

"8. The small number of military personnel in the Services who are interested in, or accurately informed about, BW should be increased by establishing a BW indoctrination course.

"9. The adoption of a positive military policy to the effect that the United States will be prepared to employ BW whenever it is militarily advantageous would serve to stimulate Service interest in the BW field and accelerate its development."

Approved by the Joint Chiefs of Staff on 25–26 February 1952 (J.C.S. 1837/29), RG218, National Archives

APPENDIX 2

U.S. Air Force Biological Warfare Program Guidance

(See p. 119.)

AFOPD–PW   17 March 1953

MEMORANDUM FOR: CHIEF, WAR PLANS DIVISION
                  CHIEF, PSYCHOLOGICAL WARFARE DIVISION

SUBJECT: (UNCLASSIFIED) Biological and Chemical Warfare

    1. The primary responsibility for actions concerning BW and CW within the Directorate of Plans will be as follows:

        a. The Psychological Warfare Division will direct and supervise covert operations in the scope of unconventional BW and CW operations and programs and the psychological aspects of BW and CW.

        b. The War Plans Division will:

            (1) Prepare and disseminate general Air Force BW and CW policy and program guidance in collaboration with the Psychological Warfare Division as applied to 1a above.

            (2) Integrate capabilities and requirements for BW and CW into war plans.

            (3) Participate in the determination of munitions requirements for BW and CW to implement approved plans.

    2. The functions outlined in paragraph 1b (2) and (3) above were previously assigned to the Psychological Warfare Division. Transferral of these functions to the War Plans Division will proceed in a manner so as not to interrupt the activities of the Directorate in these matters.

    3. This directive will supersede previous instructions on this subject with which it may conflict.

                            ROBERT M. LEE
                            Major General, USAF
                            Director of Plans

C
O
P
Y

U.S. Air Force Operations, BW/CW General Decimal Files for 1953, Entry 199, Box 5, File 337-385, RG341, National Archives

APPENDIX 3
Destroyed Evidence
(See p. 171.)

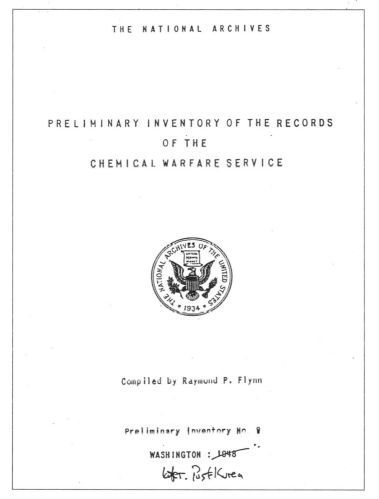

THE NATIONAL ARCHIVES

PRELIMINARY INVENTORY OF THE RECORDS
OF THE
CHEMICAL WARFARE SERVICE

Compiled by Raymond P. Flynn

Preliminary Inventory No. 8

WASHINGTON : ~~1848~~
~~later~~. Post Korea

"These lists were prepared by the Army when the records were transferred to the Records Center in 1956. They were attached to the accessioning dossiers and reflect the contents of the accession as it appeared in 1956. Between 1956 and 1969, some files were recalled by the army and others were destroyed. The records were accessioned permanently by the National Archives in 1969."

Preface to records of the Chemical Warfare Service, accession lists for 1949–1954 files, "Preliminary Inventory No. 8," compiled by Raymond P. Flynn, RG175 Indexes, v. 1, Accession 67A4900, National Archives

APPENDIX 4

M-105: Leaflet Bomb and/or Germ Bomb?
(See pp. 173–176.)

CHINA'S COMPLAINT

"In the Spring of 1952 China accused the U.S. Air Force, 3rd Bomb Wing, of using 500-lb. leaflet bombs, model number M105, for biological warfare."
People's China, No. 7 (1 Apr 1952), No.10 (16 May 1952)

M-105, similar to the M-16, leaflet bomb   NCNA PHOTO

COLONEL MOORE'S EXPLANATION

On 23 March 1953, Colonel William G. Moore, AO 418054, furnished a signed sworn statement to the inspector general of the U.S. Air Force in which he indicated that he served as commanding general of the 3rd Bomb Wing from 17 January 1952 until 29 November 1952. He said, **"The group did fly leaflet missions, the purpose of which was to warn non-combatants in the areas adjacent to military targets that those targets were subject to attacks by USAF, thus enabling civilian personnel to avail themselves of an opportunity to escape injury and fatalities."**

From "Report of Investigation of Communist Allegations That the USAF Participated in Biological Warfare in Korea," prepared by the Office of Special Investigations, the Inspector General, Headquarters, U.S. Air Force, 22 April 1953

The Actual Pattern of 3rd Bomb Wing's Attacks

U.S. Air Force records show that night after night, the 3rd Bomb Wing dropped two M105 "leaflet bombs" in the vicinity of villages and defenders located near railways after, not before, day-long attacks by squadrons of dive bomber, casting doubt on Colonel Moore's "explanation."

OPERATIONS ORDER 141-52 FOR MAY 1952 *[Extract]*
SECRET, by authority of
COMMANDING GENERAL, 5TH AIR FORCE

> *Secret*
>
> SECURITY INFORMATION

Target F-3: A mile and a half section of rail line near the village of Sainjang at map co-ordinates YD4744 to YD4846, North Korea.

TASKS FOR SUBORDINATE UNITS:

I. 136th Fighter-Bomber Wing will send 24 F84 aircraft to attack target F-3. Three flights of eight aircraft will attack at 07:15, 12:25, and 18:40.
J. 49th Fighter-Bomber Wing will send 12 F84 aircraft to attack target at 13:20.
K. 3rd Bomb Wing will despatch 30 B26 bombers to maintain continuous night coverage, of which four aircraft will attack target F-3. The last two of these aircraft will be carrying their maximum load of 500-lb general pupose bombs with 1 to 48 hour delay fuses, **with the last aircraft carrying two leaflet bombs** No. 8281 on last two stations.*(Emphasis added)*

BOMBER MISSION REPORT AND INTERROGATION
[Extract]

Date of mission: 20/21 May 52   3rd Bomb Group Mission No. 3-176433
Time over target. 02:33 [last aircraft]   Type of aircraft: B26. No. 325
Target: YD 4744 to YD 4846, railway   Pilot: Madsen   Navigator: Keegan
Armament: 4 - 500lb M64 delay fusing   Gunner: Shanke
         4 - 100lb M47 instant fusing   Type of mission: pre-briefed
         2 - 500lb M105 leaflet cannisters

> 19. Acft No Pilot Nav Bombordier VO Eng Gunner
> 325 Madsen Keegan Shanke
> 19. Interrogator's name: Hawkins A2/c
> Time and date completed 21 May 52 0535

Interrogator's name: Hawkins, A2/c
Time completed: 21 May 52, 05:35

NOTES

1. Aches and Fevers in China and Korea

1. John Burton to Stephen Endicott, 12 Apr. 1997.

2. G. B. Reed, head of the Defence Research Board, Biological Warfare Laboratory, Queen's University, Kingston, Ontario, Memorandum for Secretary of State Lester B. Pearson, "Communist Allegations of Bacteriological Warfare in Korea and China" (secret), enclosure in Escot Reid, Memorandum for the Minister, 15 May 1952, File 50208-40, Pt. 2, Vol. 5919, RG 25, National Archives of Canada [NAC].

3. Liaoning Archives (Shenyang), Volume 43, long-term preservation, Northeast Patriotic Health Campaign Committee, Reports of the Research Group of the Northeast Epidemic Disease Prevention Committee, Reports of Group Report [hereafter cited as Liaoning Archives, Reports of Research Group], No. 17, 21 Apr. 1952, "Bacteriological Examination Results." For another, slightly different version of this case, see Central Archives (Beijing), Volume 343, Office of the Northeast Bureau, "Report from the Rehe Provincial Party Committee to the Northeast Bureau and Various City, County, and Banner Party Committees on the Occurrence of Anthrax," 5 Apr. 1952.

4. Liaoning Archives, Reports of Research Group, No. 14, 10 Apr. 1952, "Recent Case of Anthrax."

5. Liaoning Archives, Reports of Research Group, No. 19, xx May 1952, "Bacteriological Examination Report," and No. 16, xx Apr. 1952, "Recent Discovery of Anthrax Patients." See also Appendix AA, pp. 361–416, with photographs, in Joseph Needham et al., *Report of the International Scientific Commission for the Investigation of the Facts Concerning Bacterial Warfare in Korea and China*, 61 pp. plus 600 pp. of appendixes (Peking, 1952) [hereafter cited as Needham Report (1952) after its principal author, Dr. Joseph Needham, FRS, biochemist, Cambridge University].

6. Liaoning Archives, Volume 43, long-term preservation, Northeast Patriotic Health Campaign Committee, Daily Reports of the Northeast Region Epidemic Disease Prevention Committee [hereafter cited as Liaoning Archives, Daily Reports], Daily Report No. 13, 16 Mar. 1952, "Luda City Epidemic Disease Prevention Committee Reporting at Midnight of 15 March." Premier Zhou Enlai personally received copies of all daily reports. Information from Mr. Shen Zhengle, archivist in charge of the Central Party and State Archives of the 1950s in Beijing. The daily reports were all labeled "Confidential document for leading cadre reference."

7. Liaoning Archives, Reports of Research Group, No. 19, xx May 1952. A Chinese Air Observer Corps report puts the date of the flight of a lone U.S. B-26

bomber over Manjing Railway Station two days earlier, on 14 March. Map printed on p. 416(d), Needham Report (1952).

8. In the summer of 1952 there were 170 cases of "forest encephalitis" in northeast China, an unusually large number, with 36 deaths. The previous year, in 1951, there had been only 3 cases of this disease, with 1 death. Liaoning Archives, Reports of Research Group, No. 24, 23 July 1952, "Forest Encephalitis Special Report," by group leader Chen Yingqian.

9. Needham Report (1952), Appendix TT, Biographical Register, p. 652.

10. Liaoning Archives, Reports of Research Group, No. 8, 14 Mar. 1952.

11. Liaoning Archives, Volume 63, permanent, Northeast Patriotic Health Campaign Committee, Central Party telegram of 19 Mar. 1952, re: Anti-bacterial warfare instructions. See also "Report on Fungus-Laden Plant Materials Dispersed by U.S. Military Planes in Northeast China and in the Northern Part of Korea," Appendix Ja, Needham Report (1952), pp. 181–189; New China News Agency [NCNA] report of 29 Feb. 1952, "U.S. Aircraft Again Drop Bacteria-Laden Insects," *Survey of China Mainland Press* [*SCMP*] (Hong Kong, 1952), No. 285, pp. 2–3.

12. "Report of the Commission of the Medical Headquarters of the Korean People's Army on the Use of Bacteriological Weapons" [hereafter Korean Medical Commission Report], pp. 3–5, in Canadian Peace Congress, "Documentation on Bacteriological Warfare, 1 April 1952" (mimeograph), File 50208-40, Pt. 1.1, Vol. 5919, RG 25, NAC.

13. Ibid., pp. 6–8.

14. Concerning the Comprehensive Situation of the Enemy's Bacterial War and the Use of Poisonous Gas," 28 Jan. to 31 Mar. 1952, by the Headquarters of the Chinese People's Volunteer Army, 5 Apr. 1952, People's Liberation Army [PLA] Archives, Beijing, JW-1, 1952, Vol. 107, Doc. 14. Albert Cowdrey, historian of the U.S. Medical Corps in the Korean War, says that since there was no history of plague in Korea, U.S. troops were not inoculated, and large stores of vaccine were not kept because immunity lasted only a few months. Cowdrey, *The Medics' War* (Washington, D.C., 1987), p. 175.

15. Korean Medical Commission Report, p. 9.

16. Cited in Qi Dexue, *Chaoxian zhanzheng juece neimu* [The Inside Story of Decision-Making in the Korean War] (Shenyang, 1991), pp. 281–282 [hereafter cited as *Jeuce neimu*].

17. Ibid., p. 282.

18. The Chinese People's Committee for World Peace and Against American Aggression, *Stop U.S. Germ Warfare!* (Peking, 1952), pp. 1–5; NCNA, 25 Feb. 1952, "Chou Enlai Issues Statement . . . ," *SCMP* (1952) No. 282, pp. 2–4.

19. Qi Dexue. *Juece neimu*, pp. 288–289.

20. Nie Rongzhen, *Nie Rongzhen junshi wenxuan* [Selected Military Writings of Nie Rongzhen] (Beijing, 1992), p. 365.

21. Qi Dexue, *Juece neimu*, p. 289.

22. "The Disease Situation of the Army," PLA Archives, JW-1, 1952, Vol. 107, Doc. 14.

23. Statistics for Anju prefecture are in *Zhongguo renmin zhiyuanjun kangmei yuanchao zhanshi* [History of the Chinese People's Volunteer Army in the Resist America, Aid Korea War], 2nd ed. (Beijing, 1990), p. 149 [hereafter cited as *Zhongguo*]. The United States acknowledged that there had been no plague re-

ported in Korea since 1912, a position that the official medical history of the war reiterated in 1987. See Cowdrey, *The Medics' War*, p. 175.

24. "The Disease Situation of the Army," PLA Archives, JW-1, 1952, Vol. 107, Doc. 14.

25. *Zhongguo*, p. 150.

26. Qi Dexue, *Juece neimu*, pp. 288–289; *Zhongguo*, pp. 151–152. Casualty figures do not include totals for Korean civilians or the North Korean People's Army, which may have been higher.

27. New China News Agency (English edition), "U.S. Invaders Extend Bacteriological Warfare to China's Northeast" (NCNA special correspondent, Mukden), 6 Mar. 1952, *SCMP* (1952), No. 290, pp. 3–4. For further eyewitness reports, see *SCMP* (1952), No. 297, p. 2; No. 300, p. 2; No. 303, p. 2; No. 304, pp. 5–6; No. 306, pp. 10–11; No. 315, p. 9; No. 319, pp. 5–6.

28. Liaoning Archives, Volume 63, permanent, Northeast Patriotic Health Campaign Committee, "Central Party telegram, instructions to various regions. Approved by Zhou [Enlai]," 19 Mar. 1952. Classification: AAAA.

29. Qi Dexue, *Juece neimu*, p. 290.

30. Liaoning Archives, Reports of Research Group, No. 13, 5 Apr. 1952; NCNA, "Sufficient Evidence on U.S. Germ War Collected in Northeast China," 26 Mar. 1952, *SCMP* (1952), No. 304, p. 5.

31. Report of the Northeast China Group of the Commission for Investigating the American Crime of Bacteriological Warfare," pp. 2–3, *Daily News Release, Supplement*, 8 Apr. 1952, NCNA.

32. Needham Report (1952), pp. 30–31, 654.

33. Liaoning Archives, Reports of Research Group, No. 13, 5 Apr. 1952.

34. Liaoning Archives, Daily Reports, No. 12, 15 Mar. 1952 (confidential document for leading cadre reference); Reports of Research Group, No. xx, 12 Mar. 1952.

35. Central Archives, Volume 271, Office of the Northeast Bureau, Liaodong Provincial Committee, "Disease Prevention Report and Comments by the Central Disease Prevention Committee," 23 Apr. 1952. Printed at the bottom of the first page is "Not to be lost. Every two months put in order and burn." It appears that Chinese authorities—no doubt on orders from Zhou Enlai, who headed the disease-prevention program—were concerned that this secret data on the results of the bacteriological warfare effort not make its way into enemy hands.

36. Liaoning Archives, Reports of Research Group, No. 14, 10 Apr. 1952.

37. Liaoning Archives, Volume 62, permanent, Telegram: "A brief report by the Central Epidemic Disease Prevention Committee on the anti–germ warfare epidemic disease-prevention work situation of May." The telegram is minuted by Chairman Mao: "This report is very good. Should circulate a notice to various regions. 14 May."

38. Liaoning Archives, Volume 68, permanent, Northeast Patriotic Health Campaign Committee, "Brief, Comprehensive Report on Epidemic Disease, March to May 1953, Presented to Vice-President Li [Xiannian]." Volume 43, long-term preservation, Daily Reports, No. 177, 3 Mar. 1953, to No. 193, 15 July 1953.

39. Liaoning Archives, Volume 68, permanent, "Brief, Comprehensive Report . . . ," May 1953. A terrible plague epidemic had killed 23,171 people in this area of northwestern Heilongjiang province in the summer of 1946, after the Japanese hurriedly destroyed their bacteria-manufacturing laboratory near Harbin and

released plague-infected animals into the countryside on the eve of liberation of the northeast in 1945. NCNA report, 16 May 1951, *SCMP* (1951), No. 105, p. 10; NCNA report from Harbin, 28 Feb. 1952, *SCMP* (1952), No. 285, p. 4. See also Sheldon Harris, *Factories of Death: Japanese Biological Warfare 1932–1945 and the American Cover-up* (London and New York, 1994), pp. 3–5.

40. Liaoning Archives, Volume 43, long-term preservation, Daily Reports, No. 11, 14 Mar. 1952.

41. Ibid., No. 8, 11 Mar. 1952.

42. Ibid., No. 12, 15 Mar. 1952.

43. Ibid., No. 14, 17 Mar. 1952.

44. Ibid., No. 12, 15 Mar. 1952, and No. 130, 18 Aug. 1952.

45. Liaoning Archives, Volume 68, permanent, Northeast Patriotic Health Campaign Committee, "Brief Comprehensive Report on Epidemic Disease, March to May 1953."

46. "Results of Scientific Tests on Germ-Laden Insects Dropped in Northeast," NCNA, Mukden, 1 Apr. 1952, *SCMP* (1952), No. 308, p. 3.

47. "Annual Historical Report 1950," 406 Medical General Laboratory, Professional Section, pp. 185–186, Historical Division, U.S. Medical Department [AMEDD] Records 1947–1961, Box 242, HD 319.19, RG 112, United States National Archives and Records Administration [NA].

48. Liaoning Archives, Volume 43, long-term preservation, Daily Reports, No. 13, 5 Apr. 1952.

49. Interview by Stephen Endicott with Colonel Qi Dexue, associate research fellow, Department of Military History, PLA Academy of Military Science, Beijing, 25 Mar. 1996, Oral History Project on the Korean War, York University. Colonel Qi wrote the chapter on biological warfare during the Korean War for the official history of the Chinese People's Volunteer Army (*Zhongguo*) and authored *Juece neimu.*

50. NCNA Peking, 14 Mar. 1952, name list of "Mission for Investigation of U.S. Bacteriological Warfare Crimes," *SCMP* (1952), No. 295, pp. 5–6.

51. Interviews with professors Qiu Weifan, Shen Qiyi, Liao Gailong, and Dr. Yan Renying by Stephen Endicott in Beijing, 21 and 23 Apr. 1994, Oral History Project on the Korean War, York University.

52. Professor Qiu Weifan's report on "Soybean Stalks and Pods Harbouring a Purple Spot Fungus Disseminated by U.S. Military Planes in the Northern Part of Korea," is in Needham Report (1952), pp. 181–183.

53. For their study on the Japanese bacteriological warfare program from the 1930s through World War II, Peter Williams and David Wallace interviewed an alleged sergeant from a battalion of the Middlesex Regiment with respect to what appeared from his description of an incident to be the use of germ warfare by the U.S. during the retreat from Kunuri in the panic of late November 1950. Peter Williams and David Wallace, *Unit 731: The Japanese Army's Secret of Secrets* (London, 1989), pp. 265–266. We conducted extensive correspondence during 1996 with about a dozen members of the regiment who were at the place of the alleged incident, from the commanding officer, Colonel A. M. Man, down through the ranks. They in turn spread our queries to others who were there via the regiment's Korea Club and the Stoke on Trent and District Branch of the Korean British Veterans' Association. One of those with the regiment in Korea and with whom

we corresponded subsequently became a military historian well versed in the detail of the regiment's Korean history. From comments in the Williams and Wallace interview, the members of the battalion narrowed down the alleged witness to one company of the battalion, a member of which corresponded with us, while others were contacted on our behalf. Nobody in the battalion who was present at the time had any knowledge of the incident, nor any idea as to who the sergeant might be. The three sergeants in the company of the alleged source had all died within a year or two preceding our correspondence.

54. Letter to us from Dr. John Burton, 14 Mar. 1996; letter with respect to a discussion with John Burton from Jaap van Ginneken, 1 Aug. 1983, in our possession. Another example of disappearing documents related to biological warfare in the Korean War apparently occurred in the Belgian archives. The Belgian chief of staff, Lt. General Piron, visited Tokyo in late February 1952 and, accompanied by the Belgian ambassador to Japan, Daufresne de la Chevalerie, had an interview with James Van Fleet, commanding general of the U.S. Eighth Army in Korea. In the course of their conversation, Van Fleet is reported by the West German news agency ADN to have said that in the war in Korea, the United States was employing "methods of mass extermination not previously used." The only record of the visit by the ambassador and the chief of staff that can be found in the Belgian archives is a courtesy letter from Van Fleet dated 29 February 1952, accompanied by two photographs of his meeting with General Piron and a cover letter from the ambassador to the Belgian foreign minister entitled "Hostilities in Korea." This document, dispatch No. 399 D.17390, 5 Mar. 1952, from Tokyo, is in the Central Archives of the Ministry of External Affairs, but does not contain any record of the ambassador's report about what was said at the meeting. The archivist at the Musée Royal de l'Armée et d'Histoire Militaire in Brussels simply says, "Nous n'avons dans nos archives aucune trace de la mission du General Piron at Tokyo." Dr. Richard Boijen to Stephen Endicott, 5 Apr. 1996. Thus the reports of conversations by Belgian officials with General van Fleet are missing from two official archives. See also Jean-Pierre Gahide, *La Belgique et la Guerre De Coree 1950 1955* (Brussels, 1991), pp. 72–73, for a defensive and unenlightening reference to this incident.

2. World War II Origins

1. The first recommendation that the Chemical Warfare Service investigate the potential of biological warfare came on 24 September 1924 from the Mechanical Division of the service's Edgewood Arsenal, Report No. 442. See p. 1 of H. I. Stubblefield, "A Resumé of the Biological Warfare Effort," 21 Mar. 1958, Record 54763, Box 2, Chemical and Biological Warfare Collection, National Security Archive, Washington, D.C. [hereafter cited as Stubblefield (1958)]. Dr. Stubblefield was BW assistant to the deputy chief chemical officer for scientific activities. Fox's article is "Bacterial Warfare: The Use of Biologic Agents in Warfare," *Military Surgeon* 72 (March 1933).

2. On World War II biological warfare development in the United States, see Sheldon H. Harris, *Factories of Death: Japanese Biological Warfare 1932–1945 and the American Cover-up* (New York and London, 1994), and Barton J. Bernstein,

"America's Biological Warfare Program in the Second World War," *Journal of Strategic Studies 2* (March 1992). For the Canadian connection, see John Bryden, *Deadly Allies: Canada's Secret War, 1937–1947* (Toronto, 1989).

Official histories to be consulted are Norman M. Covert, *Cutting Edge: A History of Fort Detrick, Maryland, 1943–1993* (Fort Detrick, Md., 1993); Richard M. Clendinin, *Science and Technology at Fort Detrick, 1943–1968* (Fort Detrick, Md., 1968); and Dorothy L. Miller, "History of Air Force Participation in the Biological Warfare Program 1944–1954," 2 vols. (U.S. Air Force, Air Materiel Command, Historical Division, Wright-Patterson Air Force Base, Ohio, 1952, 1957) [hereafter cited as Miller (1952) and Miller (1957)]. (Miller's unpublished official history was declassified in part in 1988. The footnotes remain classified. A Freedom of Information Act request that we filed to have the remainder declassified was sent by the Air Force to the Army for action, but has yet to be answered.) A valuable source from the inside is "Activities of the United States in the Field of Biological Warfare," a report to the Secretary of War by George W. Merck, Special Consultant on Biological Warfare, Entry 488, Box 182, RG 165, U.S. National Archives and Record Administration [NA]. A resumé of the Merck Report, "Official Report on Biological Warfare," appeared in the March 1946 issue of *Bulletin of the Atomic Scientists*, pp. 16–18 [hereafter cited as Merck Report (1946), resumé]. Another valuable inside history is Stubblefield (1958).

A basic source for the historical record used by Sheldon Harris is Rexmond C. Cochrane, "History of the Chemical Warfare Service in World War II (1 July 1940–15 August 1945), Biological Warfare Research in the United States," 2 vols. (Historical Section, Plans, Training and Intelligence Division, Office of Chief, Chemical Corps, November 1947, unpublished "draft" typescript, Fort Detrick Archives). Harris notes that this study is the official history of World War II biological warfare research. Norman Covert, the historian at Fort Detrick, told Harris in an interview in April 1990 that this 600-page typescript was never published, evidently because higher authorities deemed it too controversial. Harris notes that essential photographs and appendixes are missing. See also U.S. Congress, *U.S. Army Activity in the U.S. Biological Warfare Programs*, 2 vols., unclassified, presentation to Senate hearings in February–May 1977 (Washington D.C., 1977).

3. Technical Study No. 10," Chemical Warfare Service, 28 Aug. 1939. Cited in Stubblefield (1958), p. 2.

4. Colonel James S. Simmons to H. H. Bundy, 14 Aug. 1941, Entry 295A, Box 6, p. 26, WBC, 61 253, RG 175, NA. Cited in Harris, *Factories of Death*, p. 152.

5. Minutes of a Conference on Biological Warfare at 2101 Constitution Avenue," 20 Aug. 1941, Entry 295A, Box 6, RG 175, NA. Cited in Harris, *Factories of Death*, p. 153.

6. The president was Dr. Edwin B. Fred, dean of the Graduate School of the University of Wisconsin. The committee drew representatives from Yale, John Hopkins, Cornell, the University of Chicago, the Rockefeller Institute, the National Research Council, and the National Academy of Science. See Stubblefield (1958), p. 7; also Harris, *Factories of Death*, p. 153. The head of the Canadian bacteriological warfare program, Dr. E. G. D. Murray of McGill University, and the head of the bacteriological warfare laboratory at Queen's University, Dr. G. B. Reed, were present at the first meeting of the WBC Committee, which was held on 28 December 1941 at the Lord Baltimore Hotel in Baltimore. Murray's ten

pages of detailed notes on the meeting are a valuable part of the historical record. They indicate the practical, down-to-earth approach to a problem that called for fast answers to specific questions. The talk focused on the search for fast and efficient development in both countries on human, animal and plant diseases. There was discussion of botulinus toxin experiments by the U.S. Chemical Warfare Service. Rinderpest was put at the top of the list, followed by Rift Valley fever. Anthrax was considered a possibility. Other diseases discussed were foot-and-mouth disease, pleuropneumonia, African horse sickness, and glanders. A long list of anti-personnel toxins were discussed, including malaria, yellow fever carried by mosquito vectors, smallpox, psittacosis, diphtheria, tetanus, salmonella, and plague. There was interest in mosquito vectors in northern climates.

At this time Murray held out the possibility of U.S. use of the thousand-square-mile testing site to be developed with the British around Suffield, Alberta. And the WBC took up Murray's offer for a joint Canadian-American project to test rinderpest at Grosse Ile, a small island in the St. Lawrence River below Quebec City. Bryden, *Deadly Allies*, pp. 94–97.

7. Quoted by Bryden, *Deadly Allies*, p. 105.

8. Ibid., p. 107; Robert Harris and Jeremy Paxman, *A Higher Form of Killing: The Secret Story of Gas and Germ Warfare* (London, 1982), pp. 95–96.

9. Stimson to Roosevelt, 29 Apr. 1942, President's Secretary File 104, Franklin D. Roosevelt Library, as cited in Harris and Paxman, *Secret Story*, p. 154.

10. Merck Report (1946), resumé; Harris, *Factories of Death*, p. 154.

11. Stubblefield (1958), p. 8; Harris, *Factories of Death*, p. 154.

12. Stubblefield (1958), pp. 9–12.

13. For the above historical summary, see Stubblefield (1958), pp. 6, 13–20, 22–23; Merck Report (1946), resumé; Bryden, *Deadly Allies*. See also Memorandum from British Prime Minister [Winston Churchill], 7 June 1944, on coordination with the United States on the development and delivery of anthrax-filled bombs, Box 2, Chemical and Biological Warfare Collection, NSA.

14. For the interwar disarmament discussion with reference to biological warfare, see Frederic J. Brown, *Chemical Warfare: A Study in Restraints* (Princeton, N.J., 1968).

15. Truman to AEC Commissioner Thomas Murray, 19 Jan. 1953, Harry S. Truman Library, cited by Barton J. Bernstein, "Origins of the U.S. Bacteriological Warfare Program," in Susan Wright, ed., *Preventing a Biological Arms Race* (Cambridge, Mass., and London, 1990), p. 20.

16. William D. Leahy, *I Was There: The Personal Story of the Chief of Staff to Presidents Roosevelt and Truman, Based on His Notes and Diaries Made at the Time* (New York, 1950), pp. 439–440.

17. Brown, *Chemical Warfare*.

18. Theodor Rosebury, "Medical Ethics and Biological Warfare," *Perspectives in Biology and Medicine* 6 (Summer 1963): 514–515, quoted in Harris, *Factories of Death*, p. 158. Ira Baldwin, who headed the program at Camp Detrick for most of the war, expressed similar sentiments, noting, "No one I asked to join our program ever refused" (Bryden interview, *Deadly Allies*, p. 254).

Perhaps the most striking example of a doctor who let his sense of duty override the Hippocratic oath was Dr. Frederick Banting in Canada. As John Bryden demonstrates, this national icon of Canada's contribution to medical science, the Nobel Prize–winning co-discoverer of insulin, was the force behind Canada's very early entry into a bacteriological warfare program. Driven by an obsessive belief that the "Hun" was a threat to civilization, Banting called for a strategy of total war against the German population with bacteriological weapons. The Banting Institute in downtown Toronto thus became the birthplace of biological warfare research in North America. Banting's program of testing anti-personnel agents for offensive use preceded Britain's by almost a year, and that of the United States by two. The Banting Institute is best known as the site of crucial work in the development of penicillin that went on in its laboratories at the same time. A contemporary comment is the location of the University of Toronto's Institute for Bio-Ethics two buildings down the street from the Banting Institute.

The British program at Porton, Bryden concludes, was slowed for years by the chairman of the British Microbiological Warfare Committee, Lord Hankey, who, unlike most of those in a position of power, appears to have been genuinely appalled by the prospect of biological warfare and acted on his beliefs. Banting had some choice words in response to Hankey's refusal to acknowledge the merits of his attempt to put the Canadian case for biological warfare before Hankey's committee. Hankey's stall ended when Churchill, an enthusiast for just about any new weapon, including biological warfare, fired him. As a result of Banting's initiative, the Canadian War Cabinet and the Canadian Chief of Staff incorporated biological warfare into national policy in 1940. Initial work was focused at the Banting Institute, Connaught Laboratories, the University of Toronto, Queen's University, and the National Research Council of Canada, but it was quickly extended to most Canadian universities.

19. Harris, *Factories of Death*, pp. 168–170; Bryden, *Deadly Allies*, pp. 218–219.

20. The above material is from Bryden, *Deadly Allies*, pp. 90, 106, 116–117, 210–211, 214; 251, nn. 15 and 18; 292, n. 9; 294. He cites Stanley P. Lovell, *Of Spies and Stratagems* (New York, 1964), pp. 152–160; transcript of a telephone conversation between General Porter and U.S Army authorities in Germany, Autumn 1945, Box 143, p. 337, RG 175, NA; E. G. D. Murray to James Patterson, 12 Dec. 1944, C1, 4354–33–13–6, RG 24, NAC.

21. For a history of U.S. and Allied decision-making on gas warfare during World War II, see Bryden, *Deadly Allies*, pp. 60–61, 181, 185–195, n. 26; Harris, *Factories of Death*, pp. 158–159.

22. For an interesting exchange of information on the potential and development of botulinus toxin and a compatible munition see Bryden, *Deadly Allies*, p. 291, n. 5.

23. Ibid., pp. 197–199.

24. Bernstein, "The Origins of the U.S. Biological Warfare Program," p. 20. The Canadian program provided another footnote to lost opportunities by the joint Allied bacteriological warfare program to get into the war. When Japanese balloons began to drop on the Canadian Pacific coast, there was considerable concern that they might carry the products of the then-known Japanese bacteriological warfare program. The head of the Canadian program, Professor Murray, prepared for the retaliation order. With what had to be the approval of his boss, Otto Maass, and of Canadian high command, an active supporter of biological warfare from the beginning, Murray had a bomber of the Royal Canadian Air Force on standby at Uplands Airport in Ottawa, ready to begin a journey by way of Vancouver and Hawaii to drop plague bacteria on Japan. Bryden, *Deadly Allies*, pp. 219–220.

Bryden cites an interview with Dr. T. E. King of the Chemical Warfare Laboratories of the National Research Council in Ottawa.

3. The Japanese Connection

1. George Merck expressed the urgent priority that Fort Detrick scientists placed on these needs in the Merck Report of 1946: "Activities of the United States in the Field of Biological Warfare," a report to the Secretary of War by George W. Merck, Special Consultant on Biological Warfare, Entry 488, pp. 7–10, Box 182, RG 165, NA, as cited in Sheldon Harris, *Factories of Death: Japanese Biological Warfare 1932–1945 and the American Cover-up* (London and New York, 1994), p. 191. This work is the first book-length study to make full use of the relevant declassified documents in U.S. archives.

2. Sheldon Harris, "Japanese Biological Warfare Research on Humans: A Case Study of Microbiology and Ethics," *Annals of the New York Academy of Sciences* 660 (1992): 50. Harris emphasizes that it was the Joint Chiefs of Staff who pushed for the deal.

3. John W Powell, "An American Newspaperman Goes Home," in *China Monthly Review: Editors on Trial,* pamphlet, 29 pp. (Peking, 1957), p. 13.

4. It is no small irony that Alva Carpenter, who played the key role in the legal cover-up giving immunity to the Japanese biological warfare criminals, was chief counsel of the Senate Internal Security Sub-Committee (Jenner Committee), which questioned John Powell and started his problems with the government.

5. John W. Powell, "Japan's Germ Warfare: The U.S. Cover-up of a War Crime," *Bulletin of Concerned Asian Scholars* 12, no. 4 (October–December 1980). 12; Robert Gower, John W. Powell, and Bert V. A. Rolling, "Japan's Biological Weapons: 1930–1945," *Bulletin of the Atomic Scientists,* October 1981, pp. 43–53.

6. Peter Williams and David Wallace, *Unit 731; The Japanese Army's Secret of Secrets* (London, 1989), p. 301. As late as 1986, the U.S. Army's chief archivist, John Hatcher, continued to deny that the Army had ever had any files on Japanese biological warfare; Harris, *Factories of Death,* p. 223.

7. Memoranda and letters of 14 Dec. 1945, 21 Dec. 1945, 7 Jan. 1946, 6 Sept. 1947, in file ISHII, Shiro, File 201, Book I, Military Intelligence Section (G-2), General Staff, General Headquarters, Far East Command, RG 331, NA

8. Harris, *Factories of Death,* pp. 62–71; *Materials of the Trial of Former Servicemen of the Japanese Army Charged with Manufacturing and Employing Biological Weapons* (Moscow, 1950), pp. 15ff.

9. Harris, *Factories of Death,* pp. 138–146, 263, n. 69. Another death factory, Unit 100 in Changchun, was commanded by Lt. General Yujiro Wakamatsu, and was independent of Ishii.

10. Biographical Sketches of Toyoda Group," n.d., circa June 1947, ISHII, Shiro, File 201, Book I, Military Intelligence Section (G-2), General Staff, Far East Command, RG 331, NA.

11. Harris, *Factories of Death,* pp. 203, 221.

12. Ibid., p. 53; Powell, "Japan's Germ Warfare," p. 15, n. 1; Seymour Hersh, *Chemical and Biological Warfare: America's Hidden Arsenal* (New York, 1968), pp. 13–18.

13. Harris, *Factories of Death*, pp. 59, 64–65, 188, 206–207. In his search of the U.S. National Archives, Harris found all of this except the 8,000 slides.

14. Ibid., p. 66. Subsequent attempts by the Army command at Fort Detrick to downplay the materials they got is unconvincing given the interest shown and acknowledgment of the value of the information at the time; ibid., pp. 221–222.

15. Memo," Norman Fell to Chief, Chemical Corps, 20 June 1947, Fort Detrick Archives, Frederick, Md., cited by Albert E. Cowdrey, *The Medics' War* (Washington, D.C., 1987), p. 219, n. 24.

16. Williams and Wallace, *Unit 731*, pp. 26–27; Harris, *Factories of Death*, pp. 55, 68, 107, 110. The Japanese also experimented with lice as a vector; ibid., p. 107.

17. Powell says that "infecting feathers with spore diseases was one of Ishii's ideas." "Japan's Germ Warfare," p. 10.

18. Cowdrey, *The Medics' War*, pp. 64; 201–202, n. 73; 280; Powell, "Japan's Germ Warfare," p. 10; Williams and Wallace, *Unit 731*, pp. 310–313, 316; Keiichi Tsuneishi, *Kieta saikinsen butai* [The Germ Warfare Unit That Disappeared] (Tokyo: Kai-mei-sha Publishers, 1981), pp. 130–133, as cited in Harris, *Factories of Death*, pp. 64, 68, 81–82, 280, n. 73. American drawings from sketches by Ishii of seven experimental bombs are to be found in the report of the most thorough investigator, Camp Detrick's Lt. Colonel Arvo Thompson, "Report on Japanese Biological Warfare Activities," 31 May 1946, Record No. 53139, NSA.

4. The Secretary of Defense and Revival of a Program

1. The National Security Act of 1947 replaced the secretaries of war and the navy with the secretary of defense. The service secretaries remained at sub-cabinet rank. The act also attempted to coordinate military planning by creating the National Security Establishment, a body headed by the secretary of defense, who would coordinate the work of the three service secretaries and be advised by the Joint Chiefs of Staff. The secretary of defense, together with the secretary of state, the service secretaries, and other agency heads appointed at the discretion of the president, was a member of the new National Security Council, created by the act to advise the president on military policy. The service secretaries also directly advised the president and the National Security Council, while the Joint Chiefs of Staff also directly advised the president. When this spread-out organization predictably failed to empower the secretary of defense and left real power in the hands of the service secretaries and the Joint Chiefs of Staff, Congress corrected the problem with the National Security Amendment of 1949, which converted the National Military Establishment to the Department of Defense, clearly headed by the secretary of defense. The amendment demoted the service secretaries from cabinet rank by making them heads of military, not executive, departments, and clearly subordinate to the secretary of defense. The secretaries also were dropped from the National Security Council. The Joint Chiefs of Staff remained as advisors to the president, but they were represented by a new position created by the amendment, the chairman of the Joint Chiefs of Staff. The intention was that the chairman would serve as an advisor to and from the president, further shifting the

center of gravity in military policy away from the military to the civilian leadership of the president and the secretary of defense.

2. Colonel William M. Creasy, Chief, Research and Engineering Division, Office of the Chief, Chemical Corps, "Presentation to the Secretary of Defense's Ad Hoc Committee on CEBAR," 24 Feb. 1950, CCS 385.2 (12-17-43), Sec. 10 (B. P. Pt. I), Box 207, RG 218, p. 2; also to be found in the Chemical and Biological Warfare Collection, National Security Archives [NSA], Washington, D.C., Record No. 54874, 24 Dec. 1950. [Hereafter cited as Creasy Report (1950).]

3. In *Deadly Allies*, Bryden talks about how irate the head of the Canadian chemical and biological warfare program was upon reading a draft of Merck's report and finding no acknowledgment of the role that Canada played in the joint effort. He fumed and lobbied to no avail. Bryden speculates that the Canadian government, and probably Prime Minister Mackenzie King himself, did not wish public disclosure of Canada's involvement in the biological warfare program; pp. 233–234, 239.

4. "Activities of the United States in the Field of Biological Warfare," a report to the Secretary of War by George W. Merck, Special Consultant on Biological Warfare, Entry 488, Box 182, RG 165, NA. The resumé of the report released to the media is available as George W. Merck, "Official Report on Biological Warfare," *Bulletin of the Atomic Scientists*, March 1946, pp. 16–18.

5. The British Chiefs of Staff endorsed the detailed report of its joint Technical Warfare Committee, "Future Development of Biological Warfare" (6 Dec. 1945), which strongly supported development for four reasons:
"a) The probably tremendous increase in lethality of B. W. which may be produced after further research.
b) The comparative ease of production.
c) The possibility of B. W. being complementary to operations with Atomic Bombs.
d) The necessity for continuing research in B. W. potentialities, and counter measures." Chemical and Biological Warfare Collection, Box 12, Record No. 57709, NSA. For continuing cooperation with the United States, see also Records No 57679 and 55002. For the joint statement by the United States, Canada, and Great Britain, see Box 2 in this collection.

6. The board's membership continued the balance set during World War II. It was composed of three civilians and not more than two members each from the departments of the Army, Navy, and Air Force, one member nominated by the director of the U.S. Public Health Service, and one member from the Department of Agriculture. File 954/2, Joint Strategic Plans Committee [JSPC], 23 Aug. 1950, 6 (Enclosure "C"), RG 218, NA.

7. Jeanne McDermott, *The Killing Winds: The Menace of Biological Warfare* (New York, 1987), p. 163. The National Security Amendment of 1949 established the place of the Defense Department and its secretary at the head of policy development. This combination of institutional power and his personal prestige gave Marshall's endorsement of biological warfare special weight.

8. "Report of the Secretary of Defense's Ad Hoc Committee on Chemical, Biological and Radiological Warfare," 30 June 1950, CD 385 (General), RG 330; also in Record No. 54791, NSA. [Hereafter cited as Stevenson Report (1950).]

9. Ibid., pp. viii–ix.

10. Ibid., pp. 9–10.

11. Ibid., pp. 8–9.

12. Ibid., pp. 5, 21–22.

13. Ibid., p. 11. In an attempt to bolster its case, the committee speculated that the Soviet bacteriological warfare program had "probably progressed as far, if not further, than the Anglo-American one"; ibid., p. 15. At the same time it acknowledged that this was only a guess, because "intelligence on Soviet activities is limited"; ibid., p. 11.

14. Ibid., pp. 16–17.

15. Memorandum from George C. Marshall, Secretary of Defense, on "The Secretary of Defense's Ad Hoc Committee on Chemical, Biological, and Radiological Warfare," 27 Oct. 1950, to the secretaries of the Army, Navy, and Air Force, the Joint Chiefs of Staff, the chairman of the Research and Development Board, the chairman of the Munitions Board, the chairman of the Military Liaison Committee, the director of the Weapons System Evaluation Group, and the director of public information, JCS 1837/18, pp. 225–227, Enclosures C and D, RG 218. For the full range of comments endorsing the report that Marshall took under advisement, see Comments on the Stevenson Report, Doc. 941196, pp. 73–90, CD 385 (General), RG 330, NA (declassified at our request, 1996). The document is undated, but endorsements extend from July to October 1950.

16. "1951 Program Guidance Report," 15 Dec. 1950, CD 383.8 (Biological Warfare), RG 330, NA. The total expenditure for biological warfare in 1950, including overhead, was $6.6 million.

17. Dorothy L. Miller, "History of Air Force Participation in the Biological Warfare Program, 1944–54," Vol. 1, pp. 53–54. Volume 1 of this unpublished official history of USAF participation in the bacteriological warfare program was completed in 1952. Volume 2, completed in 1957, covers the period 1952–1954. They are available through the U.S. Air Force, Air Materiel Command, Historical Division, Wright-Patterson Air Force Base, Ohio [hereafter cited as Miller (1952) and Miller (1957)].

18. "Department of Defense Activities Engaged in Biological Warfare Program," Doc. 941196, p. 172, attached to "Department of Defense Directive on Chemical and Biological Warfare Readiness," 21 Dec. 1951, Acquisition No. TS-A94-0125 R1 Doc. 9, Doc. 941196, pp. 143–173 (including attachments), CD 385 (General), RG 330, NA (declassified at our request, 1996).

19. Ibid., p. 2. This directive remained in force until it was canceled by order of the new secretary of defense, Charles Wilson, shortly after the end of the Korean War; Miller (1957), p. 78.

20. Col. James Totten, Chief BW–CW Division, USAF, Memorandum for Record, 13 Feb. 1952, Folder 17, Nonlogged TS, Jan.–June, BW–CW General Decimal Files 1952 (Top Secret), Box 4, RG 341, NA.

21. Memorandum for the Secretary of Defense, 15 Dec. 1951, TAB "E," Para. 8, p. 16, attached to "Department of Defense Directive on Chemical and Biological Warfare Readiness," 21 Dec. 1951, Acquisition No. TS-A94-0125 R1 Doc. 9, Doc. 941196, pp. 143–173 (including attachments), CD 385 (General), RG 330, NA.

22. For a sense of the decision to circumvent the policy of retaliation only for a policy of first use whenever militarily advantageous, see Memorandum from Lt. Colonel C. E. Hutchin, Jr., Office of the Secretary of Defense, to Ralph N. Stohl, 4 Feb. 1952, Subject: Use of CW and BW in Retaliation Only, CD 385 (General),

RG 330, NA; National Security Council Document NSC 50621/1, March 1956; John Ellis van Courtland Moon, "Biological Warfare Allegations: The Korean War Case," *Annals of the New York Academy of Sciences* 666 (1992): 69; Statements of Policy and Directives on Biological Warfare, 11 June 1952, JCS 1837/34, p. 330, Decimal File 385.2 (Top Secret), RG 218, NA; Joint Chiefs of Staff, Decision on JCS 1837/29, 26 Feb. 1952, p. 307, and Note by the Secretaries, Decimal File 385.2 (Top Secret), RG 218, NA; Routing and Record Sheet, From: Psychological War Division, D/Plans, DCS/O, To: Director of Operations, DCS/0, Subject: (Secret) BW Plans for SAC Operations, 20 Mar. 1952, BW–CW General Decimal Files 1952 (Top Secret), File 17, Nonlogged TS Jan.–June 1952, Entry 199, Box 4, RG 341, NA; Report on Chemical and Biological Warfare Readiness, National Policy, 1 July 1952, 27–28, BW–CW Decimal Files 1952 (Top Secret), File 18, Nonlogged TS, Entry 199, Box 4, RG 341, NA; Commander in Chief, United States Air Force in Europe, to Col. Seiler, Subject: BW–CW Appendix, 25 Oct. 1952, BW–CW Decimal Files 1952 (Top Secret), File AFOAT BW TS 52/000 to 100, Box 4, RG 341, NA; Memorandum to Secretary Pace from Thomas K. Finletter, 1 Nov. 1952, BW–CW Decimal Files 1952 (Top Secret), File 15, 000/100, Entry 199, Box, 4, RG 341, NA.

For the placement of biological warfare in strategic group I, see "Decision on JCS 1862/18: A Report by the Joint Strategic Plans Committee on Research and Development Board Request for Strategic Guidance," JCS 1862/18, 11 Sept. 1951, Enclosure A, 1 Sept. 1951, Memorandum for the Chairman, Research and Development Board, Subject: Strategic Guidance for Use in Preparing a Research and Development Guidance Paper for the Department of Defense, 107, USAF-Plans, Decimal File 385.2 (Top Secret), Entry 335, Box 505, RG 341, NA; "USAF Operational Concepts for BW and CW," BW–CW Decimal Files 1952 (Top Secret), File 15, Entry 199, Box 4, RG 341, NA.

5. Research and Development, 1945–1953

1. Maj. General E. F. Bullene, speech of 8 Feb. 1952, "Chemicals in Combat," as printed in *Armed Forces Chemical Journal* 5 (April 1952): 4–7.

2. William M. Creasy, Commanding General, Chemical Corps Research and Development Command, "Biological Warfare," *Armed Forces Chemical Journal* 5 (January 1952): 16–18, 46.

3. William M. Creasy, "Presentation to the Secretary of Defense's Ad Hoc Committee on CEBAR," 24 Feb. 1950, CCS 385.2 (12-17-43), Sec. 10 (B.P. Pt. 1), Box 207, RG 218, NA; Record No. 54874, Chemical and Biological Warfare Collection, National Security Archive, Washington, D.C., p. 29. [Hereafter cited as Creasy Report (1950).]

4. H. I. Stubblefield, "A Resumé of the Biological Warfare Effort," 21 Mar. 1958, Record 54763, Box 2, Chemical and Biological Warfare Collection, National Security Archive, Washington, D.C. [hereafter cited as Stubblefield (1958)], p. 27.

5. For history and a description of Camp Detrick and the Dugway Proving Ground, see Sheldon Harris, *Factories of Death: Japanese Biological Warfare 1932–1945 and the American Cover-up* (London and New York, 1994), pp. 155ff; Jeanne McDermott, *The Killing Winds: The Menace of Biological Warfare* (New York, 1987),

pp. 139–141, 203–205. The Chemical Corps also operated arsenals capable of producing BW weaponry at Edgewood, Maryland, and after 1952 at Pine Bluff, Arkansas.

6. The Chemical Warfare Service in 1945 appointed an Advisory Committee on Research and Development, with representatives from the military services, the U.S. Public Health Service, the Department of Agriculture, and the universities. In 1946 this committee was transferred to the newly formed Joint Research and Development Board of the War and Navy departments, which in turn became the Research and Development Board of the newly organized Defense Department; Stubblefield (1958), p. 27.

7. With the surrender of Japan, the War Department directed the head of the Chemical Warfare Service to submit a bacteriological warfare program for the postwar years. Under this program, several projects from the war were scheduled to be completed, some smaller projects were consolidated, while some were abandoned. The revised 1949 program had 67 projects, down from about 200 at the end of the war (Stubblefield [1958], p. 25). The large Navy program and points of convergence with the Chemical Corps are best captured in the table of organization for the Navy bacteriological warfare program attached to Lovett's directive on bacteriological warfare readiness of 21 Dec. 1951, CD 385 (General), RG 330, NA.

8. Stubblefield (1958), pp. 25–26; Creasy Report (1950), pp. 31–32.

9. Stubblefield (1958), p. 27.

10. Ibid., pp. 25–26.

11. "Report of the Biological Department, Chemical Corps, to the Panel on Program of the Committee on Biological Warfare, Research and Development Board," October 1949, Appendixes 18, 20, Records of the Chemical Corps, Dugway Proving Ground, computerized keyword index. All top secret records of the Chemical Corps appear to be at Dugway; they remain classified and are exempted from Freedom of Information Act appeals.

12. Creasy Report (1950), p. 8.

13. Ibid., pp. 20–23, 33.

14. Ibid., p. 21.

15. Ibid., pp. 16–19, 31.

16. Ibid., pp. 3, 4, 7, 27–28, Tables I and V. The only agents for which storage problems are indicated are plant pathogens. Rust spores are noted as having a life expectancy of approximately six months. Creasy singles out anthrax and botulinus toxin for their considerable storage life, while noting that others will require refrigerated storage (pp. 25, 27). There is no indication of which three had been tested in field trials, but anthrax and botulinus had been tested during World War II, *Brucella suis* became the first standardized agent during 1950, and tularense was available to fill munitions on an emergency basis.

17. Dorothy L. Miller, "History of Air Force Participation in the Biological Warfare Program, 1944–1954," Vol. 1 (1952), U.S. Air Force, Air Materiel Command, Historical Division, Wright-Patterson Air Force Base, Ohio [hereafter cited as Miller (1952)], pp. 64–65. As an indication of the activity across a reasonably broad field, this list has changed from Creasy's top-priority list of February, which included *Brucella suis*, botulinus toxin, psittacosis virus, bacterium tularense, and *Bacillus anthracis*. Creasy Report (1950), pp. 3–4.

18. Dorothy L. Miller, "History of Air Force Participation in the Biological

Warfare Program, 1944–1954," Vol. 2 (1957), U.S. Air Force, Air Materiel Command, Historical Division, Wright-Patterson Air Force Base, Ohio [hereafter cited as Miller (1957)], p. 12.

19. A. B. Christie, *Infectious Diseases: Epidemiology and Clinical Practice*, 4th ed., Vol. 2 (Edinburgh, 1987), pp. 1133, 1135, 1142–1143.

20. Ibid., p. 1061.

21. Ibid., pp. 1052–1053.

22. Miller (1952), p. 55.

23. Ibid., p. 65; Creasy Report (1950), pp. 3–4.

24. Creasy Report (1950), pp. 5–8.

25. CD 383.8 (Biological Warfare), p. 6, RG 330, NA.

26. Creasy Report (1950), pp. 5–8.

27. Test results tables indicate the extent of the knowledge accumulated. They give heavily sanitized data on incubation period in days; casualty rate for respiratory cause by percentage; fatality rate by percentage; degree of disability by percentage and days; epidemic spread transmission from person to person; dissemination methods; persistence after dissemination in days; toxoids against and effectiveness; specific treatment; dates of readiness for specific production facilities; and stability during storage and handling. An ordering and implementation of priorities to achieve readiness was in place. "Note by the Secretaries to the Joint Chiefs of Staff on Military Priority Rating for Development of BW Agents," 3 July 1951, Appendix to "Enclosure from Research and Development Board," 2 July 1951 and 1 Sept. 1951, JCS 1837/27, pp. 236–240; "Note by the Secretaries to Holders of JCS 1837/27," 13 Sept. 1951, Enclosure B, JCS 1837/23, pp. 265–272; Memorandum for the Chairman, Research and Development Board, from the Joint Chiefs of Staff, Subject: Military Priority Rating for Development of BW Agents, 13 Sept. 1951, RG 218, NA, Top Secret Special Report No. 138, prepared by Special Operations Division and Crops Division, Biological Department, Chemical Corps, "Feathers as Carriers of Biological Warfare Agents: I. Cereal Rust Spores," 15 Dec. 1950, File 2807-T, CCS 385.2 (12 17-43), R P RG 330, NA.

28. "1951 Program Guidance Report," Committee on Biological Warfare, 5 Dec. 1950, CD 383.8 (BiologicalWarfare), RG 330, NA (declassified at our request, 1996).

29. Creasy Report (1950), pp. 16–19, 31.

30. Ibid., pp. 18, 31.

31. "1951 Program Guidance Report," pp. 2–3, 7, 12.

32. Creasy Report (1950), p. 9. In spite of its detailed nature, there is no reference in the Creasy Report to the extensive knowledge that the U.S. scientists derived from the Japanese biological warfare program. Nor is there any indication of the kind of the work being done by the other partners in the coordinated U.S.–British–Canadian programs.

33. Ibid., p. 21.

34. Ibid., p. 12.

35. Ibid., p. 22.

36. Ibid.

37. Ibid., p. 29.

38. Miller (1957), pp. 11–17. It was initially specified as an area saturation bomb to be dropped from internal carriage, but the Air Force, consistent with its

interest in the tactical as well as strategic characteristics of bacteriological weapons dating from at least 1948, expanded its requirements to include external carriage by fighter bombers; ibid., p. 13.

39. Ibid.

40. Ibid., p. 19.

41. Ibid., p. 11.

42. The quotes are from Miller (1957), pp. 11–13. For the troubled history of the development of the M33/M114 bomblet combination, dating from 1942 to its adoption, see especially Miller (1952), pp. 83–86, and Miller (1957), pp. 11–22, 85. The technical problems were that the weight of the munition required that it be carried in small numbers, which restricted the area of coverage, and that the aerosol was inefficient.

43. Miller (1952), pp. 84–86, and Miller (1957), p. 84. The technical objectives for the E61R2 were set in September 1949, the E61 designation was given 20 December 1949, and the military characteristics were issued 7 August 1950. The basic design of the E133 bomb with the E61 bomblet was in place by July 1953.

44. "1951 Program Guidance Report."

45. Miller (1952), pp. 79–81; Miller (1957), pp. 104–111, 124; Department of Defense Directive on Chemical and Biological Warfare Readiness, 21 Dec. 1951, 15 CD 385 (General), RG 330, NA. The feather bomb grew out of Air Force requirements for an anti-crop munition dating from 26 September 1947. A report on successful testing, complete with photographs of the adapted leaflet bomb and turkey feathers and maps of tests, is in Top Secret Special Report No. 138, "Feathers as Carriers of Biological Warfare Agents: I. Cereal Rust Spores." The M16 was modified so that packages containing the feathers would open and the contents discharge upon the functioning of the cluster. The feathers were washed, fluffed white turkey feathers of uniform size, averaging 3 1/2 inches long by 1 3/4 inches wide, 1,500 per pound (Figure 2). The feathers were dusted with an anti-crop agent. There is a nine-page analysis of the tests with seventeen illustrations.

46. Department of Defense Directive on Chemical and Biological Warfare Readiness.

47. Miller (1957), pp. 159–176.

48. For reference to those not mentioned previously, see Miller (1952), p. 158.

49. Department of Defense Directive on Chemical and Biological Warfare Readiness. An Air Force table of organization for bacteriological warfare is an attachment with reference number 941196-172 (declassified at our request, 1996).

50. Ibid. Attachment titled "Defense Activities Engaged in Biological Warfare, U.S. Army," with Defense Department document and page reference 941196-172 (declassified at our request, 1996).

51. AFOAT, Memorandum for the Record, Subject: OSD Conference, BW–CW Decimal Files 152 (Top Secret), File 17, Nonlogged TS, Jan.–June 1952, Entry 199, Box 341, RG 341, NA.

52. Department of Defense Directive on Chemical and Biological Warfare Readiness, attached table of organization of the Navy's bacteriological warfare program with Department of Defense document and page reference 941196-171; "Vote by the Service Secretaries to the JCS on Research Program in Biological Warfare," 28 Aug. 1952, RG 218, Appendix 362, JCS 1837/40, RG 218, NA. The Navy table of organization indicates extensive contracting out to universities and

private contractors, including a broadly based contract with the University of California "for basic research on BW agents," with specific reference to a contract for studies on *Brucella suis*. There was a contract with General Mills Corporation for the development of a dry agent airborne generator.

53. Ibid., pp. 14–15.

54. Ibid.

55. Miller (1957), p. 119.

56. For the above section, see Miller (1952), pp. 78–81, 87–90; Miller (1957), pp. 117–121. The pages of Miller's history dealing with the development of the spray tank are heavily sanitized, including all references to the agents being tested. The official history notes that the Air Force was motivated at least in part by its annoyance with the occasional "slowness of the Chemical Corps to take procurement action; and in this instance it [Air Force] had proved itself capable of producing a satisfactory end item on short notice when the urgency of the requirement demanded it." Miller (1957), p. 121.

The Air Force also attempted to create a free-floating unmanned balloon as a strategic weapon but dropped the idea amid inter-service friction after spending about one sixth of its biological warfare munitions development budget on it. Miller (1957), pp. 112–113.

57. Ibid., p. 119.

58. Dale W. Jenkins, "Defense against Insect-Disseminated Biological Warfare Agents," *Military Medicine* 128 (February 1963): 116. At that same symposium, Colonel Dan Crozier, commanding officer of the U.S. Army Medical Unit at Fort Detrick, confirmed that sufficient experimental data existed to state that the offensive use of biological agents was feasible and that insects were one of the possible means for their dissemination. Ibid., pp. 83–84.

59. William M. Creasy to Assistant Chief of Staff, G4, Department of the Army, 30 Oct. 1951, p. 6, Control No. 400.112, Entry 1B, Box 235, RG 175, NA.

60. William J. Allen, Chief, Research and Development Division, "Project Listings ... " (Secret), 6 Dec. 1951, Project No. 411-02-041, Control No. 400.112, Entry 1B, Box 235, RG 175, and "Detailed Justification for Supplemental Funds for FY-1953," for the same project with Johns Hopkins University, n.d., p. 9, Control No. 637-10-S, Entry 1B, Box 243, RG 175, NA.

61. Special Weapons, Annual Report June 1952 to June 1953," July 1953, Defense Research Board, Department of National Defense, Canada. This report turned up in recently declassified Chemical Corps papers in the U.S. National Archives, Control No. 11825, pp. 101, 103, Entry 1B, Box 255, RG 175, NA.

62. Ibid., pp. 60–61.

63. John Bryden, *Deadly Allies: Canada's Secret War, 1937–1947* (Toronto, 1989), pp. 207, 210, 224–245, 251.

64. G. B. Reed. "Present Position of Bacteriological Warfare," 16 Dec. 1947, pp. 8–12, File 54-935-302, Vol. 4152, RG 24, NAC.

65. "Special Weapons, Annual Report June 1952–June 1953," pp. 60, 61, 99; "Progress Report on 'R' Work at GIES," 10 Apr. 1952, File DRBS-1850-11, Vol. 4224, Interim Box 43, RG 24, NAC; Defense Research Board, Minutes of the Third Meeting of the Entomological Research Panel, 18 Dec. 1948, File DRBS 4-120-43-1, Vol. 4130, RG 24, NAC.

66. Defense Research Board, Minutes of the Third Meeting of the Entomological Research Panel, 18 Dec. 1948, p. 5; Minutes of the Fourth Meeting, 5 Feb.

1949, pp. 2, 4–5, Appendix A: "Preliminary Plan for Entomological Survey of the Arctic (Biting Insects)"; Colonel Francis J. Galing, Foreign Liaison Officer to A. L. Wright, Defense Research Member, Canadian Joint Staff, Washington, 21 Apr. 1949, File DRBS 4-120-43-1, Vol. 4130, RG 24, NAC.

67. Canadian Joint Staff to Chairman, Defense Research Board, "Special Weapons-Test Facilities," 7 Dec. 1951, File 700-900-267-1, Vol. 4220, Interim Box 43, RG 24F, NAC; Memo to Chief Superintendent, Suffield Experimental Station, Ralston, Alta., 27 Dec. 1951, ibid; "First Periodical Standardization Report, Canadian Army," 23 May 1949, and Appendix E, 31 Mar. 1949, File 190-0-325, Vol. 4158, Interim Box 43, RG 24F, NAC.

68. Defense Research Board Annual Report, September 1951," pp. 10–11, Speeches, etc., Vol. 2425, RG 24F, NAC.

69. Chemical Corps Medical Laboratories, "Special Report No. 34, Research Accomplishments of the Medical Laboratories, Army Medical Corps," Part II, p. 79, Nov. 1953, Control No. 24325, Entry 1B, Box 2263, RG 175, NA.

70. Ibid., p. 1.

71. Chemical Corps Medical Laboratories, "Mechanism of Entry and Action of Insecticidal Compounds and Insect Repellents," 465-20-001, 26 Oct. 1952, attached to Renewal of FY 1953 Budget, from Chief Chemical Officer to Acting Chief of Staff, G4, Entry 1B, Box 237, RG 175, NA. The Biological Laboratories project that this would support, No. 411-04-004, is the previously mentioned project on arthropod dissemination in biological warfare.

72. Memorandum for Chief Chemical Officer, Deputy Chief Chemical Officer, Subject: Research Accomplishments of the Medical Laboratories, Army Chemical Corps, Part II, "A Historical Review of the Project Program Based on Medical Laboratories Reports, 1944–1952" (MISR No. 34), 26 Jan. 1954, Control No. 2432S, Entry 1B, Box 263, RG 175, NA.

73. There is also a record of the dialogue between the medical component of the Naval Unit at Detrick and the Biological Laboratories responsible for agent development, with respect to the naval doctors' assuming responsibility, in consultation with the Biological Laboratories, for developing a testing apparatus for experimentation with agents for BW on human subjects in 1953. This document comes complete with photographs of the apparatus. From LCDR J. H. Stover, MC, USN, and LTJG W. J. Williams, MC, USNR, to Colonel G. Orth, MC USA, 7 May 1953, 15 pages, File 1497S, Entry 1B, Box 257, RG 175, NA.

74. Classified supplement to the *Monthly Newsletter to Staff Chemical Officers*, GHQ, FEC, Office of the Chemical Officer, 28 Feb. 1949, cited in Peter Williams and David Wallace, *Unit 731: The Japanese Army's Secret of Secrets* (London, 1989), p. 283.

75. Theodor Rosebury and Elvin A. Kabat, with the assistance of Martin H. Boldt, "Bacterial Warfare: A Critical Analysis of the Available Agents, Their Possible Military Applications, and the Means for Protection against Them," *Journal of Immunology* 56 (May 1947): 7, 22–25; Rosebury, "An Opinion on BW as a Weapon," to the Technical Director, Research and Development Department, Camp Detrick, Md., 8 Aug. 1946, Record No. 5700, NSA. See also n. 18 of chap. 2.

76. See chap. 3.

77. Bruce W. Rohrbacher, Comptroller, to Chief, Research and Engineering Division, Army Chemical Center, Maryland, Subject: FY 1953 Budget Jus-

tifications, 23 Oct. 1951, Control No. 110.01, Entry 1B, Box 233, RG 175, NA.

78. Miller (1952), p. 49.

79. "Report by the Joint Strategic Plans Committee to the Joint Chiefs of Staff on Chemical (Toxic) and Biological Warfare Readiness," 31 Aug. 1953, JCS 1837/50, 219, RG 218, NA.

6. Plans and Missions, 1945–1953

1. Initiating action for strategic plans could come from the Joint Chiefs, from above through the secretary of defense (before 1947 the secretary of war and the secretary of the Navy), from the Joint Strategic Planning Committee of the Joint Chiefs, or from the director of the Joint Staff, which was organized under the Joint Chiefs into the Strategic Plans Committee and its working body the Strategic Plans Group. The route to a plan's becoming guidance for doctrine was preparation by the Joint Strategic Plans Group, review by the Joint Strategic Plans Committee, and approval by the JCS. The Joint Staff was given responsibility for developing bacteriological warfare strategy. As with atomic warfare, the employment of biological warfare required presidential approval. The services and agencies such as the CIA were responsible for weapons specifications and operational readiness within their spheres of authority for land, sea, air, and covert warfare.

2. Joint Chiefs of Staff Decision on JCS 1927/3, "A Report by the Joint Strategic Plans Committee on the Employment of [sanitized] in Support of U.S. Military Position and Policy," 28 Sept. 1949, JCS 1927/3, pp. 83–92, RG 319 [Records of the Army Staff], JCS Papers maintained by the Office of the Army Deputy Chief of Staff for Operations (declassified at our request, 1996). Though JC 1927/3 was heavily sanitized to avoid revealing that it was a strategic plan for bacteriological warfare, its content is made clear by its referenced relation to a document on the "BW Cover and Deception Plan," which reads in part, " . . . the Director of the Joint Staff be authorized to implement the deception plan which the Joint Chiefs of Staff approved in JCS 1927/3" (1 Feb. 1952, Memorandum from the Chief of Naval Operations to the Joint Chiefs of Staff, Subject: Memorandum by the Director, Joint Staff on Deception in the Biological Warfare Field, no designation, but released with 3 July 1952 Memorandum by the Chief of Staff, U.S. Air Force, for the Joint Chiefs of Staff on Statements of Policy and Directives on Biological Warfare, JCS 1837/36, RG 218 [declassified 1991].

The recommendation by the Army chief of staff that the secretary of defense but not the secretary of state be included in the implementation of bacteriological warfare is an undated document titled "Deception in the Biological Warfare Field" released with the above document from the chief of naval operations dated 1 Feb. 1952. Both were released with JCS 1837/36.

On the government's acknowledgment that a doctrine of "plausible denial" existed, see Stephen Endicott, "Germ Warfare and 'Plausible Denial': The Korean War, 1952–1953," *Modern China* 5, No. 1 (1979): 79–104. CIA director William Colby stated, "I think that the basic rationale for the doctrine of plausible denial was so our Nation could deny something and not be tagged with it" (Hearings days 16–18 Sept. 1975, Senate Select Committee to Study Governmental

Operations with Respect to Intelligence Activities, Frank Church, Idaho, Chairman, Vol. 1 ("The Handling of Toxins"), p. 24).

3. Dorothy L. Miller, "History of Air Force Participation in the Biological Warfare Program, 1944–1954," Vol. 1 (1952), U.S. Air Force, Air Materiel Command, Historical Division, Wright-Patterson Air Force Base, Ohio [hereafter cited as Miller (1952)], pp. 35–36.

4. Twining to Weyland, Redline message, Hoyt Vandenberg Papers, Box 86, Library of Congress. Ninety-six of the ninety-seven boxes of these papers are declassified. They are peculiarly silent on virtually everything of interest in which Vandenberg was involved.

5. The targets were the food sheds of Shan-t'ou, Kuang-chou, and Ch'in-hsien, placed in Group A, with a readiness date of 1 February 1953; Anshan in Group B, with a readiness date of 15 March 1953; and Nanking, Su-chou, and Shang-hai in Group C, with a readiness date of 1 June 1953. See Request for Target Folders, 20 Nov. 1952, BW–CW Decimal Files 1952 (Top Secret), File 15 (000/100), Entry 199, Box 4, RG 341, NA. No targeting documents were found for STEELYARD. For STEELYARD, see Memorandum for all Branch Chiefs, BW–CW Division, Subject: (Top Secret) Use of Code Word "STEELYARD," 28 Aug 1953, BW–CW Decimal Files 1953 (Top Secret), File TS/53-300-325, Entry 199, Box 2, RG 341, NA.

6. The European theater planning document is "USAF Operational Concepts for BW and CW," BW–CW Decimal Files 1952 (Top Secret), U.S. Air Force Operations, File 15, Entry 199, Box 4, RG 341, NA. Available documents do not give the code name of the European Operations Plan, but the document trail suggests that it succeeded Plan CLASSROOM, which first appeared in available documents in 1949 (Joint Chiefs of Staff Decision on JCS 1927/3, "A Report by the Joint Strategic Plans Committee on the Employment [part of title sanitized] in Support of U.S. Military Position and Policy," 28 Sept. 1949, JCS 1927/3 (Top Secret), 83-92, RG 319). CLASSROOM was scheduled to be redesignated following its presentation to the secretaries of defense and state. CLASSROOM was the amalgamation of various BW and CW annexes. Annex A had been an emergency plan in case the Berlin Blockade led to general war; when the crisis ended, it was canceled, its relevant features incorporated into Annex B, a broader cover and deception plan which also incorporated features from a canceled Annex C, the features of which are not available. Indications are that Annex B was the cover and deception plan for BW–CW against the Soviet army.

Jeanne McDermott, in *The Killing Winds: The Menace of Biological Warfare* (New York, 1987), pp. 159, 298, suggests that a plan code-named SCHOOLYARD was a covert biological warfare plan for the Korean War. (McDermott refers to a classified document titled "Cover and Deception Plan: Deception in the Biological Warfare Field," Memorandum by the Chief of Staff, U.S. Army, JCS 1927/ JCS 1927-31 [Plan Schoolyard], n.d.). We have found no further reference to SCHOOLYARD, and at the time of writing managed to have declassified only one series 1927 document in RG 319 pertaining to cover and deception for biological warfare. The Chinese army in Korea and its rail communications in China represented a tempting experimental target for the tactical cover and deception plan, a temptation enhanced first by the crisis of U.S. and United Nations forces being driven back from the Yalu River and then by the sustained crisis of stalemate in the Korean War.

The early schedule for implementation of the tactical plan for biological warfare is found in "Tactical Air Mission Summary Statement, Biological and Chemical Warfare," 28 Oct. 1952, USAF Operations, BW–CW Decimal Files 1952 (Top Secret), Entry 199, File 15 (000-100), Box 4, RG 341, NA. That the F-86 Sabre was assigned to participate in biological and chemical warfare is indicated in AFOAT, Memorandum for Record, Subject: Briefing for Commanding General ARDC, 11 July 1952, p. 2, BW–CW Decimal Files 1952 (Top Secret), File 18, Nonlogged TS, Entry 199, Box 4, RG 341, NA.

7. Undated Memorandum from the JCS to the Chief of Staff, U.S. Army, Chief of Naval Operations, Chief of Staff, U.S. Air Force. Subject: Biological Warfare, JCS 1837/34, Enclosure, pp. 380–381, RG 218, NA.

8. "A Report by the Joint Strategic Plans Committee on Chemical, Biological, and Radiological Warfare," 21 Feb. 1951, JCS 1837/18, p. 217, RG 218, NA. The JCS response to Lovett's memo of 21 Dec. 1951 is Memorandum from JCS to the Chief of Staff, U.S. Army, Chief of Naval Operations, Chief of Staff, U.S. Air Force (undated), JCS 1837/34, Enclosure, pp. 380–381, RG 218, NA.

9. Memorandum by the Joint Advanced Study Committee for the Joint Chiefs of Staff on Biological Warfare, 21 Sept. 1951, JCS 1837/36, Enclosure, pp. 280–295, RG 218, NA. Air Force chief of staff Hoyt Vandenberg made the only modification, noting that the relatively short periods of viability for bacteriological weapons, the consequent necessity of frequent stockpile replacement, and the attendant costs of maintaining refrigerated storage for stockpiled agents might raise the cost to the levels of other weapons. He called for modified language until costs could be calculated more accurately. He also thought the report simplified postwar problems, but acknowledged that bacteriological warfare did simplify postwar economic rehabilitation. In balance, Vandenberg strongly endorsed the report: "The conclusions of the JASC . . . are generally sound and their official recognition by the Joint Chiefs of Staff would significantly aid the bacteriological warfare program." He even extended the optimism of the report in noting, "A great deal of progress in the bacteriological warfare field has occurred since the inception of the JASC study . . . certain offensive capabilities are rapidly materializing." Vandenberg also noted that the three services had already moved to remedy the indoctrination problem noted in the report by recommending the establishment of traveling teams, which he anticipated would be in place by the late fall of 1952 (15 Feb. 1952, Memorandum by the Chief of Staff, U.S. Air Force for the Joint Chiefs of Staff on Biological Warfare, JCS 1837/29, RG 218, NA, pp. 305–307). The JCS approved the report of the study committee with Vandenberg's revisions (26 Feb. 1952, Joint Chiefs of Staff, Decision on JCS 1837/19, 1837/29, attached as top sheet to 1837/29, RG 218, NA). See also Col. Arthur E. Hoffman, Deputy Chief, BW–CW Division, USAF, Memorandum for the Record, 21 Feb. 1952, USAF Operations, BW–CW General Decimal Files TS 1952 (Top Secret), Folder 17, Nonlogged TS Jan.–June 1952, Box 4, RG 341, NA.

10. For the intelligence dialogue, see "Intelligence on Soviet Capabilities for Chemical & Biological Warfare (Secret)," 16 June 1952, Joint Intelligence Committee, Joint Chiefs of Staff, Central Decimal Files 1951–1953, File 385 (1-23-43), Sec. 15, Box 152, RG 218, NA; Memorandum on Biological Warfare Intelligence, 24 Sept. 1952, Office of the Director, Central Intelligence Agency, JCS 1837/42, RG 218, NA; Report by the Joint Strategic Plans Committee to the

Joint Chiefs of Staff on Recommendations of the Air Force in BW–CW Fields, 21 Nov. 1952, Enclosure B, JCS 1837/43, pp. 376–377, RG 218, NA.

11. The memorandum also recommended that human testing be done by the U.S. Public Health Service or on contracts to universities. Memorandum on Biological Warfare, 21 Sept. 1951, JCS 1837/26, p. 292, RG 218, NA.

12. Ibid., pp. 281–285, 292, 295.

13. Ibid., pp. 288–289.

14. Ibid. The conclusion of the study, ibid., pp. 293–295.

15. Miller (1952), p. 45; Dorothy L. Miller, "History of Air Force Participation in the Biological Warfare Program, 1944–1954," Vol. 2 (1957), U.S. Air Force, Air Materiel Command, Historical Division, Wright-Patterson Air Force Base, Ohio [hereafter cited as Miller (1957)], p. 72.

16. Miller (1957), pp. 69–70.

17. Ibid., p. 4.

18. Ibid., p. 13.

19. "Report by the Joint Strategic Plans Committee to the JCS on Chemical (Toxic) and Biological Warfare Readiness," 31 Aug. 1953, JCS1837/50, p. 454, RG 218, NA. The only reference available indicates that the Air Research Development Center was issuing munitions requirements for light as well as heavy and medium bombers by October 1953. Miller (1957), p. 200.

20. A memorandum from Secretary of the Army Frank Pace, Jr., to the secretary of defense described the system in place, 23 Apr. 1952. Subject: Chemical and Biological Warfare Readiness, JSPC 954 22/D, 380.2 (12-17-45), Sec. 14, p. 70, RG 218, NA.

21. For the detailed logistical plan, see Miller (1957), pp. 30–33. The only glimpse into biological warfare plans outside the Air Force is an indication that by late 1950, the Army was studying the effectiveness of ground forces when aided or opposed by bacteriological warfare, and by 1952 it was planning a bacteriological warfare annex for the use of a tactical ground weapon. Memorandum by the Director, Weapons System Evaluation Group for JCS, Subject: Proposal and Outline for WSEG Study of "An Evaluation of the Military Worth and Effectiveness of Present and Projected Ground Force Weapons System," 16 Oct. 1950, pp. 3–5, JCS 2162, RG 218, NA; Memorandum from Frank Pace, Jr., Secretary of the Army, to the Secretary of Defense, Subject: Chemical and Biological Warfare Readiness, 23 Apr. 1952, pp. 2–4, JSPC/22/D, 382.2 (12-17-23), Sec. 14, RG 218, NA.

22. Miller (1957), pp. 71–72.

23. "WPB-55U Strategic Guidance," 9 Jan. 1953, BW–CW Decimal Files 1953 (Top Secret), AFOAT–BW TS 53/27, Entry 199, Box 1, RG 341.

24. Miller (1957), pp. 74–75.

25. "Report by the Joint Strategic Plans Committee to the JCS on Chemical (Toxic) and Biological Warfare Readiness," 31 Aug. 1953, JCS 1837/50, RG 218, NA; Arthur Radford to Charles Wilson, 11 Sept. 1953 (Top Secret), File 82301-S, Box 35, CD 385 (General), RG 330, NA (declassified at our request, 1996).

26. Remarks on BW–CW to 7th Tripartite Conference, 11 Sept. 1952, USAF Operations, BW–CW General Decimal Files 1952 (Top Secret), Folder 18, Nonlogged TS, Box 4, RG 341, NA.

27. "Report by the Joint Strategic Plans Committee to the JCS on Chemical (Toxic) and Biological Warfare Readiness"; Memorandum from Admiral Arthur

Radford, Chairman, Joint Chiefs of Staff, for the Secretary of Defense, Subject: Chemical (Toxic) and Biological Warfare Readiness, 11 Sept. 1953, p. 4, CD 385 (General), File 82301-S, Box 35, RG 330, NA.

7. Korea: A Limited War?

1. Mackinlay Cantor and Curtis LeMay, *Mission with LeMay* (New York, 1965), p. 382.

2. Robert F. Futrell, *The United States Air Force in Korea, 1950–1953* (Washington, D.C., 1983), p. 221; Dean Acheson, *Present at the Creation: My Years in the State Department* (New York, 1969), p. 463.

3. The Nuremberg Charter of 1945 declared as a war crime the "wanton destruction of cities, towns, or villages," and as a crime against humanity "inhumane acts against any civilian population." It was argued that this law was to be applied to the Nazis but not to the Allies, because the Allies had the right to use whatever force was required to put down the criminal act of aggression by an enemy which set no limits on achieving its ends in war. But the U.S. Supreme Court justice who was the United States' chief prosecutor at Nuremberg stated that these rules of war and humanity were intended to apply to the United States in the future. The legal catch, of course, was that with the general tendency toward total war in an atmosphere of intensifying ideological struggle, the winning side would always try to stick the losing side with the charge of criminal aggression, and thus exonerate itself from its own excesses in "defense of truth." General Douglas MacArthur chose the route of the warrior who had participated in both world wars, in the atomic bombing of Nagasaki and Hiroshima, and in the firebombing of Tokyo and other Japanese cities; he carefully excluded the clauses about "wanton destruction" of civilian populations from the Tokyo Charter that he established for the trial of Japanese accused of war crimes.

The Korean War found the United States still fighting under *Field Manual 27–10: Rules of Land Warfare*, as revised by the U.S. Department of Defense in 1940. Like the Nuremberg Charter, the 1940 rules paid deference to the prohibition of aerial bombardment of civilian targets. Military targets were restricted to defended places defined as "occupied by a combatant military force or through which such a force is passing." This definition of a "defended place" was not inclusive enough to justify the strategic bombing of Japan, nor most of what the U.S. did in Korea. Accordingly, when the U.S. Army revised *Field Manual 27–10* in 1956, it widened the definition of a "defended place" in such a way as to cover virtually any motive, including attrition bombing to affect civilian morale. Defended places became "factories producing munitions and military supplies, military camps, warehouses storing munitions and military supplies, and other places devoted to the support of military operations or the accommodation of troops . . . *even though they are not defended.*" (Para. 40, p. 19; emphasis added). At the same time, the revised field manual continued to pay lip service to the "generally recognized" rule of international law "that civilians must not be made the object of attack directed exclusively against them" (Para. 24, p. 16).

4. Ibid., p. 20.

5. Ibid., p. 28.

6. The most thorough, thoughtful, and scholarly treatment of the ongoing

discussion of the origins of the Korean War is Bruce Cumings, *Korea's Place in the Sun: A Modern History* (New York, 1997). Cumings comments that "civil wars do not start: they come," and they originate in multiple causes; p. 238. See also Cumings, *The Origins of the Korean War*, Vol. 2: *The Roaring Cataract, 1947–1950* (Princeton, N.J., 1990).

7. For the pro and con evidence on this, see Cumings, *Origins*, Vol. 2, pp. 615ff.

8. Robert Simmons, "Korean Civil War," in Frank Baldwin, ed., *Without Parallel: The American-Korean Relationship since 1945* (New York, 1974), pp. 151–153.

9. When the United States made requests to the UN Security Council between 25 and 27 June 1950 to authorize a "police action" to repulse the invasion of South Korea by the North, the Soviet Union was absent, boycotting the Security Council for its failure to seat the representatives of the People's Republic of China in place of Chiang Kai-shek's representative, and thus did not exercise its veto power over the U.S.-sponsored resolutions. See Donald F. Fleming, *The Cold War and Its Origins*, Vol. 2: *1950–1960* (New York, 1961), pp. 601–603; Cumings, *Origins*, Vol. 2, pp. 636–637.

10. Recently opened archives of the former Soviet Union indicate that Kim Il Sung had great difficulty getting the assurances he wanted from Stalin. The Soviet government did not wish to get drawn into World War III with the United States in Korea and dealt cautiously with the impatient North Korean leader. Eventually, according to available documents and reminiscences of participants, the Soviets agreed only to provide noncombatant military advisors and the continuation of supplies to help Kim carry out his reunification campaign. Evgeni Bajanov, "Assessing the Politics of the Korean War, 1949–1951," *Cold War in Asia Bulletin*, Winter 1995–96, pp. 54, 87–91. See also Paul Lashmar, *Timewatch: Korea—Russia's Secret War*, BBC/A&E documentary film (London, 1996). The reasons for China's entry into the Korean War remain a matter of debate among academic scholars. Opinions about Mao's motives in sending units of the Chinese army to help North Korea range from a compelling concern about the U.S. threat to China's security on the Yalu River, to a culturally based, aggressive attitude to teach the West a lesson "regardless of the high risk and cost." For a summary of viewpoints, see Zhang Shuguang, *Mao's Military Romanticism: China and the Korean War, 1950–1953* (Lawrence, Kans., 1995), pp. 1–11.

11. Zhou Enlai, "The First Year of People's China," *People's China* 2, no. 8 (1950): 7. President Truman had previously earned Zhou Enlai's condemnation for seizing Taiwan (Formosa) by placing the U.S. 7th Fleet around Taiwan on 25 June 1950, to prevent China from reasserting its control there.

12. Cumings, *Korea's Place in the Sun*, pp. 238–243, 284.

13. Fleming, *The Cold War and Its Origins*, pp. 617–18. MacArthur's air force had been reconnoitering, strafing, and bombing communications and rail centers on the Chinese bank of the Yalu River since 27 August 1950. See "Foreign Ministry Spokesman Refutes MacArthur's Distortions," 11 Nov. 1950, *People's China*, Supplement to 2, no. 11 (1 December 1950): 5.

14. Peng Dehuai, *Memoirs of a Chinese Marshal* (Beijing, 1984), pp. 474–475; *Zhongguo renmin zhiyuanjun kangmei yuanchao zhanshi* [History of the Chinese People's Volunteer Army in the Resist America, Aid Korea War] (Beijing, 1990) [hereafter cited as *Zhongguo*], Map 2, "The First Phase Offensive, October 19–25,

1950."

15. Zhang, *Mao's Revolutionary Romanticism*, p. 110; Lt. Col. Roy E. Appleman, *Disaster in Korea: The Chinese Confront MacArthur* (College Station, Tex., 1989), pp. 44–45.

16. Quoted in Appleman, *Disaster in Korea*, p. 58.

17. Ibid., pp. 58–59.

18. Ibid., pp. 40, 57.

19. Volunteers for Korea," by Qiao Guanhua, editor, *People's China* 2, No. 10 (16 November 1950).

20. For the response by peasant youth from a remote village in Sichuan province to the call to join the army in 1951, see Stephen Endicott, *Red Earth: Revolution in a Sichuan Village* (Toronto, 1989), pp. 47–48.

21. Mao Zedong, *Selected Military Writings* (Beijing, 1968), p. 137.

22. Appleman, *Disaster in Korea*, pp. 102, 104.

23. Ibid., pp. 4–5.

24. Zhang, *Mao's Revolutionary Romanticism*, p. 114. Col. Roy Appleman comments that the Chinese maneuver behind the 2nd Infantry Division "was brilliantly conceived and well executed to force the withdrawal of the Eighth Army from the Chongchon River front or to entrap large parts of its forces." Appleman, *Disaster in Korea*, p. 232.

25. *Zhongguo*, p. 43.

26. Appleman, *Disaster in Korea*, chap. 14; Anthony Farrar-Hockley, *The British Part in the Korean War*, Vol. 1 (London, 1990), pp. 333–335.

27. Appleman, *Disaster in Korea*, p. 286.

28. MacArthur, CINCUNC Tokyo to DEPTAR for JCS Wash. DC, 30 Nov. 1950, CCS 383.21, Korea (3-19-45), Box 43, Sec. 10, RG 218, NA. To reinforce his sense of crisis, MacArthur repeated this message to the Joint Chiefs of Staff four days later, 3 Dec. 1950, ibid.

29. Fleming, *The Cold War and Its Origins*, p. 623.

30. Report by the Joint Strategic Survey Committee to the JCS on the use of the atomic bomb, 4 Dec. 1950, CCS383.21 Korea (3-19-45), Enclosure A, p. 47, Sec. 10, JCS 2173/3, RG 218, NA. The dialogue between MacArthur, the Joint Chiefs of Staff, the State Department, Truman, and Attlee indicates a real sense of crisis and belies the suggestion put forward in some quarters that Truman and the U.S. military were not serious about using the atomic bomb to prevent a threat of major military disaster that was not alleviated until February 1951. See also Cumings, *Korea's Place in the Sun*, pp. 290–293, for the various occasions when the U.S. considered using atomic weapons in Korea.

31. Statement by Chou En-lai," 24 Feb. 1952, in *Stop US Germ Warfare!* (Peking, 1952), p. 1.

32. Zhang, *Mao's Revolutionary Romanticism*, p. 118; see Appleman, *Disaster in Korea*, pp. 285–289, for losses by the U.S. 2nd Division.

33. Appleman, *Disaster in Korea*, p. 17.

34. Fleming, *The Cold War and Its Origins*, p. 623; General Omar Bradley testifying at the Hearings before the Committee on Armed Services and the Committee on Foreign Relations (the MacArthur Hearings), U.S. Senate, 82nd Congress, First Session, Pt. 2, pp. 732–733, as quoted in Fleming, *The Cold War and Its Origins*, p. 641.

35. Matthew B. Ridgway, *The Korean War* (New York, 1967), pp. 264–265.

36. Lt. Colonel Roy E. Appleman, *Ridgway Duels for Korea* (College Station, Tex., 1990), pp. 576–577.

37. Quoted by John Gittings in "The War before Vietnam," in Gavan McCormack and John Gittings, eds., *Korea, North and South: The Deepening Crisis* (New York, 1978), p. 66.

38. Harry S. Truman, *Years of Trial and Hope*, pp. 460–461, as cited in Futrell, *The USAF in Korea*, p. 505.

39. Walter Hermes, *Truce Tent and Fighting Front* (Washington, D.C., 1966), pp. 500–501.

40. See Admiral C. Turner Joy, *How Communists Negotiate* (New York, 1955), p. 152, and Hermes, *Truce Tent*, pp. 500–501, for troubling questions about the high cost of winning the "voluntary repatriation" concession.

41. Peng, *Memoirs*, pp. 482–483.

42. U.S. I Corps Command Report, October 1951, Sec. I, pp. 161–167, as cited in Hermes, *Truce Tent*, p. 101.

43. Ibid., p. 192. Also UNC/FEC Command Report, Dec. 1951, as cited in ibid., pp. 180–181.

44. Ibid., pp. 186, 293.

45. General Mark Clark, UNC/FEC Message C50218, CINCFE to JCS, 15 June 1952, as cited in ibid., p. 293.

46. Zhang, *Mao's Revolutionary Romanticism*, pp. 177ff.

47. Hermes, *Truce Tent*, p. 108; Futrell, *The USAF in Korea*, pp. 406–411.

48. Redline message, 21 May 1951, Hoyt Vandenberg Papers, Box 86, Library of Congress; ibid., 22 June 1951.

49. Cited in Futrell, *The USAF in Korea*, p. 412.

50. Central Military Commission of 19 May 1951, quoted in Zhang, *Mao's Revolutionary Romanticism*, p. 171.

51. Ibid., p. 170.

52. See Phillip S. Meilinger, *Hoyt S. Vandenberg: The Life of a General* (Bloomington, Ind., 1989), pp. 187–188.

53. Miller (1957), pp. 74–75.

54. A "Daily Korean Bulletin" for 29 November to 11 December 1951 was sent to President Truman at the Florida White House. Produced by U.S. military intelligence, the bulletins show a rapid buildup of enemy forces in North Korea: from 596,000 on 30 November to 805,000 a week later, on 7 December; troops in the battle zone had increased from 213,000 to 292,000; the enemy was attacking at regimental to platoon strength; its air force now had the capability "to reach the battle line" and was performing aggressively. U.S. Government Declassified Documents Index 1988 (White House), Nos. 1333, 1334, 1337, 1340, 1342.

55. "Concerning the Comprehensive Situation of the Enemy's Bacterial War. . . . ," 28 Jan. to 31 Mar. 1952, by the Headquarters of the Chinese People's Volunteer Army, 5 Apr. 1952, JW-1, 1952, Vol. 107, Doc. 14, PLA Archives, Beijing.

56. Albert E. Cowdrey, "'Germ Warfare' and Public Health in the Korean Conflict," *Journal of the History of Medicine and Allied Sciences* 39 (1984): 157.

57. Memorandum of Conversation, 2 Mar. 1951, U.S. Government Declassified Documents Index 1978 (Department of State), No. 90B.

58. Albert E. Cowdrey, *The Medics' War* (Washington, D.C., 1987), p. 221.

59. See chap. 1.

8. Psychological Warfare and Biological Weapons

1. U.S. Government Declassified Documents Index 1988, No. 1784, p. 8.

2. Memorandum for the Record (Top Secret), 11 Aug. 1953, File 246-298A, BW–CW General Decimal Files 1953, Entry 199, Box 2, RG 341, NA.

3. Memorandum for Colonel John J. Hutchison, Chief, Psychological Warfare Division, U.S. Air Force (Secret), 17 Mar. 1953, File 337-385, BW–CW General Decimal Files 1953, Entry 199, Box 5, RG 341, NA.

4. James A. Rafferty, Operations Analyst, HQ USAF, "Diagnosis of the USAF Program in Biological and Chemical Warfare," Dec. 1952, 3 File TS53/67-99, BW–CW General Decimal Files 1953, Entry 199, Box 1, RG 341, NA.

5. Major General Robert M. Lee, Director of Plans USAF, Memorandum for Chief, War Plans Division [and] Chief, Psychological Warfare Division, 17 Mar. 1953, File 337-385, USAF-Operations, BW–CW General Decimal Files 1953, Entry 199, Box 5, RG 341, NA. This memorandum, critical for understanding the organization of U.S. covert bacteriological operations and programs, reorganizes responsibility for these activities. For earlier orders to the Psychological Warfare Division, see Lieutenant General I. H. Edwards, Deputy Chief of Staff, Operations, USAF, Memorandum on Biological and Chemical Warfare (Top Secret), 5 Dec. 1950; Major General Truman H. Landon, Director of Plans USAF, Memorandum on Biological and Chemical Warfare (Top Secret), 19 Jan. 1951, File 1, BW–CW General Decimal Files 1952, Entry 199, Box 1, RG 341, NA.

6. In the history of the 581st ARC Wing for March–April 1952, which identifies Colonel John J. Hutchison as "ARCS Deputy Commander," his name is printed as "Colonel J. J. Hutchinson." History of the 581st Air Resupply and Communications Wing, p. 7–b, Microfilm K3642, 581 ARC Wing, K318.85-581, USAF Historical Research Agency, Maxwell Air Force Base, Alabama.

7. L. Fletcher Prouty, *The Secret Team: The CIA and Its Allies in Control of the United States and the World* (Englewood Cliffs, N.J., 1973), p. 220.

8. Michael E. Haas, *Air Commando! 1950–1975: Twenty-Five Years at the Tip of the Spear* (Hurlburt Field, Fla., 1994), p. 17.

9. Ibid., p. 17.

10. U.S. Government Declassified Documents Index 1989 (White House), No. 2967, 27 May 1953.

11. History of 581st ARC Wing, July to December 1952, pp. 6–7, Microfilm Roll K3642, 581 ARC Wing, K318.85-581, USAF Historical Research Agency, Maxwell Air Force Base, Alabama.

12. Ibid., 23 July to 31 Oct. 1951.

13. "Judgement of Military Tribunal on U.S. Spies in the Arnold-Baumer Espionage Case," 23 Nov. 1954, published in Supplement to *People's China*, 16 Dec. 1954, p. 4.

14. History of 581st ARC Wing, 23 July to 31 Oct. 1951, Preface, Microfilm Roll K3642, 581 ARC Wing, K318.85-581, USAF Historical Research Agency, Maxwell Air Force Base, Alabama.

15. Joseph Needham et al., *Report of the International Scientific Commission for*

the Investigation of the Facts Concerning Bacterial Warfare in Korea and China (Peking, 1952) [hereafter cited as Needham Report (1952)], p. 181.

16. Headquarters Air Resupply and Communication Service, Washington, 21 May 1952, "Amendment of Movement Order, 581st AR&C Wing," Microfilm Roll K3643, 581 ARC Wing, K318.85-581, USAF Historical Research Agency, Maxwell Air Force Base, Alabama.

17. As cited in Alfred H. Paddock, Jr., *US Army Special Warfare: Its Origins— Psychological and Unconventional Warfare, 1941–1952* (Washington, D.C., 1982), p. 78. Other coordinating bodies with related duties were the Strategic Plans Committee of the Joint Chiefs of Staff, the Operations Coordinating Board, and the Psychological Operations Coordinating Committee (POC). For reports of some of their activities, see, for example, U.S. Declassified Documents Index 1979, No. 161-C; Index 1992 (White House), No. 2855; Index 1991 (White House), No. 3546; Index 1989 (White House), No. 2967.

18. Edward P. Lilly, Ph.D., "The Development of American Psychological Operations 1945–1951" (Top Secret), 95 pp., U.S. Government Declassified Documents Index 1988, No. 1742, pp. 93-94.

19. Minutes of the Fifteenth Meeting, Psychological Strategy Board, 11 Sept. 1952 (Top Secret), U.S. Government Declassified Documents Index 1988, No. 1779, pp. 25–27.

20. "Working Draft for the Guidance of Panel Members," Psychological Strategy Board, 17 Nov. 1952, U.S. Government Declassified Documents Index 1993, No. 1150, p. 1.

21. Minutes of General Staff Meeting, Psychological Strategy Board, 29 Aug. 1952, U.S. Government Declassified Documents Index 1988, No. 1778.

22. Memorandum on Plan Takeoff, for the Director, Psychological Strategy Board, from the Secretary of Defense, 18 Sept. 1951, PSB File 387.4 Korea, Papers of Harry S. Truman, Truman Library; William Korns, Memorandum for the Record, Subject: Operational Planning on Broadbrim [Takeoff], 26 Nov. 1951, PSB File 387.4 Korea, Papers of Harry S. Truman, Truman Library.

23. For example, in the August 1951 draft of Operation Takeoff it was stated, "In instances in which necessary concurrence between departments and agencies are not forthcoming, planning and execution problems will be referred to the Psychological Strategy Board for necessary coordination or procurement of higher level decision." James Webb, Acting Secretary of State, to Gordon Gray, Director, Psychological Strategy Board, 18 Sept. 1951, Section X, Planning, Coordination and Execution, PSB File 387.4 Korea, Papers of Harry S. Truman, Truman Library.

24. Prior to the approved Emergency Plan TAKEOFF, 18 Sept. 1951, there are drafts of the plan 4 Sept. 1951, an undated August draft, and a memorandum from Gordon Gray to Mr. John Ferguson, Brig. General John Magruder, and others, Subject: Plan TAKEOFF, 31 Aug. 1951, referring to a second draft of the plan. Secretary of Defense Robert Lovett agreed to the promulgation of the plan 18 September 1951 "in view of the urgency indicated," basing his decision on a 6 September 1951 draft. Gray sent orders to coordinate the plan to Edward W. Barrett, the assistant secretary of state for public affairs, and chairman of the Psychological Operations Coordinating Committee, on 19 September 1951. See PSB File 387.4 Korea, Papers of Harry S. Truman, Truman Library.

25. Operational coordination did not take place within Far East Command itself, as one PSB staff memo indicates:

Psywar FEC has responsibility for all strategical and tactical programs emanating from FEC [two or more sanitized sentences.] Psywar Staff [FEC] has limited representation from Navy and Air Force. Navy was never interested in Psywar and Air Force wanted to control their own program. This they could not do while operating within the area of FEC. Therefore the ARC Wing was sent to Philippines which is outside of FEC and the operation of the ARC Wing is under the Strategic Air Command. (Colonel J. Woodall Greene, Memorandum for the Record, 16 Nov. 1952, Subject: Comments on Memorandum for the Record Dated 9 Nov. 1952 from Mr. Norberg on "Broadbrim" and "Affiliate," PSB File 387.4 Korea, Papers of Harry S. Truman, Truman Library)

Col. Greene's observations in noting that Psywar FEC had responsibility for all strategical and tactical programs "emanating from" FEC may make the distinction intended by the PSB between the initiatives of competing operators in Korea and PSB initiatives from Washington, with the latter requiring PSB strategic direction and coordination.

26. Brig. General J. D. Balmer, Chief, Joint Subsidiary Plans Division of the Joint Chiefs of Staff, Memorandum for the Psychological Strategy Board, Subject: Plan "Takeoff," 14 Sept. 1951 (Top Secret), U.S. Government Declassified Documents Index 1988 (White House), No. 1502.

27. Memorandum for Mr. Gray, n.d., U.S. Government Declassified Documents Index 1988 (White House), No. 1729; Office of the Secretary of Defense, Memorandum for the Director Psychological Strategy Board, Subject: Plan "Takeoff," 18 Sept. 1951, U.S. Government Declassified Documents Index 1991 (White House), No. 3541 (also in Index 1988, No. 1503).

28. Two "Memorandum for the Record," both dated 3 Oct. 1951, U.S. Government Declassified Documents Index 1991 (White House), No. 3540. Operation Broadbrim ("Takeoff") was placed into "the green" by the Joint Subsidiary Plans Division (the Defense Department body responsible for pulling together psychological and covert warfare operations) near the end of December 1951, and was expected to receive action by the Joint Chiefs of Staff about the first week of January 1952. Edward W. Barrett, Assistant Secretary, Department of State to Gordon Gray, Director, Psychological Strategy Board, 29 Dec. 1951, PSB File 387.4 Korea, Papers of Harry S. Truman, Truman Library.

29. Memorandum for General Reuben E. Jenkins, Subject: Report on Trip to FECOM, 7 Nov. 1951, U.S. Government Declassified Documents Index 1975, No. 68 D.

30. See chap. 11.

31. Maj. General Reuben E. Jenkins, Assistant Chief of Staff G-3, Memorandum for the Chief of Staff, U.S. Army, 20 Nov. 1951, U.S. Government Declassified Documents Index 1975, No. 69-A.

32. Thomas H. Etzold and John L. Gaddis, *Containment: Documents on American Policy and Strategy, 1945–1950* (New York, 1978), p. 127.

33. William Korn, Memorandum for the Record, Subject: Operational Planning on Broadbrim ("Takeoff"), 26 Nov. 1951, PSB File 387.4 Korea, Papers of Harry S. Truman, Truman Library.

34. There are two documents laying out the objectives of Operation Hum-

mer, renamed Operation Affiliate, issued on the same date, 25 October 1951, with the same title under the same signature. There is some variation in the two texts, and the interesting moment occurs on page 8 of both documents. In a section with extensive revision from one to the other, there is sanitized from one but not from the other a reference to the possible use of novel weapons in Korea. Charles McCarthy, Addendum to Psychological Strategy Board, D-7, D-7/a, D-7/b, PSB File 387.4 Korea, 25 Oct. 1951, Papers of Harry S. Truman, Truman Library.

35. Letter from Gordon Gray to Edward W. Barrett, Assistant Secretary of State for Public Affairs, and to Chairman, Psychological Strategy Operations Coordinating Committee, 19 Sept. 1951, PSB File 4120; Letter, Edward W. Barrett to Gordon Gray, 29 Dec. 1951, PSB File 387.4 Korea, Papers of Harry S. Truman, Truman Library.

9. The CIA in the Korean War

1. CIA director William Colby testified in 1975 about the agency's relation with Fort Detrick for "the development of bacteriological warfare agents—some lethal—and associated delivery systems suitable for clandestine use." After acknowledging that many CIA records on the subject were destroyed in 1973, Colby stated that beyond one uncompleted mission, "no record can be found that these materials or devices were used for lethal operational purposes." United States Congress, *Final Report of the Senate Select Committee to Study Governmental Operations with Respect to Intelligence Activities* (The Church Committee) (Washington, D.C., 1976), Vol. 1: *The Handling of Toxins*, pp. 5–7, 22–23.

2. William Blum. *The CIA, a Forgotten History: US Global Interventions since World War 2* (London and Atlantic Highlands, N.J., 1986) pp. 211–212, 301–302, 146; "Fever Virus Sent to Cuba, Paper States," Reuters dispatch, New York, *Toronto Globe and Mail*, 10 Jan. 1977; "Cuba Denounces Biological Aggression from the United States," text of Cuban report to the UN secretary-general on the appearance of the "thrips palmi" plague, *Granma International*, June 1997, p. 3.

3. L. Fletcher Prouty, *The Secret Team: The CIA and Its Allies in Control of the United States and the World* (Englewood Cliffs, N.J., 1973) p. 221.

4. Alfred H. Paddock, Jr., *US Army Special Warfare: Its Origins—Psychological and Unconventional Warfare, 1941–1952* (Washington, D.C., 1982) pp. 73, 75–76, 79.

5. Ibid., pp. 80–81, 108–109.

6. Ibid., p. 106; Prouty, *The Secret Team*, p. 222.

7. Maj. General John K. Singlaub with Malcolm McConnell, *Hazardous Duty: An American Soldier in the Twentieth Century* (New York, 1991), p. 182.

8. Prouty, *The Secret Team*, p. 223, also pp. 138, 221–222.

9. Ibid., p. 232.

10. Ibid., p. 222.

11. Ibid., p. 138.

12. Ibid., pp. 222–223.

13. William M. Leary. *Perilous Missions: Civil Air Transport and CIA Covert Operations in Asia* (Tuscaloosa, Ala., 1984), pp. 112–113.

14. Victor Marchetti and John D. Marks, *The CIA and the Cult of Intelligence* (New York, 1980), p. 113.

15. Annis G. Thompson, *The Greatest Airlift: The Story of Combat Cargo* (Tokyo, 1954) p. 449.

16. Ibid., Acknowledgments.

17. Leary, *Perilous Missions*, p. 124.

18. "Psychological Warfare Research: A Long Range Program," Pt. 1: "Essential Background Information, March 1953," pp. 35–37, U.S. Government Declassified Documents Index 1984 (Dept. of Defense), No. 1564; Paddock, *US Army Special Warfare*, pp. 75–76; Etzold and Gaddis, *Containment*, pp. 125–128. CIA control over OPC was curtailed to the extent that the secretary of state nominated its head subject to CIA approval. The head of OPC reported to the director of central intelligence, who was both head of the CIA and responsible for the coordination of all intelligence activities. Ibid.

19. Cited in Leary, *Perilous Missions*, p. 127.

20. Frank W. Wisner, Memorandum of 1 Aug. 1949 to Colonel Yeaton of the Joint Chiefs of Staff, as cited in Paddock, *US Army Special Warfare*, p. 76. This memo reiterates the National Security Council's Directive on Office of Special Projects, NSC 10/2, 18 June 1948, in Etzold & Gaddis, *Containment*, pp. 125–127. For confirmation that these instructions were incorporated into doctrine, see Department of the Army, "The Conduct of Guerrilla Warfare Activity," Army Special Forces Program, 14 Oct. 1953, File 1573 S, Box 258, RG 175, NA.

21. U.S. Congress, *Final Report of the Senate Select Committee to Study Governmental Operations with Respect to Intelligence Activities*, p. 24.

22. See chap. 6, n. 2.

23. Leary, *Perilous Missions*, p. 116.

24. Ibid., p. 125.

25. Ibid., p. 124.

26. Prouty, *The Secret Team*, pp. 161, 221.

27. Michael E. Haas, *Air Commando! 1950–1975: Twenty-Five Years at the Tip of the Spear* (Hurlburt Field, Fla., 1994), p. 16.

28. File 385 (6-4-16), Box 151, RG 218, NA.

29. Ibid.

30. Ibid.

31. Haas, *Air Commando*, pp. 18, 22–26.

32. Ibid., p. 121.

33. U.S. Air Force, "Guerrilla Warfare and Airpower in Korea, 1950–53" (Maxwel Air Force Base, Ala., 1964), p. 175 (Microfilm Roll K2627).

34. For Air Commando clients, see Haas, *Air Commando*, p. 11.

35. Letter from Herbert A. Mason, Jr., Command Historian, Air Force Special Operations Command, Hurlburt Field, Florida, to Edward Hagerman, 9 Jan. 1997. CCRAK records that are available in the U.S. National Archives are limited to technical intelligence. Although Far East Command's G-2 may have resubordinated CCRAK activities to intelligence gathering to a degree, "Guerrilla Warfare and Airpower in Korea, 1950–53" adds to other evidence that CCRAK remained an umbrella under which the CIA effectively did its own thing when it needed the cooperation of other agencies under the Far East Command, and under which it performed missions for the Far East Command.

36. The "Kyushu Gypsies" formed the 6461 Troop Carrier Squadron (M) of the 403 Troop Carrier Wing at K-16 airport (Seoul), with twenty-one C-47 aircraft. They were also part of the Fifth Air Force 6167 Operations Squadron. See

Microfilm Roll NO 795, 483 Troop Carrier Wing (315 Air Division), KWG-483, 1953, Histories, Frame 0800, USAF Historical Research Agency, Maxwell Air Force Base, Alabama; and Stephen Pease, *PSYWAR: Psychological Warfare in Korea, 1950–1953* (New York, 1962), p. 61.

37. Thompson, *The Greatest Airlift*, p. 413; Microfilm Roll 795, 483 Troop Carrier Wing (315 Air Division), KWG-483, 1953, Histories, Frames 0185, 0720, 1613, USAF Historical Research Agency, Maxwell Air Force Base, Alabama.

38. Thompson, *The Greatest Airlift*, p. 428. See also "Guerrilla Warfare and Airpower in Korea, 1950–1953," for the role of the Kyushu Gypsies in irregular operations.

39. Haas, *Air Commando*, pp. 11–12, 21.

40. Thompson, *The Greatest Airlift*, pp. 136, 417.

41. Haas, *Air Commando*, pp. 13–14.

42. Ethel Dehaven, Helen Joiner, and Dorothy L. Miller, "History of the Air Materiel Command, 1 January–30 June 1952," Vol. 1, p. 329, Microfilm Roll K2004, Air Materiel Command, K200.01, 1950–1954, Histories, USAF Historical Research Agency, Maxwell Air Force Base, Alabama.

43. Haas, *Air Commando*, p. 33.

44. Pp. 169–175.

45. The section that follows is based on Leary, *Perilous Missions*, pp. 139–142; "Judgement of Military Tribunal on U.S. Spies in the Downey-Fecteau Espionage Case," *People's China*, No. 24, Supplement, 16 Dec. 1954; *New York Times*, 24 Nov. 1954; an interview with John Downey in *People*, 18 Dec. 1978, pp. 45–46, 49–50.

46. Leary, *Perilous Missions*, p. 138.

47. "US Agents Captured," *People's China*, No. 24 (16 Dec. 1954): 35.

48. Leary, *Perilous Missions*, p. 139.

49. Ibid., p. 140.

50. Ibid.

51. *New York Times*, 24 and 25 Nov. 1954.

52. As cited by Leary, *Perilous Missions*, p. 141. Fecteau was quietly released in 1971, two months before President Nixon's planned trip to Peking, after serving nineteen years of his sentence, but Downey had to wait until Nixon called a press conference in February 1973 to acknowledge that Downey was indeed a CIA agent who had been taken prisoner after his military aircraft was forced down in Chinese territory.

53. John Ranelagh, *The Agency: The Rise and Decline of the CIA* (London, 1986), p. 218.

54. *New York Times*, 24 Feb. 1967, 26 Dec. 1977.

55. We contacted Praeger Publishers but failed to get any background information on this book because of the alleged lack of Praeger archives.

56. Walter G. Hermes, *Truce Tent and Fighting Front* (Washington, D.C., 1966), p. 231.

57. Central Intelligence Agency Student Subsidies Bared," *Facts on File*, 9–15 March 1967, pp. 79–80; Sol Stern, "A Short Account of International Student Politics and the Cold War with Particular Reference to the NSA, CIA etc," *Ramparts* 5, No. 9 (1967): 29–38.

58. The *China Quarterly* was receiving funding from the Congress of Cultural Freedom, a Paris-based group "through which the CIA channeled the funds."

See the masthead of *China Quarterly*, No. 1 (January–March 1960); and *New York Times*, 26 Dec. 1977, p. 37.

59. John C. Clews, *Communist Propaganda Techniques*, foreword by G. F. Hudson (New York, 1964).

60. Facts Bearing on the Problem and Discussion: Study on Biological Warfare by the Joint Advanced Study Committee," 21 Sept. 1951, JCS 1837/26, 1837/29, 26 Feb. 1952; JCS 1837/34, 11 June 1952, RG 218, NA.

61. *New York Times*, 17 Sept. 1975.

62. U.S. Congress. *Final Report of the Senate Select Committee to Study Governmental Operations with Respect to Intelligence Activities* (1976), pp. 5, 22–23.

10. Insect Vectors in Occupied Japan: Unit 406

1. "Annual Historical Report 1951," 406 Medical General Laboratories, Professional Section, Introduction, Historical Unit Medical Detachments [HUMEDS], Box 163, RG 112, NA.

2. *American Men and Women of Science*, 19th ed. (New York, 1994), p. 159. See *Index Medicus* for references to numerous scientific articles published by W. D. Tigertt on medical research during the Korean War, infectious diseases, clinical pathology, immunization, the role of insect vectors, etc.

3. Reports from Unit 406 from its founding through the Korean War are conspicuous for their lack of attached distribution lists, though a study done after the war relating to overwintering mosquitoes and Japanese B encephalitis has a lengthy distribution list that includes the Medical Section at Fort Detrick. Interim Report on Japanese Encephalitis and Mosquito Vector titled "Bionics of Culex Tritaeniorhynchus," 406 Medical General Laboratory, Japan, 1959–1960, Historical Division, U.S. Medical Department [AMEDD] Records 1947–1961, File HD 319.1, Box 242, RG 112, NA.

4. Edwin W. Payne, Supply Division, Memorandum for Record, 18 June 1949, 23 Sept. 1949, 2 Dec. 1949, Supreme Commander for the Allied Powers [SCAP] Documents, GHQ–SCAP, Public Health and Welfare Section, RG 331, NA. The organization supplying Unit 406 with its animals—the Saitama Experimental Animal Research Institute—was headed by Mr Ichisaburo Ozawa, formerly associated with General Shiro Ishii's germ war activities.

5. "Annual Historical Report 1947," p. 3, 406 Medical General Laboratory, HUMEDS, Box 162, RG 112, NA.

6. "Annual Historical Report 1948," p. 8, 406 Medical General Laboratory, HUMEDS, Box 486, RG 112, NA.

7. Sheldon H. Harris, *Factories of Death: Japanese Biological Warfare 1932–1945 and the American Cover-up* (London and New York, 1994), chap. 10; and Peter Williams and David Wallace, *Unit 731: The Japanese Army's Secret of Secrets* (London, 1989), p. 279.

8. ISHII, Shiro, File 201, Book 1, Military Intelligence Section, General Staff, General Headquarters, Far East Command, n.d., RG 331, NA; Nippon TV 1995, *The Bacteriological Warfare Is Still Alive*, a documentary featuring Professor Keiichi Tsuneishi on this topic.

9. "Annual Report of Medical Service Activities 1951," pp. 13–15, Adminis-

trative Section, 406 Medical General Laboratory, Tokyo, RG 112, Surgeon General, Historical Division, AMEDD Records 1947–1961, HD 319.1, Box 242.

10. "Annual Historical Report 1946," p. 19, 406 Medical General Laboratory, HUMEDS, Box 162, RG 112, NA.

11. Unit 406's work on mosquitoes and Japanese B encephalitis can be followed in "Annual Historical Report 1947," pp. 47, 49–50, 52–56, 59–61, HUMEDS, Box 162, RG 112; Annual Historical Report, Professional Section, 1949, Box 163, RG 112; "Annual Historical Report," Professional Section, 1950, pp. 155–186, AMEDD Records 1947–1961, File HD391.1, Box 242, RG 112; "Annual Report of Medical Service Activities 1951," pp. 9, 14–15, 49–50, ibid.; "Interim Report, 1959–1960," AMEDD Records, File HD 319.1, Box 242, RG 112, NA.

12. According to the official wording, the Ecology Section was "assigned the mission of determining the biologic characteristics of insects suspected of being vectors of Japanese B. Encephalitis and was established to initiate studies to be carried on by the proposed Far East Medical Research Unit to be activated at a future date." "Annual Report of Medical Service Activities 1951," p. 3, Administrative Section, 406 Medical General Laboratory, Far East 1951–1952, AMEDD Records 1947–1961, File HD 319.1, Box 242, RG 112, NA.

13. "Annual Historical Report 1950," p. 202, Professional Section, Historical Division, 406 Medical General Laboratory, AMEDD Records 1947–61, File HD 319.1, Box 242, RG 112, NA. The "Annual Historical Report 1949" of Unit 406, pp. 197–199, includes a bibliography on mosquitoes and encephalitis with fifteen references to works by Japanese scientists; HUMEDS, Box 163, RG 112, NA.

14. "Monthly Technical Report for September 1951," p. 12, 406 Medical General Laboratory, Box 163, HUMEDS, RG 112, NA.

15. "Annual Historical Report 1953," pp. 2–5, 406 Medical General Laboratory, Department of Entomology, Taxonomic Entomology Section, pp. 1–7, HUMEDS, Box 163, RG 112, NA.

16. Records of Unit 406 projects are generally to be found in the monthly technical reports of HUMEDS, Boxes 162–163, and the AMEDD Records 1947–1961, File HD 319.1, Box 242, RG 112, NA. For early reports, see GHQ–SCAP, Box 9341, RG 331, NA.

17. "Annual Report of Medical Services Activities 1951"; "Annual Report 1952," 406 Medical General Laboratory, Administrative Section, AMEDD Records 1947–1961, File HD 319.1, Box 242, RG 112, NA.

18. As a Unit 406 annual report noted, "Throughout the year there was a continuous flow of military and civilian personnel through this organization. These people arrived in the Far East Command for periods ranging between fifteen days and indefinite temporary duty for the purpose of investigating or consulting on special medical problems." Those passing through the epidemic hemorrhagic fever unit included people from the Army Medical Service Graduate School, the Walter Reed Army Medical Center, the Brooke Army Medical Center, the Rockefeller Foundation, the Harvard School of Public Health, the U.S. Public Health Service, and the University of Kansas—altogether nineteen people. "Annual Report of Medical Service Activities 1952," AMEDD Records 1947–1961, File HD 319.1, Box 242, RG 112, NA.

19. Memo to File: Progress Report on "R" Work at GIES, 10 Apr. 1952, File DRBS-1820-11, Vol. 4224, Interim Box 43, RG 24F, NAC.

20. Memorandum for the Officer in Charge, 14 Dec. 1945, Subject: Memorandum from Japanese Communist Party, File 201 (ISHII, Shiro, #700196), Book I, Military Intelligence Section, General Staff, GHQ, Far East Command, RG 331, NA. (Declassified in February 1992.)

21. Harris, *Factories of Death*, pp. 175–176.

22. "Monthly Technical Report for August 1951," 9 Oct. 1951, 406 Medical General Laboratory, HUMEDS, Box 163, RG 112, NA.

23. "Annual Historical Report 1946," p. 9, 406 Medical General Laboratory, HUMEDS, Box 162, RG 112, NA.

24. Pamphlet distributed by the Japanese delegation to the Vienna Congress of the Peoples for Peace, Dec. 1952; New China News Agency, dispatch of 11 Mar. 1953; *Survey of China Mainland Press [SCMP]* No. 530, 1953.

25. Ms. Fuyuko Nishisato, freelance research worker, information given to Stephen Endicott in Tokyo, 5 Apr. 1994.

26. "Annual Historical Report 1951," pp. 266–271, 406 Medical General Laboratory, Professional Section, AMEDD Records 1947–1961, File HD 319.1, Box 242, RG 112; "Report of Activities of Epidemic Hemorrhagic Fever Field Unit, 14 July 1952," p. 12, HUMEDS, Box 163, RG 112, NA; Harris, *Factories of Death*, p. 206.

27. "Annual Report of Medical Services Activities 1951," p. 36, 406 Medical General Laboratory, Administrative Section, AMEDD Records 1947–1961, File HD 319.1, Box 242, RG 112, NA.

28. Lt. Col. R. L. Hullinghorst and Lt. Col. Arthur Steer, Department of Pathology, 406 Medical General Laboratory, "Pathology of Epidemic Hemorrhagic Fever," *Annals of Internal Medicine* 38 (1953): 101; "Foreword," *American Journal of Medicine* 16 (1954): 617. See Williams and Wallace, *Unit 731*, p. 338, n. 78, and pp. 276–277, 283.

29. "Monthly Technical Report for August 1951," 9 Oct. 1951, 406 Medical General Laboratory, HUMEDS, Box 163, RG 112, NA.

30. This data is to be found in "Annual Historical Report 1952," 406 Medical General Laboratory, HUMEDS, Box 163, RG 112, NA.

31. "Far East Command Conference on Hemorrhagic Fever: Introduction," cited in Williams and Wallace, *Unit 731*, p. 283.

32. Williams and Wallace, *Unit 731*, pp. 338–339, nn. 78, 80, 83; Hullinghorst and Steer, "Pathology of Epidemic Hemorrhagic Fever," pp. 77–79, 101, and "Foreword," *American Journal of Medicine*, p. 671; Col. Charles L. Leedham, Medical Consultant, Far East Command, "Epidemic Hemorrhagic Fever: A Summarization," *Annals of Internal Medicine* 38 (1953): 106.

33. Albert E. Cowdrey, *The Medics' War* (Washington, D.C., 1987), p. 175.

34. "Report by Brigadier General Crawford F. Sams, MC, Chief, Public Health and Welfare Section, SCAP to Chief of Staff, Far East Command," Subject: "Special Operations in North Korea," 17 Mar. 1951, File, Special Operations in North Korea–General Sams, Box 3179 (Public Health and Welfare, Medical Section FEC, Korea, Reports to Korea–Sanitation), RG 338, NA. A document titled "Complete Discussion, Classification of Sams Report" was declassified 25 October 1977. This document, in our possession courtesy of John W. Powell, is from the National Archives, though there is no reference number attached.

35. A. V. Hardy, R. P. Mason, and G. A. Martin, "The Dysenteries in the Armed Forces," *Journal of Tropical Medicine and Hygiene*, January 1952, pp. 171–

175. There are reports of this same epidemic in *Tropical Medicine and Hygiene News* ("Dysentery among Enemy Prisoners Cut," February 1952) and in the *Journal of the American Medical Association* of 28 Mar. 1953, pp. 1055–1059, and 4 Apr. 1953, pp. 1157–1159.

36. File CD 383.8 (Biological Warfare), p. 5, RG 330, NA (declassified at our request, 1996).

37. G. B. Reed, "Present Position of Bacteriological Warfare," 16 Dec. 1947, p. 8, under cover, From: DRCS Washington, To: DRB (Action), July 1949, File 54-935-302, Vol. 4152, RG 24, NAC.

38. From: Medical Section to G-2, 12 Dec. 1950, Far East Command Medical Section, General Correspondence, File 312.3, Box 76, RG 338, NA.

39. See chap. 7.

40. See chap. 11.

11. The Flyers

1. See chap. 1.

2. Interview with Professor Zhu Chun, Deputy General Secretary, China Institute for International Strategic Studies, conducted by Stephen Endicott in Beijing, 27 Mar. 1996, for the Oral History Project on the Korean War, York University.

3. Interview with Howard B. Hitchens, Jr., conducted by Edward Hagerman in Sarasota, Florida, 26 Jan. 1996, for the Oral History Project on the Korean War, York University. Sworn statements of Lieutenants Quinn, Enoch, Kniss, O'Neal, Strieby, and Stanley, Colonels Schwable, Mahurin, and Evans, and Major Bley deposited with the United Nations Secretariat by U.S. delegate Henry Cabot Lodge, Jr., in October 1953, UN Secretariat Documents, A/C 1L66, 1953.

4. Farrar-Hockley interviewed in *Korea: The Unknown War*, Thames Television in cooperation with WGBH, Boston, produced and directed by Phillip Whitehead.

5. Anthony Farrar-Hockley, *The Edge of the Sword* (London, 1954/1981), pp. 222–223.

6. Hitchens interview.

7. Eugene Kinkead, *In Every War but one* (New York, 1959), p. 17, and chap. 2, "Why They Collaborated."

8. Twenty-five of them were printed in English in *People's China* in 1952 and 1953; we obtained two additional statements by Capt. Robert J. Burns, 45th Squadron, 67th Tactical Reconnaisance Group, and 1st Lieutenant Thomas L. Eyres, 19th Bomb Group, 20th Air Force, Kadena Air Base, Okinawa, from the Central Archives in Beijing in March 1996, courtesy of the State Archives Bureau. Although these last two are marked "top secret," they are similar in nature to the POW statements that were published in Beijing in 1952 and 1953.

9. Deposition by Col. Walker M. Mahurin, 10 Aug. 1953, in *Depositions of Nineteen Captured U.S. Airmen on Their Participation in Germ Warfare in Korea*, Supplement to *People's China* (Peking), 1 Dec. 1953, p. 14.

10. Colonel Andrew J. Evans Jr., 34, a pilot, was deputy commanding officer of the 49th Fighter Bomber Wing. He was shot down and captured in Korea on

26 March 1953. He had been a professional officer all his life, trained in air-ground operations and the use of atomic energy, and had served in such capacities as deputy secretary of the Air University, joint secretary of the JCS Logistics Plans Group, assistant to the executive of the chief of staff of the Air Force, and a member of the War Plans Division of the Air Force. Although he managed to omit the last point from the biography he gave the Chinese, they nevertheless had reason to believe that he was knowledgeable about high-level decisions. *Depositions of Nineteen US Airmen*, p. 4; "Sworn Statement" (typewritten) to Special Agent, Office of Special Investigations, Far East Air Force, 13 Sept. 1953, UN Secretariat Documents, A/C 1L66, 1953.

11. Colonel Frank H. Schwable, "Statements of Colonel Frank H. Schwable, U.S. Marine Corps," Supplement to *New Times*, No. 10 (4 Mar. 1953: 5–6.

12. *Depositions of Nineteen U.S. Airmen*, pp. 43, 41.

13. Ibid., pp. 5–6, 33, 34, 37.

14. Ibid., pp. 11, 43.

15. Ibid., pp. 6, 43, 49.

16. Ibid., pp. 6, 44.

17. Ibid., pp. 16, 22, 29, 41.

18. Schwable, "Statements," p. 8.

19. *New York Times*, 6 Sept. 1953.

20. Colonel Frank Hawse Schwable, born in Norfolk, Virginia, in 1908, the son of a Marine colonel who fought in the Boxer Rebellion and in the suppression of insurrection in the Philippines in 1900, joined the Marines in 1929. He received four Distinguished Flying Crosses in World War II and a Gold Star for "exceptionally meritorious achievement" in the Korean War, and was considered one of the most promising senior officers of the Marines. The Marine Corps was stunned by Schwable's confession of germ warfare to the Chinese. The transcript of his court of inquiry runs 1,200 pages. In the end he was promoted one rank and allowed to retire. When contacted many years later for an interview by Ken Kann, researcher for the authors (in the Oral History Project on the Korean War, York University), General Schwable declined, saying he did not wish to reopen "old wounds." Elie Able, New York Times Service, Washington, *Toronto Globe and Mail*, 22 Feb. 1954; John W. Powell to Stephen Endicott, 2 Mar. 1978, 9 Sept. 1979.

21. Walker M. Mahurin, *Honest John: The Autobiography of Walker M. Mahurin* (New York, 1962), pp. 283–284, 287, 288; *New York Times*, 15 Aug. 1953

22. Enclosure in Memorandum of 15 Sept. 1953 by General G. B. Erskine, USMC (Ret), Assistant to the Secretary of Defense (Special Operations), to the U.S. Air Force and the U.S. Marine Corps, CD 385 (Biological Warfare), RG 330, NA.

23. Meeting of POW Working Group, Operations Coordinating Board, Washington, D.C., 13 Nov. 1953, p. 4, U.S. Government Declassified Documents Index 1992 (White House, Secret), No. 2855.

24. UN Secretariat Documents, A/C 1L66, 1953, 23 Sept.–26 Oct. 1953.

25. Ibid.

26. "Protest Statement," 8 Mar. 1952; *Stop U.S. Germ Warfare!* (Peking, 1952), p. 8.

27. See chap. 6.

28. "Report of Investigation of Communist Allegations That the USAF Par-

ticipated in Biological Warfare in Korea," 22 Apr. 1953, pp. 5–6, Office of Special Investigations, Records of the Office of the Inspector General, USAF, File K-142.7691-1, RG 341, NA (declassified 21 Nov. 1977).

29. James Angus MacDonald, Jr.. *The Problems of US Marine Corps Prisoners of War in Korea*, Occasional Paper. History and Museums Division, Headquarters, U.S. Marine Corps (Washington D.C., 1988), pp. 157–158.

30. "Sworn Statement to Summary Court Official, Henry R. Petersen," 19 Sept. 1953, p. 3, UN Secretariat Documents, A/C 1L66, 1953.

31. We tried to contact fourteen of the former POWs. We, or our research assistants, spoke to Howard Hitchens, Paul Kniss, Walker Mahurin, Vance Frick, Bobby Hammett, Frank Schwable, Warren Lull, Robert Lurie, and Floyd O'Neal and were successful in arranging interviews with five—Hitchens, Lull, Lurie, Kniss, and Mahurin. See Oral History Project on the Korean War, York University.

32. The following information about Mahurin is taken from his autobiography, *Honest John;* his "Sworn Statement to Summary Court Official, Henry R. Petersen," excerpts of which were printed in the *New York Times*, 1 Nov. 1953; his deposition in *Depositions of Nineteen U.S. Airmen*, pp. 43–72; and an interview with history professor Mark Selden, then of Washington University, made at Mahurin's home on 28 July 1976, for the Oral History Project on the Korean War, York University.

33. Mahurin, *Honest John*, p. 13.

34. Ibid., pp. 70, 72, 84.

35. Ibid., p. 69.

36. Ibid., p. 68.

37. Lester B. Pearson, Secretary of State for External Affairs, to Hume Wrong, Canadian ambassador to Washington (Top Secret), 29 May 1952, and Wrong to Pearson, 5 June 1952, External Affairs Records, Vol. 35, MG 26 N1, National Archives of Canada.

38. W. G. Nixon, interviewed by Carl Dow in Calgary, 7 July 1976, for the Oral History Project on the Korean War, York University.

39. Hume Wrong to Lester Pearson, 5 June 1952, External Affairs Records, Vol. 35, MG26 N1, NAC.

40. "Sworn Statement," subscribed and sworn aboard MSTS *Howze*, before summary court official Henry R. Petersen, 19 Sept. 1953, p. 3, UN Secretariat Documents, A/C 1L66, 1953.

41. U.S. Marine Corps, Marine Aircraft Group-33, Historical Diary for March 1952, Appendix 2, S-2 Report, p. 2; Marine Aircraft Group-33, Command Diary for April 1952, Appendix 2, S-2 Report, p. 2. See photograph of "Burn Barrel" in this book. Acquisition No. 65A-4620, Box 58, RG 127, Federal Records Center, Suitland, Md.

42. Headquarters UN Command, Far East Command, Command Report (RSC) CSGPO-28RI, 1st Quarter FY 57, July–Sept. 1956 (declassified 1980), as cited by Paul Cassell in the *Stanford Law Review* 35, no. 259 (January 1983): 271. (This document originally comes from ACC61A-1606, Box 3, FEC Reports 1956, RG 334, Suitland Records Center.) These orders were in spite of an official government statement that U.S. bacteriological capabilities were "retained only within the continental United States." Seymour Hersh, *Chemical and Biological Warfare: America's Hidden Arsenal* (New York, 1968), p. 20. We found evidence that nineteen "Secret" Far East Command documents in the Chemical Corps files had in

fact been removed and/or destroyed following the Far East Command's 1956 order. We discovered this by comparing an inventory prepared by Raymond P. Flynn of documents in the category "Miscellaneous File Secret 1952," originally in Accession 67A4900, 1949–1954, RG 175, with the documents that remained in those files when they were declassified in 1996. An archivist's note on Flynn's initial inventory says that the original lists "were prepared by the Army when the records were transferred to the Records Center in 1956." The inventory lists attached to the accessioning dossiers "reflect the contents of the accession as it appeared in 1956." Between 1956 and 1969, however, "some files were recalled by the Army and others were destroyed." The archivist notes, finally, that the records were not accessioned permanently by the National Archives until 1969. See "The National Archives, PRELIMINARY INVENTORY OF THE RECORDS OF THE CHEMICAL WARFARE SERVICE," compiled by Raymond P. Flynn, Preliminary Inventory No. 8, WASHINGTON: post-Korea.

43. See, for example, 3rd Bomb Group, Combat Mission Reports Nos. 3-19614 to 3-19617 of 31 July 1952, Box 155; Nos. 3-19683 to 3-19685 of 3–4 Aug. 1952, Box 156; and Nos. 3-20907 to 3-20908 and 3-20915 to 3-20916 of 26–27 Sept. 1952, Box 159, Mission Reports of U.S. Air Force Units during the Korean War Era, RG 342, NA.

44. 3rd Bomb Group Combat Mission No 14524, of the night of 13–14 January 1952, was shot down, and Quinn and Enoch were captured very early in the alleged bacteriological warfare campaign. All the reports of combat missions they flew prior to being captured, beginning with Mission No. 14210 of 1 January 1952, were removed from the files on 23 March 1952, according to a penciled note by Lt. Colonel Leo H. Johnson of the Office of Special Investigations, and are not available for scrutiny. 3rd Bomb Group, Korean War Era, Combat Mission Reports, January 1952, Box 140, RG 342, NA.

45. U.S. Fifth Air Force, Operations Order 141–52 for 20 May 1952 (Secret), U.S Marine Corps, 1st Marine Air Wing, Korean War Era, Accession List 65A-4620, Location 002/36-02-7, Box 8, RG 127, Federal Records Center, Suitland, Md.

46. See *Depositions of Nineteen U.S. Airmen*, pp. 178, 187, 201, for reference to "duds" and "no visible results" as codes for reporting germ bombs. Declassified U.S. military records reveal that as early as December 1950, the M16 leaflet bomb was successfully adapted to carry feathers as a vector for biological warfare. Special Report No. 138, B.P. CCS385.2 (12-17-43), 15 Dec. 1950, RG 218, NA.

47. Deposition by 1st Lt. William L. Fornes, 27 Aug. 1952, *Depositions of Nineteen U.S. Airmen*, p. 103, and Hsinhua News Agency, Introduction, ibid., p. 7.

48. "Report of Investigation of Communist Allegations That the USAF Participated in Biological Warfare in Korea," 22 Apr. 1953, pp. 2, 5, and 15 on the allegations of Lts. Quinn and Enoch. It is worth noting that the Office of Special Investigations report, perhaps quite innocently but by its own admission, was not a "normal objective investigation" because of the "predetermined fact" of the untruth of the germ war allegations. Thus the "object of the investigation was to develop information that would refute, beyond all reasonable doubt, the allegations that the USAF had participated in biological warfare in Korea." For this reason, "only those leads essential to the fulfillment of the objective were developed." Preface, pp. 1–2. Office of Special Investigations, Records of the Office of the Inspector General, USAF Headquarters, File K-142.7691, RG 341, NA.

49. Fifth Air Force, Operations Order 141-52 for 20 May 1952 (Secret), U.S. Marine Corps, 1st Marine Air Wing, Korean War Era, Accession List 65A-4620, Box 8, RG 127, Federal Records Center, Suitland, Md.

50. 17th Bomb Wing (Lt), Combat Mission Reports for May and June 1952, Mission Reports of U.S. Air Force Units during the Korean War Era, Boxes 166–167, RG 342, NA.

51. 17th Bomb Wing (Lt), Combat Mission Reports for May 1952, Mission Reports of U.S. Air Force Units during the Korean War Era, Box 166, RG 342, NA.

52. 17th Bomb Wing (Lt), Combat Mission Reports for 1952, teletype of 30/31 May, Mission Reports of U.S. Air Force Units during the Korean War Era, Box 166, RG 342, NA.

53. General Barcus officially replaced General Everest as commanding general of the Fifth Air Force in Korea on 1 June 1952; Robert F. Futrell, *The United States Air Force in Korea, 1950–1953* (Washington, D.C., 1983), p. 483. Fifth Air Force, Operation Order No. 153-52, U.S. Marine Corps, Acc. 65A-4620, Box 8, RG 127, Federal Records Center, Suitland, Md.

12. Conclusion

1. Colonel Arthur P. Long, "An Analysis of the 'Report of the International Scientific Commission for the Investigation of the Facts Concerning Bacterial Warfare in Korea and China,'" 1 Dec. 1952, pp. 3–5, File HQ770.6-2, Bacterial Warfare in Korea 52, Box 336, Office of the Surgeon General, U.S. Medical Department [AMEDD], RG 112, NA.

2. James Ellis van Courtland Moon, "Biological Warfare Allegations: The Korean War Case," *Annals of the New York Academy of Sciences* 666 (1992): 69–71.

3. Lt. Col. George A. Carruth, Office of the Deputy Chief of Staff for Operations and Plans, U.S. Army, *U.S. Army Activity in the U.S. Biological Warfare Programs*, presented to U.S. Congress, Hearings of the Senate Subcommittee on Health and Scientific Research, chaired by Edward Kennedy, 24 Feb. 1977. U.S. Senate Committee on Human Resources, 95th Congress, 1st Session 32 (1977), 292 pp. (Washington, D.C., 1977). This oft-cited history seeks to minimize the scope of U.S. biological warfare activity during 1950–53 and employs half-truths, weasel words, and omissions to this end. When it is placed beside the documentary record, it is obvious that this official accounting before the Senate was a public relations cover-up directed at both Congress and the American public. In her book *Preventing a Biological Arms Race* (Cambridge, Mass., 1990), Susan Wright relies heavily on Carruth's presentation to the Senate committee. She also quotes, on p. 28, the U.S. Army's *Field Manual 27-10: The Law of Land Warfare*, "1954 edition," as evidence that no first use of biological warfare was allowed. Wright's statement is wrong on several counts. In the first place, there was no 1954 version or revision of *Field Manual 27-10*; secondly, the governing text during the Korean War (1950–53) was the 1940 revision. On this question, the 1940 revision said that although the United States had signed the Geneva Protocol "for the prohibition of the use in war of asphyxiating, poisonous, or other gases, and of bacteriological methods of warfare," on 17 June 1925 the U.S. Senate had failed to ratify the Protocol, and *"it is accordingly not binding on this country"* (Para. 29, pp. 8–9,

1940 revision; emphasis added). The same wording is repeated in the next revision of the field manual, published in 1956 (Para. 38, pp. 18–19). In other words, the United States was not party to any treaty that prohibited or restricted the use of bacteriological warfare, nor, according to the Army field manuals, did it have any domestic law to that effect. This state of affairs changed only in 1972, when, under President Nixon, the U.S. signed and ratified the international Biological Weapons Convention. The 1972 revision of *Field Manual 27–10: The Law of Land Warfare* asserted that the United States would not use biological weapons in a first or second strike offensive.

4. National Security Council document NSC5062/1, of 15 Mar. 1956, which said, "The decision as to their use will be made by the President"; Moon, "Biological Warfare Allegations," p. 69.

5. Statements of Policy and Directives on Biological Warfare," 11 June 1952, JCS 1837/34, 330 (Top Secret), Decimal File 385.2, RG 218, NA.

6. Joint Chiefs of Staff, "Decision on JCS 1837/29," 26 Feb. 1952, p. 307, and "Note by the Secretaries" (Top Secret), Decimal File 385.2, RG 218, NA.

7. Carruth, *U.S. Army Activity*, p. iii: "some of the detailed working papers have been destroyed." CIA director William Colby, under cross-examination before a Senate Select Committee on 16 September 1975, revealed that in 1952 the CIA entered into an agreement with the U.S. Army Bacteriological Warfare Laboratory at Fort Detrick to develop bacteriological agents and delivery systems, and he acknowledged that because of the paucity of written records, "some of which were destroyed in 1973," he could not rule out that bacteriological weapons had been used for aggressive operations. U.S. Congress, *Final Report of the Senate Select Committee to Study Governmental Operations with Respect to Intelligence Activities*, Vol. 1: *The Handling of Toxins* (Washington, D.C., 1976), pp. 5–7, 22–23.

8. See chap. 11, n. 41.

9. Committee on Biological Warfare, "1951 Program Guidance Report," 5 Dec. 1950, Office of the Secretary of Defense, File CD 383.8 (Biological Warfare), RG 330, NA.

10. Robert M. Lee, Major General USAF, Director of Plans, Memorandum on Biological and Chemical Warfare, 17 Mar. 1953 (Secret), BW–CW General Decimal Files 1953, File 337-385, Entry 199, Box 5, RG 341; also Truman H. Landon, Major General, USAF, Director of Plans, to Deputy Chief of Staff, Operations, Memorandum, Subject: Biological and Chemical Warfare (Top Secret), 19 Jan. 1951, File 1, BW–CW General Decimal Files 1952, Entry 199, Box 5, RG 341, NA.

11. Michael E. Haas, *Air Commando! 1950–1975: Twenty-Five Years at the Tip of the Spear* (Hurlburt Field, Fla., 1994), p. 17.

12. Joint Strategic Plans Committee to Joint Chiefs of Staff, "Report on Chemical (Toxic) and Biological Warfare Readiness," 31 Aug. 1953, p. 454, JCS 1837/50 (Top Secret), RG 218, NA (declassfied 1993).

13. U.S. Congress, *Final Report of the Senate Select Committee to Study Governmental Operations with Respect to Intelligence Activities*, Vol. 1, pp. 5–6.

14. Memoranda by the Chief of Staff, U.S. Army, and the Chief of Naval Operations to the Joint Chiefs of Staff on "Deception in the Biological Warfare Field," 1 Feb. 1952, JCS 1927/3, released with JCS 1837/36 (declassified in 1991), RG 218, NA. A further glimpse into the level of cover for the secretary of state is found in a document pertaining to the biological warfare plan against the Soviet

Union in 1949; if the Berlin Blockade developed into general war, State Department concurrence was to be sought through *oral* communication. This document, though partially sanitized, is referred to and identified with the above memorandum, on "Deception in the Biological Warfare Field," JCS 1927/3, 28 Sept. 1949, p. 89, RG 319, NA. For William Colby's comments on plausible denial, see U.S. Congress, *Final Report of the Senate Select Committee to Study Governmental Operations with Respect to Intelligence Activities* (1976), Vol. 1, p. 24.

15. Conversation with Stephen Endicott, 25 Mar. 1996, in Beijing. Colonel Qi, Associate Research Fellow at the Department of Military History, PLA Academy of Military Science, authored *Chaoxian zhanzheng juece neimu* [The Inside Story of Decision-Making in the Korean War] (Shenyang, 1991).

16. For the educational and professional background of the Chinese and Korean scientists, see "Biographical Register of Chinese and Korean Scientists and Medical Men," in Joseph Needham et al., *Report of the International Scientific Commission for the Investigation of the Facts Concerning Bacterial Warfare in Korea and China* (Peking, 1952) [hereafter cited as Needham Report [1952]), Appendix TT, pp. 635–665.

17. Stephen Endicott's conversations in Beijing in April 1994 with professors Qiu Weifan, Shen Qiyi, and Dr. Yan Renying, who took part in the investigations into biological warfare in 1952. See Oral History Project on the Korean War, York University.

18. Needham Report (1952), p. 8. When the accusation about U.S. use of biological warfare in the Korean War arose in 1952, the USSR fully endorsed the Chinese and North Korean claims. This support was expressed by Professor N. N. Zhukov-Verezhnikov, a bacteriologist and vice-president of the Soviet Academy of Medicine who had taken part as a medical expert in the Khabarovsk Trial of the Japanese ex-servicemen accused of participating in biological warfare in World War II. The Soviet professor took part in the International Scientific Commission to Investigate the Facts Concerning Bacterial Warfare in China and Korea in 1952; he signed the report, which concluded that "the peoples of Korea and China have indeed been the objective of bacteriological weapons . . . employed by units of the U.S.A. armed forces" (Needham Report, p. 60).

Seventeen years later, in 1969, a United Nations–sponsored document appeared which suggested that the Soviet government had changed its mind and had reversed its stand. At this time, when Sino-Soviet relations were at their lowest ebb, and when Presidents Nixon and Brezhnev were trying to promote a climate of disarmament agreements including the eventual Biological Warfare Convention of 1972, O. A. Reutov, member of the Soviet Academy of Science and professor of chemistry at Moscow State University, joined with U.S. and other counterparts in declaring that "there is no clear evidence that these [biological warfare] agents have ever been used as modern military weapons" and that there is "no military experience of the use of bacteriological (biological) agents as weapons of war" (*Chemical and Bacteriological [Biological] Weapons and the Effects of Their Possible Use,* UN Document E 69.1.24 [New York: Ballantine Books, 1970], pp. 3, 20). This reversal of opinion from 1952 and implicit exoneration of the United States and Japan was not explained at the time and passed virtually unnoticed. Meantime both the People's Republic of China and North Korea were excluded from membership in the United Nations.

Later, after the collapse of the Soviet Union and the opening of its archives, more documents began to appear. The Japanese press has reported the existence of Soviet archival documents of the 1950s suggesting that the Chinese and North Korean charges against the United States were fabricated (*Sankei Shinbun*, 8 Jan. 1998). In 1992, British historian Jon Halliday interviewed two former Soviet officers, General Selivanov and General Sasanov, who had been advisors to the North Korean government from 1950 to 1952. "We never saw it," they told Halliday, and they did not beleive that a biological warfare attack had taken place (personal communication from Jon Halliday). Some Western academics are actively searching the Soviet archives on this topic, with as yet inconclusive results.

It is partly in response to these developments that the Chinese authorities decided to open up the Liaoning Archives and other repositories of documents so that we could examine their evidence more fully and reach our own conclusions. We have presented the results of our research in China in chapter 1, as well as our judgment that the Chinese scientists and government were prudent and responsible in making their accusations—which they continue to maintain to this day.

19. Dr. Needham is widely recognized as one of the great scientific minds of the twentieth century. See his obituary in *The Independent* (United Kingdom), 27 Mar. 1995.

20. See the material in Vols. 5959 and 5920 of recently declassified documents on the Canadian biological warfare program in the papers of the Department of External Affairs, RG 25, National Archives of Canada, Ottawa.

21. Hume Wrong, Canadian ambassador in Washington, to Lester B. Pearson, Secretary of State for External Affairs, Subject: Possible Prosecution of Dr. Endicott, 17 May 1952 (Secret), File 50208-40, Pt. 2, Vol. 5920, RG 25, NAC. Wrong wrote to Pearson, "I have been given a clear impression that the United States officials have grave doubts that they will be able to furnish satisfactory evidence from United States sources that would prove in a Canadian court that the allegations of Dr. Endicott are false." Canadian diplomats in Tokyo and Canberra were telling the Department of External Affairs that people whom they considered credible observers of the germ warfare debate, including an Indian diplomat, a former head of the Australian Foreign Service, and "an eminent Scandinavian jurist," were not convinced that the charges of germ warfare were untrue. Tokyo dispatch, 8 Dec. 1953, Minutes on dispatches Nos. 366 and 367 of 6 and 10 June 1952 from Canberra, Subject: Dr. J.W. Burton, File 50208-40, Pt. 2-1, Vol. 5920, RG 25, NAC.

22. Canadian Scientists Refute Germ War Charges," *External Affairs* 4, No. 7 (July 1952): 249–252.

23. The records of the Defense Research Board of the Canadian Department of Defense indicate that none of the three scientists—W. H. Brittain (McGill University), C. E. Atwood (University of Toronto), and A. W. Baker (Ontario Agricultural College)—were members of the government's biological warfare panel. Notice of Meeting, 6 May 50, File 4-935-43-1, Vol. 4133, Interim Box 43, RG 24F, NAC.

24. Reed told Pearson, "The Communist propaganda has been carefully prepared and there are no obvious impossibilities with regard to the diseases and the carriers with which they were supposed to be associated. . . . The dropping of insects from the air is entirely feasible. Such objects as rotten fish and bags of pork are rather unorthodox B. W. weapons but again they are not entirely impossible. The use of feathers has been experimented with in Canada, although anthrax,

which the Communists link with them was not used in our experiments." Memorandum, Communist Allegations of Bacteriological Warfare in Korea and China, enclosure in Escot Reid, Memorandum for the Minister, 15 May 1952, File 50208-40 Pt. 2, Vol. 5919, RG 25, NAC.

25. Canadian Peace Congress, "Documentation on Bacteriological Warfare, 1 April 1952" (mimeograph), in File 50208-40, Pt. 1.1, Vol. 5919, RG 25, NAC.

26. Dale W. Jenkins, "Defense against Insect Disseminated Biological Warfare Agents," *Military Medicine* 128 (February 1963): 116.

27. William M. Creasy, Revised Research and Development Project Listing (Secret), 30 Oct. 1951, Project No. 411-04-004, Arthropod Dissemination [of BW], Control No. 400.112, Entry 1B, Box 235, RG 175, and Henry H. Rogers, Chief, Research Branch, "Index and Classification . . . in D/A Research and Development Program," 12 Mar. 1953, p. 6, Control No. 154-3-S, Entry 67A-4900, Box 246, RG 175, NA. William J. Allen, Chief, Research and Development Division, "Project Listings . . . " (Secret), 6 Dec. 1951, Project No. 411-02-041, "Mosquito Vectors and Encephalomyelitis Viruses as Agents for BW," Control No. 400.112, Entry 1B, Box 235, RG 175, and "Detailed Justification for Supplemental Funds for FY-1953," for the same project at Johns Hopkins University, n.d., p. 9, Control No. 637-10-S, Entry 1B, Box 243, RG 175, NA.

28. Department of State, Memorandum of Conversation, 27 June 1952, p. 1, and Statement on Bacteriological Warfare, for use by Ambassador Cohen, p. 2, in Army G-3, Deputy Chief of Staff, Operations, General Decimal File 1952 (Secret), Box 314, RG 319, NA; Memorandum on Proposed Message from the Secretary of State to the ICRC to Counteract Communist Propaganda Campaign on Biological Warfare, 10 Mar. 1952 (Secret), Army G-3, Deputy Chief of Staff, Operations, Decimal File 385, ibid.; Steering Group for Eighteenth International Red Cross Conference, "Communist Bacteriological Warfare Propaganda," 16 June 1952, File 50208-40, Pt. 6 FP1, Vol. 5921, RG 25, NAC; Isabel Vincent, *Hitler's Silent Partners: Swiss Banks, Nazi Gold, and the Pursuit of Justice* (New York, 1977), pp. 125–126, 295–297.

29. Paul G. Cassell, "Establishing Violations of International Law: 'Yellow Rain' and the Treaties Regulating Chemical and Biological Warfare," *Stanford Law Review* 35 (January 1983): 259–295.

30. George Wald to Stephen Endicott, 15 Mar. 1979.

31. Needham Report (1952), pp. 14–17, Appendixes B, C, D, Gb, H, HH; Liaoning Archives, Volume 63, permanent, Northeast Patriotic Health Campaign Committee, Central Party telegram instructions to various regions, 19 Mar. 1952.

32. Walker M. Mahurin, *Honest John: The Autobiography of Walker M. Mahurin* (New York, 1962), pp. 250, 252; Mahurin, "Sworn Statement," *New York Times*, 1 Nov. 1953; Stephen Endicott, "Germ Warfare and 'Plausible Denial,': The Korean War, 1952–1953," *Modern China* 5, No. 1 (1979): 99–100.

33. Jenkins, "Defense against Insect-Disseminated Biological Warfare Agents," p. 116.

34. William M. Creasy to Assistant Chief of Staff G4, Department of the Army, 30 Oct. 1951, p. 6, Decimal File 400.112, Entry 1B, Box 235, RG 175, NA; H. I. Stubblefield, "A Resumé of the Biological Warfare Effort," 21 Mar. 1958, Record No. 54763, Chemical and Biological Warfare Collection, Box 2, National Security Archive, Washington, D.C., pp. 14, 16, 25; "Defense against Biological

Warfare: A Symposium," *Military Medicine*, February 1963, pp. 84, 116–118; John Bryden *Deadly Allies: Canada's Secret War, 1937–1947* (Toronto, 1989), pp. 207, 210, 224–225, 246, 251.

35. Needham Report (1952), Appendixes F, V-7, AA-1; Liaoning Archives, Volume 43, long-term preservation, Reports of Research Group, No. 13, 5 Apr. 1952.

36. Department of Defense, "Chemical and Biological Warfare Readiness," 21 Dec. 1951, Top Secret 3145.1-TS, 15, Office of the Secretary of Defense, File CD 385 (General), RG 330, NA.

37. Central Party telegram, instructions to various regions, approved by Zhou Enlai, Classification AAAA, 19 Mar. 1952, Liaoning Archives, Volume 63, permanent, Northeast Patriotic Health Campaign Committee, Reports of Research Group, No. 13, 5 Apr. 1952.

38. Theodor Rosebury and Elvin A Kabat, "Bacterial Warfare: A Critical Analysis of the Available Agents, Their Possible Military Applications, and the Means for Protection against Them," *Journal of Immunology* 56 (May 1947): 32–33.

39. The U.S. 500-lb.-size propaganda leaflet bomb is identified by the code M16 and was adapted as a BW feather bomb coded E73R/M115. The code M105 on the same type of bomb may appear as an anomaly. Records of the 3rd Bomb Group of the U.S. Fifth Air Force in Korea, however, show that 500-lb. size leaflet bombs marked M105 were dropped at the conclusion of heavy bombing raids on railways (U.S. Fifth Air Force, 3rd Bomb Group, 90th Squadron, Mission No. 3-17643, 20/21 May 1952, Box 149, RG 342, NA). The Chinese claimed that these M105 "leaflet" bombs released infected insects as part of the U.S. biological warfare experiments.

40. Needham Report (1952), pp. 37–44.

41. Rosebury and Kabat, "Bacterial Warfare," pp. 7–89.

42. Photographs (Secret), File 1280S 1953, Box 256, RG 175, NA.

43. *People's China*, No. 18 (17 Sept. 1952).

44. Memo for Record, Subject: ISHII, Shiro, 6 Sept. 1947 (Secret); Summary of Information, Subject: ISHII, Shiro, former Lt. General, CG Kwantung Army Water Purification Unit, 10 June 1947 (Secret) (declassified 19 Feb. 1992), General Headquarters Far East Command, Military Intelligence Section, General Staff, Civil Intelligence Section, Counter Intelligence Division, Subject: ISHII, Shiro, 7009196, File 201, Book 1, RG 331, NA.

45. Minutes of the thirteenth meeting of the Psychological Strategy Board, 12 June 1952, U.S. Government Declassified Documents Index 1988 (White House, Top Secret), No. 1770.

46. Memorandum for the Under-Secretary: United States Proposal Regarding Affidavits Stating That the Chinese Communists Have Extracted False Confessions from Their Prisoners under Duress, 4 Nov. 1952, Defense Liaison, File 50208-40, Pt. 4.1, Vol. 5920, RG 25; Hume Wrong, Ambassador in Washington, to L. B. Pearson, Secretary of State for External Affairs, 4 Mar. 1953, File 50208-40, Pt. 4.2, Vol. 5920, RG 25, NAC.

47. The popularization of the idea that the flyers were "brainwashed" grew out of a widely read book of the time by Edward Hunter, titled *Brainwashing in Red China* (1951). A few years later, after the results of a mammoth U.S. Army

study were known, the U.S. Defense Department concluded that American POWs had not been subject to brainwashing, merely hardship, stress, and duress. The results of the Army study are summarized in Eugene Kinkead, *In Every War but One* (New York, 1959). Other follow-up studies, mostly sponsored by the Army, are Albert D. Biderman, "Further Analysis of POW Follow-up Study Data," Final Technical Report (Washington, D.C., 7 Apr. 1965); E. H. Schein, W. E. Cooley, and M. T. Singer, *A Psychological Follow-up of Former Prisoners of War of the Chinese Communists*, Pt. 1: *Results of the Interview Study* (Cambridge, Mass., 1960); E. H. Schein, W. F. Hill, H. L. Williams, and A. Lubin, "Distinguished Characteristics of Collaborators and Resistors among American Prisoners of War," *Journal of Abnormal and Social Psychology* 55 (1957): 197–201; J. Segal, "Factors Related to the Collaboration and Resistance Behavior of US POWs in Korea" (Washington, D.C., 1965); Robert J. Lifton, "Home by Ship: Reaction Patterns of American Prisoners of War Repatriated from North Korea," *American Journal of Psychiatry* 10 (April 1954): 732–737.

48. George A. Morgan, acting director, Psychological Strategy Board Working Committee, to The Honorable Allen W. Dulles, Director of Central Intelligence, 5 Mar. 1953, p. 2, U.S. Government Declassified Documents Index 1988 (Top Secret), No. 521; C. D. Jackson to General Wilton B. Parsons, 11 May 1953, Index 1985, No. 618.

49. George A. Morgan, 5 Mar. 1953, ibid.

50. Meeting of POW Working Group, Friday, 13 Nov. 1953, Operations Coordinating Board, 16 Nov. 1953, U.S. Government Declassified Documents Index 1992 (White House), No. 2855, p. 4.

51. Charles R. Norberg, Chairman, POW Working Group, Operations Coordinating Board, Washington D.C., Minutes of Meeting, 13 Nov. 1953, and Memorandum for the Acting Deputy Executive Officer, 13 Oct. 1953, U.S. Government Declassified Documents Index (White House) 1992, No. 2855, and Index 1979, No. 161C. The USAF Office of Special Investigations hearings to refute the confessions also strain credibility because "only those leads essential to the fulfillment of the objective . . . were developed." See "Report of the Investigation of Communist Allegations That the USAF Participated in Biological Warfare in Korea," prepared by the Office of Special Investigations, the Inspector General, Headquarters USAF, 22 Apr. 1953, RG 341, NA.

52. Needham Report (1952), p. 60.

53. *Ethics and International Affairs* 3 (1989): 204.

SOURCES CITED

Chinese and Korean Sources

The Chinese attach great importance to their archives and devote much attention to their preservation, arrangement, and description. The volumes are often sewn together by hand to avoid losses, a labor-intensive process that requires a great deal of time and effort. Foreign scholars' access to China's archives is governed by the Archives Law of the People's Republic of China of 1 January 1988, and by Implementing Order No 3. of the State Archives Bureau, "Trial Procedures for Foreign Organizations and Individuals to Use Chinese Archives," effective 1 July 1992.

William W. Moss, Emeritus Archivist of the Smithsonian Institute, who has made extended tours of archives in China and prepared a special study of these procedures, has useful advice about what to expect: broad, exploratory research in post–1949 archives does not exist; usually scholars do not examine the original documents directly; users must justify their need for access to the archives, and the archivist decides, "from the users' definition of research scope and focus in their application, which record groups, folders and documents are pertinent to their topic." Moss says that unless there is "an extraordinary understanding and communication between the user and the archivist, many pertinent materials may escape attention." However, he believes that it is possible, even for foreigners, to have productive relations with archive service staff based "in part on mutual respect of each other's expertise and in part on patient explanation and negotiation."*

Our experience confirms these observations. We were received by Mr. Liu Guoneng, deputy director of the State Archives Bureau, and by members of his staff on three occasions during three separate visits to Beijing in 1992, 1994, and 1996, where we made known our research needs. Mr Liu apologetically said that it would take time to locate these historical documents. As a result of our first conversations, Mr. Shen Zhengle, senior archivist in charge of the Central Party and State Council archives for the 1950s, came up with fourteen documents which he felt gave the truth of the general picture. He said that he saw others but thought they were "not so useful." These documents were declassified for our use, and permission was given to quote them. The second time we asked permission to

---

*William W. Moss, "Dang'an: Contemporary Chinese Archives," *China Quarterly*, March 1996, pp. 122–123. The duty to preserve the national heritage, according to Moss, has led the Chinese archives to an extraordinary records retention rate of between 50 and 100 percent of working unit files, compared to the U.S. federal government's retention rate of about 2 percent.

visit the Liaoning Provincial Archives in Shenyang and Dalian. This was discouraged because it would be a waste of our time: the relevant documents are still classified and are mixed in volumes with other classified documents so that it would not be possible for us to go and pick them out for ourselves. Instead, Mr. Leng Baocun, department head of the All-China Supervision Department for Archival Institutions and Record Offices, personally went to Liaoning to collect documents. He came back with a large number which he said had been declassified for us, following our request and the approval of the relevant authorities. "I got them all," he said. "As department head in charge of all state archives in the country, nothing would be hidden from me." We appreciated his energetic efforts on our behalf and his confidence, but we noticed and pointed out to him that from the numbering system of the documents, there were some fairly large gaps. Whether the local archivists thought that they had produced enough material to establish the truth of the broad picture, whether they had provided everything they could find—perhaps all the records that have survived—we cannot profess to know. In any case, we greatly appreciated the treasure trove of daily reports, telegrams, instructions, and research analysis of epidemic diseases from the border area to Korea that came our way.

Apart from the above, we had some modest success in gaining access to the archives of the People's Liberation Army, the first foreigners to be given that opportunity. Because of some misunderstanding, we did not receive the materials we had requested, but we did see other valuable documents of the Chinese People's Volunteer Army in Korea that were on our topic.

Manuscript Sources
CHINA
Central Archives (Beijing)

Office of the South Central [Party] Bureau, Vol. 124
Office of the Northeast Bureau, Vols. 271, 343
Office of the North China Bureau, Vol. 290
Office of the East China Bureau, Vol. 389

Liaoning Archives (Shenyang and Dalian)

Daily Reports of the Northeast Region Epidemic Disease Prevention Committee, 1952–1953, Vol. 43, long-term preservation
Reports of the Northeast Administrative Committee, Vol. 38, permanent
Reports of the Research Group of the Northeast Patriotic Health Campaign Committee, 1952–1953, Vol. 43, long-term preservation; Vols. 62, 63 and 68, permanent

People's Liberation Army Archives (Beijing)

Government Publications
CHINA

Depositions of Nineteen Captured U.S. Airmen on Their Participation in Germ Warfare in Korea. 201 pp. Peking: The Chinese People's Committee for World Peace, 1953.

Korean Armistice Agreement and Other Documents. 31 pp. *People's China*, Supplement, 1 Aug. 1953.

Report of the International Scientific Commission for the Investigation of the Facts Concerning Bacterial Warfare in Korea and China. 61 pp. plus 600 pp. of appendixes. Peking, 1952. Members of the commission were Dr. Andrea Andreen (Sweden), Mons. Jean Malterre (France), Dr. Joseph Needham (UK), Dr. Oliviero Olivo (Italy), Dr. Samuel B. Pessoa (Brazil), and Dr. N. N. Zhukov-Verezhnikov (USSR). Dr. Needham was the principal author of the final report, which is cited in the notes as Needham Report (1952).

Stop U.S. Germ Warfare! Pamphlet. Peking: The Chinese People's Committee for World Peace and Against American Aggression, 1952.

The Struggle for the Armistice in Korea: Selected Documents. 148 pp. Peking: The Chinese People's Committee for World Peace, September 1953.

The Struggle for Peace in Korea: Selected Documents. Revised ed. 76 pp. Peking: The Chinese People's Committee for World Peace, June 1953.

United Nations POWs in Korea. 92 pp. Peking: The Chinese People's Committee for World Peace, 1953.

Zhongguo renmin zhiyuanjun kangmei yuanchao zhanshi [History of the Chinese People's Volunteer Army in the Resist America, Aid Korea War]. 2nd ed. Beijing: Academy of Military Science and the Military History Research Institute, 1990.

Zhongguo renmin zhiyuanjun kangmei yuanchao zhanzheng zhengzi gongzuo [Political Work of the Chinese People's Volunteer Army in the Resist America, Aid Korea War]. Beijing: People's Liberation Army Press, 1985.

KOREA

"Report of the Commission of the Medical Headquarters of the Korean People's Army on the Use of Bacteriological Weapons." Canadian Peace Congress, "Documentation on Bacteriological Warfare, 1 April 1952." (mimeograph), File 50208-40, Pt. 1.1, Vol. 5919, RG 25, NAC.

The History of the United Nations Forces in the Korean War. Vol. 5. Seoul: Ministry of National Defense, Republic of Korea, 1976.

Newspapers and Magazines

New China News Agency [NCNA], Beijing, *Daily News Release.* Translated in *Survey of China Mainland Press* [*SCMP*]. Hong Kong: U.S. Consulate General.

People's China, 1950–1958 (Beijing, semi-monthly)

Renmin Ribao [People's Daily]

Books

Mao Zedong. *Selected Military Writings.* Beijing, 1968.

Nie Rongzhen. *Nie Rongzhen junshi wenxuan* [Selected Military Writings of Nie Rongzhen]. Beijing: PLA Publishing House, 1992.

Peng Dehuai. *Memoirs of a Chinese Marshal.* Beijing: Foreign Languages Press, 1984.

Qi Dexue. *Chaoxian zhanzheng juece neimu* [The Inside Story of Decision-Making in the Korean War]. Shenyang, 1991.

Xu Yen. *Diyici jiaoliang* [The First Trial of Strength]. Beijing: China Radio and Television Publishing House, 1990.

Oral Interviews

Liao Gailong, research professor, Chinese Academy of Social Sciences
Qi Dexue, colonel, Department of Military History, PLA Academy of Military Science, Beijing
Qiu Weifan [W. F. Chiu], professor, Beijing Agricultural University
Shen Qiyi, professor, China Association for the Dissemination of Scientific Knowledge
Yan Renying, physician, Beijing Medical University
Zhu Chun, professor, China Institute for International Strategic Studies

Western Sources

The portions of this book dealing with the development of U.S. biological warfare after 1945 rely mainly on the manuscript collections in the U.S. National Archives. Among the more useful are the subject files on "Manner and Methods of Conducting Warfare" of the Office of the Secretary of Defense, in Record Group 330; the chronological biological warfare files of the Joint Chiefs of Staff, in Record Group 218, File JCS 1837; the Secret declassified files of the U.S. Army Chemical Corps, in Record Group 175, including "A Resumé of the Biological Warfare Effort" by H. I. Stubblefield, M.D. (1958); the Biological and Chemical Warfare subject files of the U.S. Air Force, Operations Division, in Record Group 341; and, finally, the Air Materiel Command's unpublished "History of Air Force Participation in the Biological Warfare Program, 1944–1954" by Dorothy L. Miller.

Not so helpful are such reports by the Army as "U.S. Army Activity in the U.S. Biological Warfare Programs," presented to hearings of the Subcommittee on Health and Scientific Research of the Senate Committee on Human Resources in 1977, or the section on biological warfare in *The History of the Joint Chiefs of Staff*; they are concerned more with public relations and deflecting public attention than with serious knowledge of the U.S. biological warfare program.

For the part of the book that deals with the Korean War, it is not possible to point to some document collections as being more important than others. They all may have significance. Many of the operations in that war were of a covert and "need to know" kind, the records pertaining to which were either destroyed, lost, hidden or remain classified.* Clues to covert biological warfare activity are scattered in many places—a letter giving the command structure, a chance remark, a picture here, a piece of machinery there, a bombing pattern—and gain significance

---

*For example, when portions of the files of the U.S. Army Chemical Corps (the body chiefly responsible for the development of biological warfare) for 1949–1954 were turned over to the Federal Records Center in 1956, a preliminary inventory was made describing the content of all the files ("Preliminary Inventory of the Records of the Chemical Warfare Service," compiled by Raymond P. Flynn, RG 175, National Archives Index, Vol. 1, Accession 67A4900). A subsequent note by archivists at the U.S. National Archives says that "between 1956 and 1969, some files were recalled by the Army and others were destroyed."

when pieced together and compared to evidence that appears in the Chinese sources. The researcher looking in historical archives for concrete evidence of U.S. covert biological warfare during the Korean War must follow the advice of the person who grew up on a farm and said, "I learned that if there are rabbit tracks around the haystack, if you look hard enough, there'll be a little rabbit sitting around there somewhere on his cottontail."

Manuscript Sources

CANADA

National Archives of Canada

Record Group 24, Department of National Defence
Record Group 24E, Defense Research Board
Record Group 25, Department of External Affairs, Top Secret File on BW, Vols.
 5919–5921, December 1944–July 1963

GREAT BRITAIN

London Public Record Office

DEFE Chiefs of Staff

UNITED STATES

Declassified Documents Index, 1974–1996 (White House, Departments of
 Defense and State)

Dugway Proving Ground, Utah

Record Group 175, Army Chemical Corps (including the "Top Secret" files)

Federal Records Center, Suitland, Maryland, and Marine Historical Section, Navy Yard, Washington, D.C.

Record Group 127, U.S. Marine Corps

Harry S. Truman Library

Psychological Strategy Board Records

(*continued*) The RG 175 records, except for those at Dugway and possibly other places, were accessioned permanently by the National Archives in 1969 and made fully open to the public in 1997. A comparison of the communications listed in the preliminary inventory as "Miscellaneous File, Secret" from the Far East Command in 1952 with those of that category that can now be found in RG 175 shows that twenty out of twenty-five (80 percent) of such documents were removed by the Army between 1956 and 1969. The request to remove these documents was made by the U.S. Army Far East Command. The remaining five documents deal with such matters as riot tear gas, flame throwers, smoke, and gas masks. Another example of the heavy censorship surrounding U.S. biological warfare activity is the fact that the portion of Dorothy L. Miller's "History of Air Force Participation in the Biological Warfare Program" covering the years 1952–1954 has 75 of its 226 pages either entirely or partially sanitized, and the endnotes remain classified.

Library of Congress

Hoyt Vandenberg Papers

Maxwell Air Force Base, Alabama

USAF Historical Research Agency, microfilms of unit histories during the Korean War

National Archive II, College Park, Maryland

Record Group 94, Adjutant General Command reports 1949–1954
Record Group 111, Signal Corps (Photographs)
Record Group 112, Surgeon General, AMEDD and HUMED files; 406th Medical General Laboratory
Record Group 175, U.S. Army, Chemical Corps
Record Group 218, Joint Chiefs of Staff
Record Group 319, Army Staff
Record Group 330, Office of the Secretary of Defense
Record Group 331, GHQ–SCAP (Japan)
Record Group 334, Records of the Interservice Agencies
Record Group 338, U.S. Army Commands (Far East Command)
Record Group 341, U.S. Air Force, Headquarters Records
Record Group 342, U.S. Air Force, Commands, Activities and Organizations

National Security Archive, Georgetown University, Washington, D.C.

Chemical and Biological Warfare Collection. This broad-ranging collection provides easy access to basic documents dealing with policy, including reports by George Merck, William Creasy, and Earl Stevenson, and the difficult-to-find "A Resumé of the Biological Warfare Effort," 21 Mar. 1958, by H. I. Stubblefield.

Wright-Patterson Air Force Base, Ohio

U.S. AIR FORCE, AIR MATERIEL COMMAND, HISTORICAL DIVISION
Miller, Dorothy L. "History of Air Force Participation in the Biological Warfare Program, 1944–1954," Vols. 1 (1952) and 2 (1957). Unpublished and heavily censored.
Dehaven, Ethel; Helen Joiner; and Dorothy L. Miller. "History of the Air Materiel Command 1 January–30 June 1952," Vol. 1: "Narrative" (1953, unpublished). Available through the Historical Research Agency, Maxwell Air Force Base. ("Highly classified" projects of the period are not included.)

Government Publications

Great Britain

Farrar-Hockley, Anthony. *The British Part in the Korean War.* 2 vols. London: HMSO, 1990, 1995.

Soviet Union

Materials of the Trial of Former Servicemen of the Japanese Army Charged with

Manufacturing and Employing Biological Weapons [Khabarovsk Trial]. Moscow: Foreign Languages Publishing House, 1950.

United Nations

Health Aspects of Chemical and Biological Weapons. Geneva: World Health Organization, 1970.
UN Secretariat Documents, A/C 1L66, 1953. Sworn statements of ten U.S. airmen who were formerly POWs in Korea.
Yearbook of the United Nations: 50th Anniversary Special Edition, pp. 151–153. London, 1995.

United States Congress

Final Report of the Senate Select Committee to Study Governmental Operations with Respect to Intelligence Activities (the Church Committee). 7 vols. Washington, D.C., 1976.
U.S. Army Activity in the U.S. Biological Warfare Programs. Vol. 1, 24 Feb. 1977. 297 pp. Washington, D.C.: U.S. Government Printing Office, 1977. A report by Lt. Col. George A. Carruth to hearings held by the Subcommittee on Health and Scientific Research, Senate Committee on Human Resources, 95th Congress, 1st Session, p. 32.

United States Consulate General, Hong Kong

Survey of China Mainland Press [SCMP]. A translation service.

U.S. Air Force

Futrell, Robert F. *The United States Air Force in Korea, 1950–1953.* Revised ed. Washington, D.C., 1983.
"Guerilla Warfare and Airpower in Korea, 1950–1953." Microfilm Roll 2627. Concepts Division, Aerospace Institute, Air University, Maxwell Air Force Base, Ala., 1964.
Haas, Col. Michael E. *Air Commando! 1950–1975: Twenty-Five Years at the Tip of the Spear.* Hurlburt Field, Fla.: Special Operations Command, 1994.

U.S. Department of the Army

Covert, Norman M. *Cutting Edge: A History of Fort Detrick, Maryland, 1943–1993.* Fort Detrick, Md., 1993.
Cowdrey, Albert E. *The Medics' War.* Vol. 4 of *United States Army in the Korean War.* Washington, D.C., 1987.
Hermes, Walter G. *Truce Tent and Fighting Front.* Vol. 3 of *United States Army in the Korean War.* Washington, D.C., 1966.
Paddock, Alfred H., Jr. *US Army Special Warfare: Its Origins—Psychological and Unconventional Warfare, 1941–1953.* Washington D.C.: National Defense University, 1982.
Sandler, Dr. Stanley. *A History of US Army Combat Psychological Operations.* Fort Bragg, N.C.: Special Operations Command, 1996.
Treaties Governing Land Warfare. Army pamphlet No. 27-1, 1956.

U.S. Department of Defense

Field Manual 27–10: Rules of Land Warfare. Revised 1940, 1956, and in 1972 as *The Law of Land Warfare.*

U.S. Joint Chiefs of Staff

Schnabel, James F., and Robert J. Watson. *The Joint Chiefs of Staff and National Policy: The Korean War.* Vol. 3 of *The History of the Joint Chiefs of Staff.* Wilmington, Del., 1979.

U.S. Marine Corps

MacDonald, James Angus. *The Problems of US Marine Corps Prisoners of War in Korea.* Occasional Paper, History and Museums Division, Washington, D.C., 1988.
Meid, Lt. Col. Pat, and Major James M. Yingling. *Operations in West Korea.* Vol. 5 of *US Marine Operations in Korea, 1950–1951.* Washington, D.C., 1979.
Montrose, Lynn; H. D. Kuokka; and N. W. Hicks. *The East-Central Front.* Vol. 4 of *US Marine Operations in Korea.* Washington, D.C., 1962.

U.S. Department of the Navy

Field, James A., Jr. *History of United States Naval Operations: Korea.* Washington, D.C., 1962.

Additional U.S. Government Publications

Biderman, Albert D., principal investigator. "Further Analysis of POW Follow-up Study Data, Final Technical Report." Period covered 1 Apr. 1963 to Feb. 1965. Washington, D.C.: Bureau of Social Science Research, Inc.; Alexandria, Va.: Defense Documentation Center for Scientific and Technical Information, Cameron Station.
Segal, J. "Factors Related to the Collaboration and Resistance Behavior of US POWs in Korea." Washington, D.C.: Human Resources Research Office, George Washington University, 1965. UumRRo Technical Report No. 33.

Books, Articles, and Reports

Acheson, Dean. *Present at the Creation: My Years in the State Department.* New York, 1969.
Alexander, Bevin. *Korea: The First War We Lost.* New York, 1986.
Ambrose, Stephen E. *Ike's Spies: Eisenhower and the Espionage Establishment.* Garden City, N.J., 1981.
Appleman, Lt. Col. Roy E. *Disaster in Korea: The Chinese Confront MacArthur.* College Station, Tex., 1989.
Appleman, Lt. Col. Roy E. *Ridgway Duels for Korea.* College Station, Tex., 1990.
Bajanov, Evgeni. "Assessing the Politics of the Korean War, 1949–1951." *Cold War in Asia Bulletin,* Winter 1995–96, pp. 54, 82–91. Cold War International History Project, Woodrow Wilson International Center for Scholars, Washington, D.C.

Baldwin, Frank, ed. *Without Parallel: The American-Korean Relationship since 1945.* New York, 1974.

Bank, Colonel Aaron. *From OSS to Green Berets: The Birth of Special Forces.* New York, 1986.

Bernstein, Barton J. "America's Biological Warfare Program in the Second World War." *Journal of Strategic Studies* 2 (March 1992).

Biderman, Albert D. "Social-Psychological Needs and Involuntary Behavior As Illustrated by Compliance in Interrogation." *Sociometry* 23 (June 1960): 120–147.

Blum, William. *The CIA, a Forgotten History: US Global Interventions since World War Two.* London and Atlantic Highlands, N.J., 1986.

Brown, Frederic J. *Chemical Warfare: A Study in Restraints.* Princeton, N.J., 1968.

Bryden, John. *Deadly Allies: Canada's Secret War, 1937–1947.* Toronto, 1989.

Bullene, Major General E. F. "Chemicals in Combat." *Armed Forces Chemical Journal* 5 (April 1952): 4–7.

Cantor, Mackinlay, and Curtis LeMay. *Mission with LeMay.* New York, 1965.

Carruth, George A. *U.S. Army Activity in the U.S. Biological Warfare Programs.* Vol. 1, 24 Feb. 1977. 297 pp. Washington, D.C., 1977.

Cassell, Paul. "Establishing Violations of International Law: 'Yellow Rain' and the Treaties Regulating Chemical and Biological Warfare." *Stanford Law Review* 35 (January 1983): 259–295.

Christie, A. B. *Infectious Diseases: Epidemiology and Clinical Practice.* Edinburgh, 1987.

Clendinin, Richard M. *Science and Technology at Fort Detrick, 1943–1968.* Fort Detrick, Md., 1968.

Clews, John. *The Communists' New Weapon: Germ Warfare.* London, 1952.

Clews, John C. *Communist Propaganda Techniques.* Foreword by G. F. Hudson. New York, 1964.

Cookson, John, and Judith Nottingham. *A Survey of Chemical and Biological Warfare.* London, 1969.

Covert, Norman M. *Cutting Edge: A History of Fort Detrick, Maryland, 1943–1993.* Fort Detrick, Md., 1993.

Cowdrey, Albert E. "'Germ Warfare' and Public Health in the Korean Conflict." *Journal of the History of Medicine and Allied Sciences* 39 (1984): 153–172.

Cowdrey, Albert E. *The Medics' War.* Vol. 4 of *United States Army in the Korean War.* Washington, D.C., 1987.

Creasy, William M. "Biological Warfare." *Armed Forces Chemical Journal* 5 (January 1952): 16–18, 46.

Creasy, William M. "Presentation to the Secretary of Defense's Ad Hoc Committee on CEBAR." 24 Feb. 1950. Record No. 54874, Chemical and Biological Warfare Collection, National Security Archive, Georgetown University, Washington, D.C.

Cumings, Bruce. *Korea's Place in the Sun: A Modern History.* New York, 1997.

Cumings, Bruce. *The Origins of the Korean War.* Vol 2: *The Roaring Cataract, 1947–1950.* Princeton, N.J., 1990.

Dando, Malcolm. *Biological Warfare in the Twenty-First Century: Biotechnology and the Proliferation of Biological Weapons.* London, 1994.

"Defense against Biological Warfare: A Symposium." *Military Medicine* 128 (January 1963): 81–146.

Endicott, James G. *I Accuse!* Pamphlet. 36 pp. Toronto, 1952.

Endicott, Stephen. "Germ Warfare and 'Plausible Denial': The Korean War, 1952–1953." *Modern China* 5, No. 1 (1979): 79–104.

Endicott, Stephen. *Red Earth: Revolution in a Sichuan Village*. Toronto, 1989.

Etzold, Thomas H., and John L. Gaddis. *Containment: Documents on American Policy and Strategy, 1945–1950*. New York, 1978.

Fain, Tyrus G., ed. *The Intelligence Community: History, Organization and Issues*. With an introduction by Senator Frank Church. New York, 1977.

Falk, Richard. "Inhibiting Reliance on Biological Weaponry: The Role and Relevance of International Law." *Ethics and International Affairs*, No. 3 (1989): 183–204.

Farrar-Hockley, Anthony. *The British Part in the Korean War*. 2 vols. London, 1990, 1995.

Farrar-Hockley, Anthony. *The Edge of the Sword*. London, 1954/1981.

Field, James A. *History of United States Naval Operations: Korea*. Washington, D.C., 1962.

Fleming, Donald F. *The Cold War and Its Origins*. Vol. 2: *1950–1960*. New York, 1961.

Fox, D. C. "Bacterial Warfare: The Use of Biologic Agents in Warfare." *Military Surgeon* 72 (March 1933).

Futrell, Robert F. *The United States Air Force in Korea, 1950–1953*. Washington, D.C., 1983.

Gahide, Jean Pierre. *La Belgique et la Guerre de Coree, 1950–1955*. Brussels, 1991.

Geissler, Erhard, and Robert H. Haynes. *Prevention of a Biological and Toxin Arms Race and the Responsibility of Scientists*. Berlin, 1991.

Goncharov, Sergei N.; John Lewis; and Xue Litai. *Uncertain Partners: Stalin, Mao and the Korean War*. Stanford, 1993.

Gower, Robert; John W. Powell; and Bert V. A. Rolling. "Japan's Biological Weapons, 1930–1945." *Bulletin of the Atomic Scientists*, October 1981.

Haas, Michael E. *Air Commando! 1950–1975: Twenty-Five Years at the Tip of the Spear*. Hurlburt Field, Fla., 1994.

Harris, Robert, and Jeremy Paxman. *A Higher Form of Killing: The Secret Story of Gas and Germ Warfare*. London, 1982.

Harris, Sheldon H. *Factories of Death: Japanese Biological Warfare 1932–1945 and the American Cover-up*. London and New York, 1994.

Harris, Sheldon. "Japanese Biological Warfare Research on Humans: A Case Study of Microbiology and Ethics."*Annals of the New York Academy of Sciences* 666 (1992): 21–52.

Harvey, A. V.; R. P. Mason; and G. A. Martin. "The Dysenteries in the Armed Forces." *Journal of Tropical Medicine and Hygiene*, January 1952, pp. 171–175.

Hermes, Walter G. *Truce Tent and Fighting Front*. Washington, D.C., 1966.

Hersh, Seymour. *Chemical and Biological Warfare: America's Hidden Arsenal*. New York, 1968.

Hersh, Seymour. "Germ Warfare: For Alma Mater, God and Country." *Ramparts* 8, No. 6 (1969): 21–28.

Hershberg, James G., ed. *The Cold War in Asia*. Woodrow Wilson International Center for Scholars, Cold War International History Project Bulletin, Washington, D.C., Winter 1995/1996.

Hullinghorst, Lt. Colonel R. I., and Lt. Colonel Arthur Steer. "Foreword." *American Journal of Medicine* 16 (May 1954).

Hullinghorst, Lt. Colonel R. I., and Lt. Colonel Arthur Steer. "Pathology of Epidemic Hemorrhagic Fever." *Annals of Internal Medicine* 38 (1953).

Hunter, Edward. *Brainwashing in Red China.* New York, 1951.

Jenkins, Dale W. "Defense against Insect Disseminated Biological Warfare Agents." *Military Medicine* 128 (February 1963): 116–118.

Joy, Admiral C. Turner. *How Communists Negotiate.* New York, 1955.

Kinkead, Eugene. *In Every War but One.* New York, 1959.

Kutler, Stanley I. *The American Inquisition: Justice and Injustice in the Cold War.* New York, 1982.

Leahy, William D. *I Was There: The Personal Story of the Chief of Staff to Presidents Roosevelt and Truman, Based on His Notes and Diaries Made at the Time.* New York, 1950.

Leary, William M. *Perilous Missions: Civil Air Transport and CIA Covert Operations in Asia.* Tuscaloosa, Ala., 1984.

Leary, William M., ed. *The Central Intelligence Agency: History and Documents.* Tuscaloosa, Ala., 1984.

Leitenberg, Milton, "Allegations of Biological Warfare in China and Korea, 1951–1953." In Stockholm International Peace Research Institute, *The Problem of Chemical and Biological Warfare*, Vol. 5: *The Prevention of CBW.* New York, 1971.

Lifton, Robert J. "Home by Ship: Reaction Patterns of American Prisoners of War Repatriated from North Korea." *American Journal of Psychiatry* 110 (April 1954).

MacDonald, Callum A. *Korea: The War before Vietnam.* London, 1986.

MacDonald, James Angus. *The Problems of US Marine Corps Prisoners of War in Korea.* Occasional Paper, History and Museums Division, Headquarters, U.S. Marine Corps, Washington, D.C., 1988.

Mahurin, Walker M. *Honest John: The Autobiography of Walker M. Mahurin.* New York, 1962.

Marchetti, Victor, and John D. Marks. *The CIA and the Cult of Intelligence.* New York, 1980.

McCormack, Gavan, and John Gittings, eds. *Korea, North and South: The Deepening Crisis.* New York, 1978.

McCune, George M. *Korea Today.* Cambridge, Mass., 1950.

McDermott, Jeanne. *The Killing Winds: The Menace of Biological Warfare.* New York, 1987.

Meid, Pat, and James M. Yingling. *Operations in West Korea.* Vol. 5 of *US Marine Operations in Korea, 1950–1951.* Washington, D.C., 1979.

Meilinger, Phillip S. *Hoyt S. Vandenberg: The Life of a General.* Bloomington, Ind., 1989.

Merck, George W. "Official Report on Biological Warfare." *Bulletin of the Atomic Scientists*, March 1946, pp. 16–18. This article is a resumé of Merck's report to the secretary of war, "Activities of the United States in the Field of Biological Warfare" (1946). U.S. National Archives, Entry 488, Box 182, RG 165.

Miller, Dorothy L. "History of Air Force Participation in the Biological Warfare Program, 1944–1954." 2 vols. U.S. Air Force, Air Materiel Command, Historical Division, Wright-Patterson Air Force Base, Ohio, 1952, 1957.

Montrose, Lynn; H. D. Kuokka; and N. W. Hicks. *The East-Central Front*. Vol. 4 of *US Marine Operations in Korea, 1950–1951*. Washington, D.C., 1962.

Moon, John Ellis van Courtland. "Biological Warfare Allegations: The Korean War Case." *Annals of the New York Academy of Sciences* 666 (1992): 53–83.

Needham, Joseph, et al. *Report of the International Scientific Commission for the Investigation of the Facts Concerning Bacterial Warfare in Korea and China*. 61 pp. plus 600 pp. of appendixes. Peking, 1952.

Paddock, Alfred H. *US Army Special Warfare: Its Origins—Psychological and Unconventional Warfare, 1941–1952*. Washington, D.C., 1982.

Pate, Lloyd W., as told to B. J. Cutler. *Reactionary!* New York, 1956.

Pease, Stephen E. *PSYWAR: Psychological Warfare in Korea, 1950–1953*. New York, 1992.

Poupard, James A., and Linda A. Miller. "History of Biological Warfare: Catapults to Capsomeres." *Annals of the New York Academy of Sciences* 666 (1992): 9–19.

Powell, John W. "An American Newspaperman Goes Home." In *China Monthly Review: Editors on Trial*. Pamphlet. 29 pp. Peking, 1957.

Powell, John W. "Japan's Germ Warfare: The US Cover-up of a War Crime." *Bulletin of Concerned Asian Scholars* 12, No. 4 (1980): 2–17. A shorter version appeared in *Bulletin of the Atomic Scientists*, October 1981, pp. 43–53.

Prados, John. *Presidents' Secret Wars: CIA and Pentagon Covert Operations*. New York, 1986.

Prouty, L. Fletcher. *The Secret Team: The CIA and Its Allies in Control of the United States and the World*. Englewood Cliffs, N.J., 1973.

Ranelagh, John. *The Agency: The Rise and Decline of the CIA*. London, 1986.

Rees, David. *Korea: The Limited War*. London, 1964.

Ridgway, Matthew B. *The Korean War*. New York, 1967.

Rosebury, Theodor. *Peace or Pestilence: Biological Warfare and How to Avoid It*. New York, 1949.

Rosebury, Theodor, and Elvin A Kabat, with the assistance of Martin H. Boldt. "Bacterial Warfare: A Critical Analysis of the Available Agents, Their Possible Military Applications and the Means for Protection against Them." *Journal of Immunology* 56 (May 1947): 7–89.

Ryan, Mark. *Chinese Attitudes toward Nuclear Weapons: China and the US during the Korean War*. Armonk, N.Y., 1992.

Sandler, Stanley. *A History of US Army Combat Psychological Operations*. Fort Bragg, N.C., 1966.

Schein, E. H.; W. E. Cooley; and M. T. Singer. *A Psychological Follow-up of Former Prisoners of War of the Chinese Communists*. Pt. 1: *Results of the Interview Study*. Cambridge, Mass., 1960.

Schein, E. H.; W. F. Hill; H. L. Williams; and A. Lubin. "Distinguished Characteristics of Collaborators and Resistors among American Prisoners of War." *Journal of Abnormal and Social Psychology* 55 (1957): 197–201.

Schnabel, James F., and Robert J. Watson. *The Joint Chiefs of Staff and National Policy: The Korean War*. Vol. 3 of *The History of the Joint Chiefs of Staff*. Wilmington, Del., 1979.

Sherry, Michael. *In the Shadow of War*. New Haven, Conn., 1995.

Singlaub, Maj. General John K. *Hazardous Duty: An American Soldier in the Twentieth Century*. New York, 1991.

Stevenson, Earl. "Report of the Secretary of Defense's Ad Hoc Committee on Chemical, Biological and Radiological Warfare." 30 June 1950. Record No. 54791, Chemical and Biological Warfare Collection, National Security Archive, Georgetown University, Washington, D.C.

Stubblefield, H. I. "A Resumé of the Biological Warfare Effort." 21 Mar. 1958. Record No. 54763, Chemical and Biological Warfare Collection, National Security Archive, Georgetown University, Washington, D.C.

Thompson, Capt. Annis G. *The Greatest Airlift: The Story of Combat Cargo.* Tokyo, 1954.

Thompson, Arvo T. "Report on Japanese Biological Warfare Activities." 31 May 1946. Record No. 53139, Chemical and Biological Warfare Collection, National Security Archive, Georgetown University, Washington, D.C.

Tigertt, W. D. "The Initial Effort to Immunize American Soldier Volunteers with Typhoid Vaccine." *Military Medicine,* May 1959, pp. 342–349.

Tigertt, W. D. "Japanese B Encephalitis." *American Journal of Public Health,* June 1957, pp. 713–718.

Tigertt, Col. W. D., M.C. "Medical Research in Korean Conflict." *Texas State Journal of Medicine,* August 1953, pp. 622–626.

Tigertt, W. D. "Status of the Medical Research Effort." *Military Medicine,* Symposium on Defense against Biological Warfare, February 1963, pp. 81–146.

Tigertt, W. D. "Studies on Q Fever in Man." *Transactions of the Association of American Physicians* 69 (1956): 98–104.

Tiggert, W. D.; T. O. Berge; K. F. Burns; and J. P. Saterwhite. "Evaluation of Japanese B. Encephalitis Vaccine IV: Pattern of Seriological Response to Vaccination over a Five Year Period in an Endemic Area," *American Journal of Hygiene* 63 (1956): 238–249.

Tigertt, W. D., and A. B. Sabin. "Evaluation of Japanese B. Encephalitis Vaccine I: General Background and Methods." *American Journal of Hygiene* 63 (1956): 217–223.

Toland, John. *In Mortal Combat.* New York, 1991.

Truman, Harry S. *Memoirs.* 2 vols. New York, 1955–56.

Vincent, Isabel. *Hitler's Secret Partners: Swiss Banks, Nazi Gold, and the Pursuit of Justice.* New York, 1997.

White, W. L. *The Captives of Korea.* Westport, Conn., 1957.

Williams, Peter, and David Wallace. *Unit 731: The Japanese Army's Secret of Secrets.* London, 1988.

Winnington, Allan. *Breakfast with Mao.* London, 1986.

Winokur, George, M.D. "The Germ Warfare Statements: A Synthesis of a Method for the Extortion of False Confessions." *Journal of Mental and Nervous Diseases* 122 (July 1955).

Wise, David. *The Politics of Lying: Government Deception, Secrecy and Power.* New York, 1973.

Wright, Susan, ed. *Preventing a Biological Arms Race.* Cambridge, Mass., 1990.

Zhang Shuguang. *Mao's Military Romanticism: China and the Korean War, 1950–1953.* Lawrence, Kans., 1995.

Zilinskas, Raymond A., ed. *The Microbiologist and Biological Defense Research: Ethics, Politics and International Security. Annals of the New York Academy of Science* 666 (1992).

Oral Interviews

York University. Archives and Special Collections. Oral History Project on the Korean War. This collection includes interviews by the authors, Mark Seldon, Ken Kann, and Carl Dow with Crawford Sams of the U.S. Army; U.S. Air Force flyers Howard B. Hitchens, Jr., Paul Kniss, Warren W. Lull, Robert C. Lurie, and Walker M. Mahurin; RCAF flyers William Nixon and Douglas Lindsay; Professors Zhu Chun, Qiu Weifan, Shen Qiyi, Liao Gailong, and Dr. Yan Renying; and Col. Qi Dexue.

Documentary Films

Korea, the Unknown War. Thames TV/ WGBH Boston. Philip Whitehead, producer and director (ca. 1991).
The Bacteriological Warfare Is Still Alive. Nippon TV, 1995.
Lashmar, Paul. *Timewatch: Korea- -Russia's Secret War*. BBC/A&E, 1996.

INDEX

Stephen Endicott was born in Shanghai of missionary parents and grew up in China before the Communist revolution. His family lived in Sichuan province for three generations, where he returned to teach in the 1980s. Dr. Endicott, who is a graduate of the University of Toronto, has received the Killam Senior Fellowship and other academic awards while teaching East Asian history at York University in Toronto. His books include *Diplomacy and Enterprise: British China Policy, 1933–1937; James G. Endicott: Rebel out of China;* and *Red Earth: Revolution in a Sichuan Village.*

Edward Hagerman is a member of the history faculty of York University in Toronto. He has published many articles on the origins of modern war and modern total war, and has contributed to textbooks for the U.S. Military Academy at West Point, the U.S. Army Command and General Staff college, the U.S. Air Force Academy, and the Air War College of the U.S. Air Force. He is author of *The American Civil War and the Origins of Modern Warfare.*